CHICKEN SOUP FOR THE CAT & DOG LOVER'S SOUL

Celebrating Pets as Family with Stories About Cats, Dogs and Other Critters

Jack Canfield
Mark Victor Hansen
Marty Becker, D.V.M.
Carol Kline

Health Communications, Inc.
Deerfield Beach, Florida

www.hci-online.com
www.chickensoup.com

We would like to acknowledge the many publishers and individuals who granted us permission to reprint the cited material. (Note: The stories that were penned anonymously, that are in the public domain, or that were written by Jack Canfield, Mark Victor Hansen, Marty Becker, D.V.M., and Carol Kline are not included in this listing.)

Rescued by Love. Reprinted by permission of Lisa Duffy-Korpics. ©1999 Lisa Duffy-Korpics.

Bumpus. Reprinted by permission of Janine Adams.©1999 Janine Adams.

Agnes and Mattie. Reprinted by permission of Shari Smyth. ©1999 Shari Smyth.

Friends in Arms. Reprinted by permission of Rosamond Young. ©1999 Rosamond Young.

The Yorkshire Christmas Cat. Copyright ©1976, 1977 by James Herriot. From *All Things Wise and Wonderful* by James Herriot. Reprinted by permission of St. Martin's Press, LLC and David Higham Associates.

Princess Was a Nuisance. Reprinted by permission of Carol Ann Baum. ©1999 Carol Ann Baum.

(Continued on page 404)

Library of Congress Cataloging-in-Publication Data

Chicken soup for the cat & dog lover's soul: celebrating pets as family with stories about cats, dogs, and other critters / [edited by] Jack Canfield . . . [et al.].
    p. cm.
ISBN 1-55874-711-7 (hardcover). —ISBN 1-55874-710-9 (trade paper)
1. Cats Anecdotes. 2. Dogs Anecdotes. 3. Pets Anecdotes. 4. Pet owners Anecdotes. 5. Human-animal relationships Anecdotes.
I. Canfield, Jack, date.
SF445.5.C46 1999   99-33710
636.0188'7—dc21   CIP

Publisher: Health Communications, Inc.
            3201 S.W. 15th Street
            Deerfield Beach, FL 33442-8190

Cover photo © Barbara Campbell
Cover design by Lisa Camp
Typesetting by Lawna Patterson Oldfield

This book is dedicated with love to
the millions of people around the world who treat
their pets—cats, dogs and other critters—
like family members, doing whatever it takes to make
sure their beloved pets are happy, healthy and
live full lives. And to the world's pets who fortify us
with their daily gifts of love and loyalty,
and make us laugh.

We also dedicate this book to the veterinary
profession, whose skillful, compassionate service has
earned the public's admiration, trust and respect.

And to our heroes, the people who work
tirelessly and without fanfare in their communities
to help homeless, sick or injured pets. You have our
profound, eternal gratitude for making
a difference, one pet at a time.

Finally, we dedicate this book to God,
who, through his grace and compassion, has given
us the special love of animals to bless
our hearts and homes.

CITIZEN DOG BY MARK O'HARE

Contents

3. PETS AS HEALERS

4. PET-POURRI

8. SAYING GOOD-BYE

9. ON COMPANIONSHIP

Acknowledgments

Putting together a book like this takes the help of many people. We want to acknowledge our families, friends, staff, business partners colleagues and others who contributed to make *Chicken Soup for the Cat & Dog Lover's Soul* happen!

First, a huge thank you to our families!

To Jack's family, who, in the midst of the pressure-filled weeks it takes to finish a book like this, constantly reminded him to slow down, smell the roses, "purr the cats" and pet the bunnies. To Jack's mother, Ellen, who instilled in him a love for all creatures big and small, and whose stepfather, Fred, worked so hard to purchase, house and feed them—from the purebreds to the numerous strays that inevitably appeared on their doorstep.

To Mark's wife, Patty, who has the biggest heart for animals of almost anyone we know in the whole world; and to his daughter, Elisabeth, who often declares that she is going to become an animal chiropractor, and to his daughter, Melanie, who has decided that one of her chief missions in life is to help save the elephants on the planet.

To Marty's cherished wife, Teresa, and his beloved children, Mikkel and Lex, whose love, loyalty, laughter and vitality ignite Marty's desire to tackle many projects and fuel his daily walk. To Virginia Becker and the late Bob Becker, who passed on the DNA that says, "Love pets like family." To Teresa's family—Valdie, Jim and Rocky Burkholder—whose rock-solid support and avalanche of goodwill have allowed Marty the freedom to globetrot in pursuit of helping pets and people, with the blessing of returning to a hometown oasis of beauty, simplicity and serenity.

To Carol's husband, Larry, for his seemingly endless strength, kindness and support. Without him, this book could not have been written. And to Carol's stepchildren, Lorin and McKenna, two fantastic people who inspire her constantly with their creativity, humor and enthusiasm. To Carol's lovely mother, Selmajean Schneider, for her constant encouragement and to Carol's father, Raymond Zurer, who lives on in the hearts of his family. To her wonderful brothers and sisters and their families, Jim— "Mr. Internet"—and Diana, cheerleaders Barbara and Wilbur, fellow pet-lovers Burt, Pam and Rachel, and the ever-charming and delightful Holly.

Special thanks go to Marci Shimoff, whose generosity and brilliance is unparalleled. Your friendship is so precious to us. We love you, Marci.

Grateful thanks go to Heather McNamara, our senior editor, whose skill and steadiness make her such an invaluable asset. To Nancy Autio, for her hard work and patience getting all the permissions we needed and for miraculously keeping all of the simultaneous "book action" straight. To Leslie Forbes, for her help with permissions, for forwarding e-mails and cartoons, and keeping this book on track. And to Patty Aubery, who astounds us with her ability to get everything done with warmth, humor and skill. You go girl!

A large round of applause goes to the incredible Linn Thomas, whose dedication, hard work and considerable talents are only matched by his enormous heart. And to Anne Sellaro, our publicity and public relations expert whose boundless energy, creativity, enthusiasm and dogged determination have allowed us to reach millions of pet lovers; Anne, you are a sparkling fountain of dynamism, beauty and bright ideas.

Thanks go to:

Kimberly Kirberger, for her ongoing support of this project; Ro Miller, Veronica Romero, Lisa Williams, Laurie Hartman, Robin Yerian and Teresa Esparza, for holding down the fort while the rest of us wrote and edited.

Beverly Merson, for her constant encouragement and valuable assistance, as well as her empathy and charm; Bryan Aubrey, an impeccable editor and brilliant mind. Your feedback was useful beyond measure and your assistance made the whole thing fun as well. Well done, old chap; Cindy Jevne Buck, a great collaborator, whose thoughtful and deft editing was greatly appreciated; Betsy Hinchman, a mega-animal-lover and dear friend, for much-needed input and help with story selection and editing; Teresa Williams, Natalie Cleeton and Ruthie Hutchings for superb editing work; Karie Hansen, Carol's office angel, for her important assistance with everything and Craig Herndon, our trusty computer whiz; Jim Rubis, for going the extra mile; the Fairfield Printing crew for their professional friendly service; Sherry, Tom and all the other kind faces at the post office.

Fred C. Angelis, Jack's stepfather, who read and commented on every story in the book. Your thoughtful feedback was extremely useful.

Joel Goodman and Hanoch McCarty for taking the time to send us funny pet cartoons.

We thank some key partners, Bayer Animal Health and Hill's Pet Nutrition, for supporting this book—first as pet lovers, and second as companies that have devoted incredible resources over many years to helping pets live happier, healthier, fuller lives. We would like to single out John Payne from Bayer, and Gilles Guillemette, Blake Hawley, Paula Stack, Dorset Sutton, Chuck Wayner and Bob Wheeler from Hill's, for special recognition. They are extraordinary friends, good stewards of the resources at their disposal and special shepherds of The Bond.

Thanks to all of the people who agreed to dedicate a few weeks to evaluating, commenting upon and improving the stories you see in this book. Their feedback was priceless. The panel of readers included: Fred C. Angelis, Bryan Aubrey, Virginia Becker, Carol J. Benson, Elizabeth Brown, Valdie Burkholder, Joanne Clevenger, Tom Colvin, Wallace L. Croskey, Sharon DeNayer, Robin Downing, D.V.M., Lisa Drucker, Thales Finchum, Mary Gagnon, Elinor Hall, Betsy Hinchman, Allison Janse, Bud and Phyliss Johnston, Bettie Kapiloff, Rita M. Kline, Christi Leahs, M. B. Leininger, D.V.M., Barbara Lomonaco, Ariane Luckey, Holly Moore, Jana Murphy, Janice Phillips, Alisa Pucher, Mary Rubis, Marci Shimoff, Sarah Skoglund, Sharon Cuddy Somers, Laura May Story, C.V.T., Carolyn Strickland, Jan Sturges, Celeste Wallace, Luree Welch, and Mark Wood, D.V.M.

All the people at our publisher, Health Communications, Inc.—especially Peter Vegso, for his guidance and support, and for getting the book into the hands of millions of readers.

Christine Belleris, Matthew Diener, Allison Janse and Lisa Drucker, our skilled and dedicated editors at Health Communications; Randee Feldman, our dear friend and *Chicken Soup for the Soul* product manager; and Tom Sand, who helps us make sure our books are sold worldwide. And, to our hard-working publicists, Kim Weiss and Larry Getlen, who were always there to support us and give us words of encouragement along the way.

Claude Choquette, who manages year after year to get each of our books translated into over twenty languages around the world.

All of Marty's veterinary colleagues who have helped shine energizing light on the sanctity and precious nature of The Bond including: R. K. Anderson, Michael Blackwell, Scott Campbell, Tom Catanzaro, Robin Downing, Steve Garner, Roger Kuhn, Kathy Mitchener, Greg Ogilvie, Peg Rucker, Jack Stephens, Rolan Tripp, Chuck Wayner, Jim Wilson, and the late Leo Bustad and Jan Wolf.

Other pet-partners who have inspired us or helped us in some special way that contributed directly and significantly to the success of this book and the causes it promotes: Kathleen Gilligan, *Spokesman-Review*; Stephanie Hargreaves, *Amazon.com*; Lyn Henderson, *Petsburgh USA/Animal Planet*; Ken Leonardo and Shawn Walker, *Animal Planet*; Ann Oldenberg, *USA Today*. A huge hug and special thanks to our special friend, Patty Neger of *Good Morning America*, who blasts through mountains to help us help pets.

We also wish to thank the more than three thousand people who took the time to submit stories, poems and other pieces for consideration. All of the stories we received were special, but unfortunately the book could only be so long and most could not be included.

Because of the enormity of this project, we may have left out names of some people who helped us along the way. If so, we are sorry. Please know that we really do appreciate all of you.

Introduction

You hold in your hands the ticket for a very special journey: *Chicken Soup for the Cat & Dog Lover's Soul.* This collection of true stories about cats, dogs (and other critters) is guaranteed to warm your heart and lift your spirits—in the same way that our pets cheer and inspire us daily. In fact, those of us who live with cats and dogs know that our animal companions *are* "Chicken Soup for the Soul."

Cat lovers will tell you that cats are poetry in motion, living sculptures at rest, and that the warm weight of a purring cat on your lap is a surefire cure for what ails you.

Dogs also have a tremendous talent for melting our hearts with their unquestioning devotion and unbridled enthusiasm for us, their people. Dog lovers can attest that sharing your life with a dog, or two, can be as entertaining as it is comforting.

In today's crazy, busy world, pets, perhaps more than anything else, teach us to appreciate the simple joys of life.

It all started a long, long time ago, when one day a human reached down and patted a dog or cat as a reward for helping with the hunt, guarding a home or polishing off pesky rodents. In that instant, something magical happened—the human-animal bond was born.

It was then the dog, tail wagging, and the cat, madly purring, joined mankind at the fireside. A new covenant was formed—and since then, mankind has benefited from having a genuine, mutually supportive, and loving relationship with animals.

Today's cat and dog owners love their pets—and they also love to share stories about them. We received thousands of story submissions for this book from cat and dog lovers around the world. It was terribly difficult to choose which stories to include, but finally, we selected the ones that we hoped would deepen people's respect, compassion and appreciation for the entire animal kingdom, as well as for the cats and dogs who share our homes.

We have divided these stories into chapters that encompass the large variety of ways cats, dogs and other animals impact people's lives. We have chapters on love and companionship, on pets as teachers, as healers and as heroes, plus a chapter on saying good-bye to our pets when it comes their time to pass on. Taken together, the stories are powerful proof that the animals in our lives significantly contribute to our happiness and well being.

For truly, our pets lend a touch of grace to our lives. They teach us the real meaning of unconditional love and bring out the kindest and most generous impulses of humanity.

As you read, you may notice that some of the stories in this book are written by well-known celebrities, while others are by individuals who are famous only within the smaller circle of friends and family. But every one of the contributors to this book knows well the power and magic of the human-animal bond. It is our sincere hope that the extraordinary stories in the book will offer inspiration and insight into discovering and receiving the special love of pets, who provide each and every one of us with a little bit of heaven right here on Earth.

Share with Us

We would love to hear your reactions to the stories in this book. Please let us know what your favorite stories were and how they affected you.

Also, please send us stories about pets and animals you would like to see in future editions of *Chicken Soup for the Soul.* You can send us stories you have written or stories written by others you have read and liked.

Send your stories to:

Animal Stories
Chicken Soup for the Soul
P.O. Box 30880
Santa Barbara, CA 93130
Fax: 805-563-2945
e-mail: *stories@canfieldgroup.com*
Web site: *www.chickensoup.com*

We hope you enjoy reading this book as much as we enjoyed compiling, editing and writing it.

You can also visit the *Chicken Soup for the Soul* site on America Online at keyword: chickensoup. The site offers news, chats, excerpts and contests.

1

ON LOVE

Until one has loved an animal, a part of one's soul remains unawakened.

Anatole France

THE FAMILY CIRCUS® **By Bil Keane**

"I like dogs 'cause if you're doing something stupid,
they don't yell at you. They do it with you."

Rescued by Love

On most days you could find him sitting on the wall in front of Saint Mary's Church next to the sign that read "Saint Mary's—A Church for Everyone." No doubt the pastor had meant to attract a larger membership with this billboard invitation, but I'm not sure he was prepared for Bobby. A towering six-footer, weighing in at over two hundred pounds, Bobby was, at twenty-something, a very large child. He spent most of his time waving and smiling at the people driving by, and shouting, "Hey, pal!" to those he recognized.

Bobby called me Goldilocks. He knew me because, as the police department's Animal Control Officer, I was as visible around town as he was. My regular duties were to uphold the leash law, patrol for loose dogs and issue tickets. Bobby had appointed himself my unpaid assistant, and he took his job seriously. Once he waved me down in traffic, ran over to the patrol car and banged on the hood.

"Goldilocks, there's a big dog up the street gonna get hit by a car! You gotta go get 'im now!"

Another time he found a litter of newborn kittens in a garbage can and made it his job to find a home for all of them—including the last one which, at his insistence, I ended up taking home myself!

At first I had loved being the "dog catcher," but as time went by, the job began to get me down. It wasn't the animals—it was the people. I dreaded having to deal with negligent owners. Especially those who no longer wanted their dogs.

In our town the city provided a dog-surrender service with the local SPCA. For a ten-dollar fee, I'd pick up a dog whose owner could no longer keep him, and, more importantly, I'd collect information about him (good with children, medical history, favorite toys, etc.) that would make it easier for him to be adopted.

Unbelievably, sometimes the people most capable of paying this fee chose not to, and abandoned the dog to be picked up as a stray instead. They gave up their best opportunity to increase the dog's chances of finding another home—just to save a measly ten dollars. At first I felt crushed by this kind of behavior, but as time passed I toughened up. Lately, I felt so cynical I was afraid of what was happening to me.

One October when the nights were already dropping below freezing, it occurred to me that I hadn't seen Bobby for a while. He usually spent his nights at the Salvation Army in the winter, so I stopped by and asked about him. No one had seen him. I looked at the phone call log at headquarters to see if he had been making his usual calls to report animals—or just talk. No calls were recorded.

A week later I got a call at headquarters. "Goldilocks," he rasped, "I need you to come." He had a bad cold.

"Bobby! Where are you? Everyone's been looking for you!"

"I'm okay. I'm out in back of the chair factory."

Within a few minutes, I was turning the car off the main street onto a gravel road behind the old chair factory. All at once the road stopped and I was in a large field strewn with debris. In the middle of the field, a rusting station wagon sat on cement blocks.

I approached the car, bent over and knocked lightly on the passenger window. Bobby was curled up tightly in the front seat with his windbreaker thrown over him. Lying next to him was a chocolate Labrador puppy with long gangly legs and ears that he had yet to grow into.

The dog looked up at my knock with bright eyes and a thumping tail. I peered in to get a closer look. The front of the car was filled with empty Styrofoam cups and potato-chip bags. The back of the wagon was covered in soft blankets. Neatly stacked boxes of dog biscuits and a bag of dog food were lined up next to two jugs of bottled water and two chewed rubber balls.

"Bobby, are you okay?" His eyes fluttered open.

"Goldilocks," he croaked. He struggled to sit up and get his bearings. He looked at me and I could see his nose was red and his eyes bleary. He untangled himself and climbed from the car, wincing as he stood.

"Come on with me, Bobby. Get in the patrol car and I'll bring you to the Salvation Army, or the medical center. Okay? It's warm there." I urged.

"No, I'm okay. Social Service says I'm gonna lose my check if I don't go into housing. You gotta take Brownie."

It was true. I couldn't think of a single facility that would allow him to keep his dog. He was only out here in the cold because the Salvation Army didn't allow pets. He started unloading the puppy's supplies and carrying them over to the patrol car. Brownie watched every move he made with adoring eyes. I grabbed a jug of water out of the car and started to help, feeling helpless all the same.

Everything was packed up, except for Brownie. Bobby knelt down and put his hands on each side of the puppy's head. They looked at each other for a long moment and then Brownie started to lick Bobby's face. In one quick movement, the man picked him up and placed him gently in the front seat of the patrol car. He turned to me, his eyes even redder than before.

"Here," he said, handing me a ten-dollar bill. "For the dog pound." I stared open-mouthed at the money. I couldn't believe it. Bobby was paying the surrender fee, though it was probably all the money he had in the world.

I put out my hand and grabbed his arm, "Bobby, don't worry about any fee. They'll understand."

He looked at me. "No, Goldilocks. You told me ten dollars to get a good home, 'member? A home with a kid to play with would be good for Brownie."

He turned from me suddenly and started to walk back toward the rusty station wagon. I knew better than to try to convince him to come with me. He had a mind of his own and treasured his independence, often at the expense of his health and safety.

"Bobby! I'll find him a great home," I called after him, my voice catching in my throat.

He made a noise, but didn't turn around.

As I drove away, Brownie put his muzzle on my lap and fell asleep. There were times I couldn't see the road through my tears.

Brownie was taken home that evening by a police officer who fell in love with him the moment he saw me carry him into the precinct. A year later his Christmas photos showed his little boy and Brownie sitting together in front of a fireplace.

I tried to return Bobby's money, but the station wagon was always empty. Later, I heard that he had gone to a group home in another city and was doing fine. I dropped the ten-dollar bill into the Salvation Army donation box.

I missed my assistant and wished I could have told Bobby what a wonderful job he'd done. He had rescued cats and dogs—and my faith in people, too.

Lisa Duffy-Korpics

Bumpus

There is indeed, no single quality of the cat that man could not emulate to his advantage.

Carl Van Vechten

The big, Maine-coon-type cat was found by firefighters on Father's Day 1996, his long orange fur matted and scorched. He lay, barely alive, in the charred remains of the wildfires that plagued Alaska that year. Even though he must have been in great pain, the cat purred the moment he was touched. When the vet first saw the badly burned cat, he began to cry. He had never seen a living animal with such extensive injuries. The fire had claimed his rear feet and all his front toes. The vet was afraid this latest fire victim might not live long.

But the cat was a survivor. Bumpus, as he came to be called, seemed unaware of the odds against him. Once he began to heal, Bumpus struggled persistently to learn to walk again. Eventually, to everyone's astonishment, the cat succeeded.

Bumpus became a favorite with the rescue volunteers who helped the clinic staff care for him. After facing so much ruin, devastation and death left in the wake of the fires, the presence of this friendly, spirited cat boosted morale and helped the rescuers continue their work.

One of the volunteers, a woman named Sharon, fell in love with the big orange cat. When she was finished in Alaska, she couldn't face leaving him behind, so when Bumpus was well enough to travel, he came home to live with her in Missouri.

Besides doing emergency rescue work, Sharon volunteered at her local humane society. Her specialty was fostering sick or injured kittens in her home and nursing them back to health.

Not long after Bumpus came to live with her, Sharon took in a litter of badly wounded kittens who required special medical attention—two of them eventually needed to have a leg amputated. After the surgery, one of the two-month-old kittens, a female named Minus, came home from the vet, charged out of her carrier and jumped right up on the bed. She didn't even seem to notice she was missing a front leg.

But her brother, Cheerio, named for the circular patterns on his solid orange coat, was traumatized by the operation. Unlike other amputees Sharon had fostered, Cheerio seemed depressed at having lost a limb. He cried constantly, and when he tried to walk, Cheerio always fell and ended up doing a somersault. He took his frustration out on the carpeting, biting and growling at anything around him. At other times, he hid under the bed, refusing to come out.

When Sharon saw how depressed Cheerio was—even his eyes were dull—she worried he might sicken and die. She had to do something, but what? Her eyes fell on Bumpus, serenely grooming himself in a sunny spot on the floor. *He's been through this,* she thought. *Maybe he could help.*

Sharon had isolated the injured kittens in one room in an attempt to keep them less active. When she opened the door to the kittens' room for Bumpus, he made a beeline for the crying kitten, quietly talking to him the whole way. He walked right up to the kitten and, wrapping his furry front paws around Cheerio's damaged little body, held him like a child holds a doll. Then Bumpus began rubbing his head against Cheerio's head and licking the kitten's face. Immediately the crying stopped—and the purring began. The little three-legged kitten, who could not warm to the love of a human, immediately responded to the love of another orange cat—a larger version of himself—who had suffered in this way, too.

Over the next few days, Cheerio and Bumpus became inseparable. Though Cheerio didn't want his littermates around, he stuck close to Bumpus. Often when Sharon looked in on them, she found Bumpus and the kitten curled up together on the bed—the same bed that Cheerio had refused to jump on, hiding under it instead.

Thanks to Bumpus's therapy, Cheerio regained his cheerful disposition and eventually went to live with a devoted new family.

Since then, Bumpus has become Sharon's secret weapon. Any time she has a problem with a kitten, she sends the big cat in and waits for the inevitable miracle.

Bumpus works his magic on people as well. Sharon often takes him to visit children in the pediatric oncology ward at a local hospital. The children are deeply affected when they see what the fire did to Bumpus and witness how his strong will to live has helped him. They reach out eagerly to pet the big, brave cat. And his purring presence seems to quiet their fears.

Sharon doesn't wonder how Bumpus does it, because she's always known. This wonderful cat possesses an enormous quantity of the healing spirit—more than enough to share.

Janine Adams

Agnes and Mattie

The heart that loves is always young.

Greek Proverb

In her ninety-third summer, Agnes, her mind still sharp as an eagle's eye, was wheeled down the dim hall of the nursing home to the last room on the left. Number 109.

"It's a good room, Auntie," her niece, one of two living relatives, said softly. "Nice and clean."

Agnes took in the white walls, the gray linoleum floor and was silent. That night, as she lay on the strange bed, trying to shut out the sounds of the TV from the room next door, she felt as if her real life had ended in that careless moment when she'd tripped over a tree root, shattering her hip and her freedom.

She hung her wooden crucifix above the metal nightstand. Into the top drawer she stuffed old letters, pictures, a box of candy and a broken old dog biscuit she found in the bottom of her purse. In her real life, she'd walked every day, and the neighborhood dogs greeted her eagerly, just as her own dog Rusty used to. She couldn't bear to throw out the biscuit.

Agnes refused to leave her room. She refused to make this place home.

This is not my home, she thought fiercely. *This is nothing like my home.*

She read. She napped. She traveled a worn path in memory back over the years to the big yellow house at the end of the street. Rusty always trotted at her heels as she strolled. She saw the towering shade trees that her beloved Papa had planted as saplings for her and her husband Jack when they first got married.

She and Jack had enjoyed a good marriage. There'd been no children. Just the dogs. The last was Rusty, a tall, proud mutt, who was with her when Jack died of pneumonia. Rusty had slept on the floor by her side of the bed, and every morning she'd reach down first thing to pet him. Now, curled in her bed, she hung an arm over the mattress; for a heart-stopping second, she thought she felt Rusty's mink-soft head and heard the thump of his long, fringed tail. Then the clanging of the meal carts and the bland smell of institutional food brought her back to reality. She cried into her pillow.

The activities director of the nursing home, a woman named Ronnie, was concerned about Agnes. There must be a way to reach her, she thought. Every day Ronnie came to Number 109, pulled up a chair and showed Agnes the activities schedule.

"Look at this," Ronnie would say, her finger sliding down the list. "We have current events, bingo, women's issues, music, sweet memories. Won't you just try one? Or maybe you'd like to go down the hall and meet some people?"

But the elderly lady with the girlish bangs shook her head. "I'm fine," she said, her eyes cloudy with sadness.

One day, in late autumn, Ronnie walked into Agnes's room and spied a dog calendar on top of the nightstand.

"What a handsome dog," Ronnie said, tapping the picture. For the first time she saw a spark in the faded blue eyes.

"I love dogs," Agnes said.

Ronnie's mind started racing. She'd tried in the past to arrange for a dog to visit the nursing home, but it had never worked out. Now it was time to try again. Back in her office, she dialed the number of a local shelter and talked to the shelter director, a woman named Mimi. Halfway through Ronnie's story, Mimi broke in and said, "We have the perfect dog. Her name is Mattie."

For weeks Mimi had been wondering what to do about Mattie. She thought back to the blustery winter night when Mattie, a large black mutt, had been brought in as a stray. She shivered in the doorway, her coat mud-caked and wet. Despite her appearance, she was dignified, like a lady who'd fallen on hard times.

"Here, girl," Mimi called. Shyly the dog came, placing a dirty paw on Mimi's knee, then removing it, as if to say, "I'm sorry. I forgot about the mud."

They bathed her and combed out the mats, from which they took her name—Mattie. No one claimed her. She lived in a kennel run with four to five other dogs, waiting to be adopted. Months turned to years. Each time people came to look, competing canines raced to the gate, barking and furiously wagging their tails. Mattie trailed modestly behind, shyly raising trusting brown eyes. Like a gem that doesn't shine, she was passed over. She became a lonely, institutional survivor. Like Agnes.

Now, Mimi walked down the long, noisy kennel aisle to a large run. "Mattie," she called into the maze of barking, wriggling canines. The big, long-haired mutt padded to the gate, calmly easing herself through the crush of younger, excitable dogs. She pressed her setter-type nose into the wire mesh.

"Hey, old girl," Mimi said, getting down to eye level. "A lady named Agnes needs you." Mattie's ears perked.

Not many days later, Mimi walked Mattie down the dim hall of the nursing home to the last room on the left. Number 109. The dog was freshly bathed and groomed. Her ears were erect, and her tail was raised high with anticipation. They turned the corner of the doorway and Mattie's nails clicked on the gray linoleum. Agnes looked up from her chair; the book she'd been reading slipped off her lap. Her mouth dropped. Tears filled her eyes and spilled down her cheeks.

"I thought I'd never see a dog again," she sobbed.

"Her name's Mattie," Mimi said.

"Here, Mattie. Here, girl," Agnes called. Mattie trotted over, leash dragging, waving her long, fringed tail just as Rusty used to. Agnes buried her face in the soft fur. Mattie scrunched as close as she could get and placed a paw on Agnes's lap. She looked up adoringly, her eyes begging friendship.

Agnes stroked her silky head, whispering, "Hello, Mattie, girl. There's a good girl." Her wizened face was soft and glowing. Mattie laid her head in Agnes's lap and sighed as Agnes scratched behind her ears.

Suddenly, Agnes remembered something. With the aid of her walker, she hobbled eagerly to the nightstand, Mattie trotting at her heels. The old lady opened the drawer, retrieving the crumbling dog biscuit she hadn't been able to throw away. Mattie's ears lifted. Daintily she took the biscuit, then cleaned the crumbs from the floor.

Before they left, Mimi promised Agnes they'd come every week. Agnes flipped through the dog calendar, marking in all the Tuesdays with Mattie's name.

Now when Mattie arrived for her visits, the drawer of the metal cabinet was always stocked with favorite treats. Ever the lady, Mattie would ask politely by sniffing the drawer, then sitting and waiting. She never had to wait long.

As the months went by, Agnes began to show an interest in the events around her. Soon Mattie was accompanying Agnes to drawing classes, flower-arranging workshops and gospel songfests. She sat with her head in Agnes's lap as Agnes talked with friends, and she thumped her tail at Agnes's happy chuckle.

Encouraged by the change in Agnes, Mimi took Mattie to visit residents at other nursing homes. Mattie's days became full as well. Before long, many volunteers were taking dogs to visit old people and children throughout the area. The successful Golden Outreach Program was officially launched.

When Agnes celebrated her one-hundredth birthday, Mattie, herself a senior citizen and still a regular visitor, came to celebrate. As Agnes ate her cake and visited with her many guests, she stroked the now-grizzled head resting in her lap and frequently returned the old dog's devoted gaze. Finding each other had transformed their lives, as well as the lives of others through Golden Outreach—a program born of the love between one elderly lady and a gentle dog.

Shari Smyth

Friends in Arms

"Have you a pet who would make a good War Dog?"

The message went out by radio and newspapers to citizens of England in July 1942 at the height of the Allied struggle with Germany during World War II. "The British War Office needs strong, intelligent dogs to be trained for guard and patrol duty, rescue work, as messengers and mine detectors," the message continued. "If you have such a dog and would consider lending him to the service of your country, please call the war office."

Eight-year-old Barry Railton heard the appeal at his home in Tolworth, Surrey. He looked at his six-year-old cream-colored German shepherd Khan, whom he had owned since the dog was a puppy. "Would you like to be a War Dog?" he asked Khan.

He went to his father, Harry Railton. "Could I volunteer Khan to be a War Dog?"

Railton had heard the radio appeal. "Are you sure you want to volunteer Khan? He is intelligent enough and has always been eager to learn, but remember, he would be gone for a long time."

"How long?"

Railton shook his head. "Who knows when this war will

end? I can't say how long he would be gone."

Barry patted the dog's head. "Khan is smart. If the country needs him, I think he should go."

"Think about this, Barry. He might not come back."

"He'll come back, all right." Barry spoke with the optimism of a child.

Harry Railton phoned the war office, and soon papers arrived for him to fill out. In a few weeks, it was time for Khan to leave his Norfolk home for the War Dog Training School. Barry kissed the top of Khan's head and cried as he said good-bye, but the boy remained steadfast in his confidence that Khan would return.

The training school requirements were a breeze for Khan, and on graduation he was assigned to the 6th Battalion Cameronians, based in Lanarkshire, Scotland.

Corporal Jimmy Muldoon was assigned to work with Khan. Right from the beginning, they became good friends. They worked together on guard patrol for two years.

Then in 1944, Kahn and Muldoon were assigned to take part in the Allied forces invasion of German-held western Europe. In boats, men of the 6th Battalion were to outflank a causeway leading to a Dutch island and then wade ashore along a mile-long stretch of mud bank.

An assault craft, packed with men and equipment, was launched at high tide, in the early hours of the morning. As the boat approached the shore, enemy guns fired. A shell hit the boat amidship and men, dogs and equipment catapulted into the air. Muldoon and Khan were thrown into the icy water as the boat, riddled by gunfire, broke in two and sank.

Men struggled to keep afloat and hold their rifles above the water. Khan rose to the surface and swam toward the lights on the shore. When the dog neared the bank, he sank into the mud, but he was able to scramble up onto firmer ground. He stopped and stood still.

The flash of searchlights and the blasts of gunfire raked the struggling men in the mud. In spite of the cracking of artillery and the screams of injured and dying men, Khan must have heard the voice of Johnny Muldoon calling to him. Unable to swim, Muldoon was desperately battling to stay afloat two hundred yards from the shore. Khan plunged back into the frigid water and, guided by Muldoon's calls, swam to his master. Grabbing the collar of Muldoon's tunic, Khan paddled through the water and mud and at last dragged Muldoon to the shore. Man and dog collapsed on the bank.

Litter bearers found Muldoon and carried him to a field hospital. Khan stayed right beside his bed the entire time the corporal was in hospital. When Muldoon and Khan returned to the regiment, the battalion commander nominated Khan for the Dickin Medal, named for Maria Dickin, founder of the People's Dispensary for Sick Animals, a British charitable organization. The Dickin Medal was awarded to eighteen dogs, eight horses, thirty-seven pigeons and one cat during World War II and its aftermath for service to the armed forces or civil defense.

Khan's medal was presented March 27, 1945, by the commanding officer at a full battalion parade. The citation on the medal read, "For rescuing Corporal Muldoon from drowning under heavy shell fire of the assault at Walcheren November 1944, while serving with the 6th Cameronians."

Corporal Muldoon wrote many letters to the war office, asking to be allowed to keep Khan after the war ended. The Railton family, however, asked for their dog to be returned.

When the war ended, Corporal Muldoon was demobilized, and he returned to civilian life in Strathaven, Scotland. Khan was sent for six months to the quarantine station not far from the Railton's home in Surrey. Barry Railton, now twelve, visited the quarantined Khan three times a week. At the end of six months, Khan returned to the Railton home.

The following year, Khan was invited to participate in the National Dog Tournament. Harry Railton wrote to Muldoon, asking him to lead Khan in the Special War Dog Parade.

Muldoon was ecstatic at the thought of seeing Khan again, even if only for a little while. Two hundred of the most intelligent, skillful dogs in Great Britain, including sixteen Dickin medalists, were to appear in the parade.

On the day of the parade, Khan was one of a huge crowd of dogs milling around on the grounds. Suddenly he stopped, lifted his head, his ears at the alert. He sniffed the air. His legs tensed. He jerked the leash from Mr. Railton's hand and bolted, a streak of fur, across the parade grounds, barking loudly.

Ten thousand people in the spectator stands saw the joyful reunion of man and dog. Applause thundered as Muldoon and Khan took their places in the parade line.

Afterwards Harry Railton searched out Muldoon in the crowd. He watched as Muldoon, tears bathing his cheeks, buried his head in the dog's fur. Sobbing, he held out the leash to Railton.

Railton shook his head. "Barry and I talked it over during the parade," he said. "Tell him, Barry."

"We think Khan belongs with you," said Barry, the tears shining in his own eyes. "He's yours. Take him home."

A grateful Muldoon left with Khan on the overnight express for Glasgow. Next morning when they left the train, they were welcomed at the station by a crowd of press members. At the end of the interview, Johnny Muldoon told the reporters, "Pray God we will live out our lives together."

His prayer was answered.

Rosamond Young

The Yorkshire Christmas Cat

My strongest memory of Christmas will always be bound up with a certain little cat. I first saw her when I was called to see one of Mrs. Ainsworth's dogs, and I looked in some surprise at the furry black creature sitting before the fire. "I didn't know you had a cat," I said.

The lady smiled. "We haven't, this is Debbie."

"Debbie?"

"Yes, at least that's what we call her. She's a stray. Comes here two or three times a week and we give her some food. I don't know where she lives but I believe she spends a lot of her time around one of the farms along the road."

"Do you ever get the feeling that she wants to stay with you?"

"No." Mrs. Ainsworth shook her head. "She's a timid little thing. Just creeps in, has some food, then flits away. There's something so appealing about her, but she doesn't seem to want to let me or anybody into her life."

I looked again at the little cat. "But she isn't just having food today."

"That's right. It's a funny thing but every now and again she slips through here into the lounge and sits by the fire for a few minutes. It's as though she was giving herself a treat."

"Yes . . . I see what you mean." There was no doubt there was something unusual in the attitude of the little animal. She was sitting bolt upright on the thick rug which lay before the fireplace in which the coals glowed and flamed. She made no effort to curl up or wash herself or do anything other than gaze quietly ahead. And there was something in the dusty black of her coat, the half-wild scrawny look of her, that gave me a clue. This was a special event in her life, a rare and wonderful thing. She was lapping up a comfort undreamed of in her daily existence.

As I watched she turned, crept soundlessly from the room and was gone. "That's always the way with Debbie," Mrs. Ainsworth laughed. "She never stays more than ten minutes or so, then she's off."

Mrs. Ainsworth was a plumpish, pleasant-faced woman in her forties and the kind of client veterinary surgeons dream of—well off, generous, and the owner of three cosseted Basset hounds. And it only needed the habitually mournful expression of one of the dogs to deepen a little and I was round there post-haste. Today one of the Bassets had raised its paw and scratched its ear a couple of times and that was enough to send his mistress scurrying to the phone in great alarm.

So my visits to the Ainsworth home were frequent but undemanding, and I had ample opportunity to look out for the little cat that had intrigued me. On one occasion I spotted her nibbling daintily from a saucer at the kitchen door. As I watched she turned and almost floated on light footsteps into the hall and then through the lounge door. The three Bassets were already in residence draped snoring on the fireside rug, but they seemed to be used to Debbie because two of them sniffed her in a bored manner and the third merely cocked a sleepy eye at her before flopping back on the rich pile.

Debbie sat among them in her usual posture; upright,

intent, gazing absorbedly into the glowing coals. This time I tried to make friends with her. I approached her carefully but she leaned away as I stretched out my hand. However, by patient wheedling and soft talk I managed to touch her and gently stroke her cheek with one finger. There was a moment when she responded by putting her head on one side and rubbing back against my hand, but soon she was ready to leave. Once outside the house she darted quickly along the road then through a gap in a hedge, and the last I saw was the little black figure flitting over the rain-swept grass of a field.

"I wonder where she goes," I murmured half to myself.

Mrs. Ainsworth appeared at my elbow. "That's something we've never been able to find out."

It must have been nearly three months before I heard from Mrs. Ainsworth, and in fact I had begun to wonder at the Bassets' long symptomless run when she came on the phone.

It was Christmas morning and she was apologetic. "Mr. Herriot, I'm so sorry to bother you today of all days. I should think you want a rest at Christmas like anybody else." But her natural politeness could not hide the distress in her voice.

"Please don't worry about that," I said. "Which one is it this time?"

"It's not one of the dogs. It's . . . Debbie."

"Debbie? She's at your house now?"

"Yes . . . but there's something wrong. Please come quickly."

Driving through the marketplace, I thought again that Darrowby on Christmas Day was like Dickens come to life; the empty square with the snow thick on the cobbles and hanging from the eaves of the fretted lines of roofs; the shops closed and the colored lights of the Christmas trees winking at the windows of the clustering houses, warmly inviting against the cold white bulk of the fells behind.

Mrs. Ainsworth's home was lavishly decorated with tinsel and holly, rows of drinks stood on the sideboard and the rich aroma of turkey and sage-and-onion stuffing wafted from the kitchen. But her eyes were full of pain as she led me through to the lounge.

Debbie was there all right, but this time everything was different. She wasn't sitting upright in her usual position; she was stretched quite motionless on her side, and huddled close to her lay a tiny black kitten.

I looked down in bewilderment. "What's happened here?"

"It's the strangest thing," Mrs. Ainsworth replied. "I haven't seen her for several weeks then she came in about two hours ago—sort of staggered into the kitchen, and she was carrying the kitten in her mouth. She took it through the lounge and laid it on the rug, and at first I was amused. But I could see all was not well because she sat as she usually does, but for a long time—over an hour— then she lay down like this and she hasn't moved."

I knelt on the rug and passed my hand over Debbie's neck and ribs. She was thinner than ever, her fur dirty and mud-caked. She did not resist as I gently opened her mouth. The tongue and mucous membranes were abnormally pale and the lips ice-cold against my fingers. When I pulled down her eyelid and saw the dead white conjunctiva, a knell sounded in my mind. I palpated the abdomen with a grim certainty as to what I would find and there was no surprise, only a dull sadness as my fingers closed around a hard lobulated mass deep among the viscera. Massive lymphosarcoma. Terminal and hopeless. I put my stethoscope on her heart and listened to the increasingly faint, rapid beat then I straightened up and sat on the rug looking sightlessly into the fireplace, feeling the warmth of the flames on my face.

Mrs. Ainsworth's voice seemed to come from afar. "Is she ill, Mr. Herriot?"

I hesitated. "Yes . . . yes, I'm afraid so. She has a malignant growth." I stood up. "There's absolutely nothing you can do. I'm sorry."

"Oh!" Her hand went to her mouth and she looked at me wide-eyed. When at last she spoke her voice trembled. "Well, you must put her to sleep immediately. It's the only thing to do. We can't let her suffer."

"Mrs. Ainsworth," I said. "There's no need. She's dying now—in a coma—far beyond suffering."

She turned quickly away from me and was very still as she fought with her emotions. Then she gave up the struggle and dropped to her knees beside Debbie. "Oh, poor little thing!" She sobbed and stroked the cat's head again and again as the tears fell unchecked on the matted fur. "What she must have come through! I feel I ought to have done more for her."

For a few moments I was silent, feeling her sorrow, so discordant among the bright seasonal colors of this festive room. Then I spoke gently. "Nobody could have done more than you," I said. "Nobody could have been kinder."

"But I'd have kept her here—in comfort. It must have been terrible out there in the cold when she was so desperately ill—I daren't think about it. And having kittens, too—I . . . I wonder how many she did have?"

I shrugged. "I don't suppose we'll ever know. Maybe just this one. It happens sometimes. And she brought it to you, didn't she?"

"Yes . . . that's right . . . she did . . . she did." Mrs. Ainsworth reached out and lifted the bedraggled black morsel. She smoothed her finger along the muddy fur and the tiny mouth opened in a soundless miaow. "Isn't it strange? She was dying and she brought her kitten here. And on Christmas Day."

I bent and put my hand on Debbie's heart. There was no beat.

I looked up. "I'm afraid she's gone." I lifted the small body, almost feather light, wrapped it in the sheet which had been spread on the rug and took it to the car. When I came back Mrs. Ainsworth was still stroking the kitten. The tears had dried on her cheeks and she was bright-eyed as she looked at me. "I've never had a cat before," she said.

I smiled. "Well it looks as though you've got one now."

And she certainly had. The kitten grew rapidly into a sleek, handsome cat with a boisterous nature which earned him the name of Buster. In every way he was the opposite to his timid little mother. Not for him the privations of the secret outdoor life; he stalked the rich carpets of the Ainsworth home like a king and the ornate collar he always wore added something more to his presence.

On my visits I watched his development with delight, but the occasion which stays in my mind was the following Christmas Day, a year from his arrival.

I was out on my rounds as usual. I can't remember when I haven't had to work on Christmas Day because the animals have never got around to recognizing it as a holiday; but with the passage of the years the vague resentment I used to feel has been replaced by philosophical acceptance. After all, as I tramped around the hillside barns in the frosty air I was working up a better appetite for my turkey than all the millions lying in bed or slumped by the fire; and this was aided by the innumerable aperitifs I received from the hospitable farmers. I was on my way home, bathed in a rosy glow. I had consumed several whiskies—the kind the inexpert Yorkshiremen pour as though it was ginger ale—and I had finished with a glass of old Mrs. Earnshaw's rhubarb wine which had seared its way straight to my toenails. I heard the cry as I was passing Mrs. Ainsworth's house. "Merry Christmas, Mr. Herriot!" She was letting a visitor out of the front door and she waved at me gaily. "Come in and have a drink to warm you up."

I didn't need warming up, but I pulled in to the curb without hesitation. In the house there was all the festive cheer of last year and the same glorious whiff of sage and onion which set my gastric juices surging. But there was not the sorrow; there was Buster.

He was darting up to each of the dogs in turn, ears pricked, eyes blazing with devilment, dabbing a paw at them, then streaking away.

Mrs. Ainsworth laughed. "You know, he plagues the life out of them. Gives them no peace."

She was right. To the Bassets, Buster's arrival was rather like the intrusion of an irreverent outsider into an exclusive London club. For a long time they had led a life of measured grace; regular sedate walks with their mistress, superb food in ample quantities and long snoring sessions on the rugs and armchairs. Their days followed one upon the other in unruffled calm. And then came Buster.

He was dancing up to the youngest dog again, sideways this time, head on one side, goading him. When he started boxing with both paws it was too much even for the Basset. He dropped his dignity and rolled over with the cat in a brief wrestling match.

"I want to show you something." Mrs. Ainsworth lifted a hard rubber ball from the sideboard and went out to the garden, followed by Buster. She threw the ball across the lawn and the cat bounded after it over the frosted grass, the muscles rippling under the black sheen of his coat. He seized the ball in his teeth, brought it back to his mistress, dropped it and waited expectantly. She threw it and he brought it back again. I gasped incredulously. A feline retriever!

The Bassets looked on disdainfully. Nothing would ever have induced them to chase a ball, but Buster did it again and again as though he would never tire of it.

Mrs. Ainsworth turned to me. "Have you ever seen anything like that?"

"No," I replied. "I never have. He is a most remarkable cat."

She snatched Buster from his play and we went back into the house where she held him close to her face, laughing as he purred and arched himself ecstatically against her cheek.

As I looked at him, a picture of health and contentment, my mind went back to his mother. Was it too much to think that that dying little creature, with the last of her strength, had carried her kitten to the only haven of comfort and warmth she had ever known in the hope that it would be cared for there? Maybe it was.

But it seemed I wasn't the only one with such fancies. Mrs. Ainsworth turned to me and though she was smiling her eyes were wistful. "Debbie would be pleased," she said.

I nodded. "Yes, she would. . . . It was just a year ago today she brought him, wasn't it?"

"That's right." She hugged Buster to her again. "The best Christmas present I ever had."

James Herriot, D.V.M.

Princess Was a Nuisance

She was only a mixed-breed scrap of a dog. Her colors were black and tan, but her eyes were what made me take her. They were warm and had gold flecks in them. Other than that, she was nothing unusual, or as my father put it, "A damn nuisance." I called her Princess.

Dad preferred his hunting dog, a massive hound named Rudy, who followed him everywhere. Rudy had status; Princess was barely tolerated. At mealtimes, she would wait until Rudy ate, then settle for scraps. She slept beside my bed, content that at least one person loved her.

One day Princess started barking like mad near the railroad tracks that ran beside our house. We realized something was wrong when Dad said Rudy had gotten loose. We followed Princess, who led us to Rudy's lifeless body beside the tracks. His neck was broken.

Dad stumbled back to the house in shock. The task of burying the huge dog fell to me. As I dug, Princess sat next to the body with a perplexed look in her eyes. When I lowered Rudy into the grave, she showed alarm. When I began to cover him with dirt, she became visibly agitated, so much so that I hurriedly unburied Rudy and made certain he was dead.

When I finished, Princess tried to unbury him. I chased her away. She tried again. I held her to me and told her through my tears that her friend was gone. An odd expression came over her features, and she walked over to the grave and lay across Rudy's final resting place.

That night, I tried to get her inside, but she wouldn't budge. I tried to get her to eat, but she ignored the bowl. Next day, the same thing. That night, a howling rainstorm roared in. She was still there the following morning and kept her vigil throughout the rainy day. I told Dad I was worried, but he said, "She'll be in when she gets hungry and wet enough." He clearly wasn't concerned over what he considered an inferior animal. More important, he was doing his own grieving. Until then, he had not been able to even look at his pet's grave.

The next morning, Princess was still in place. I ran downstairs, determined this time to drag her off. I stopped when I saw Dad emerge from the parlor carrying his buffalo-robe blanket. No one was ever allowed to touch that blanket. He told me to stay put. I watched from the window as he shook out the blanket above Princess's soaked form, wrapped her up, and lifted her into his arms like a child. He told us to get towels and warm soapy water. My sister and I wanted to care for her, but he wouldn't allow it. Never looking up as he worked on the bedraggled animal, he said the job was his alone.

He cleaned off the mud and dried her shivering body. Then he took her in his lap.

For a long time he sat there, tears running down his cheeks, the only sound in the room the rain beating on the windows. Finally, he said quietly that he had never known such loyalty from man or beast.

And so for as long as she lived, Princess sat at his feet, slept on his bed and ate from his plate—an honored member of our family.

Carol Ann Baum

A Horse and His Boy

When Wayne, my oldest son, turned two, I bought a four-year-old, black Appaloosa gelding named Sonny. The two quickly bonded. Even though Wayne was too small to ride Sonny, the two were inseparable. We installed a fence around our well-grassed sideyard and allowed Sonny to graze freely. He often came right up to the house. In fact, Sonny hadn't been with us long when he ripped the screen off Wayne's bedroom window. After that, I'd often find my son reaching out the window to pet Sonny or to give him food. And I'd even see Sonny's black head inside the window, snoozing, while my son slept in his bed.

One day, I put Wayne to bed for his midday nap and busied myself with my vegetable canning. Time slipped past until I glanced at the clock. Wayne hated naptime and usually slept for only an hour or so. I suddenly realized he'd been quiet for nearly two. I walked to his bedroom and peered around the door. The bed was empty.

I called his name but heard no reply or noises of his playing. I searched under the bed and in his closet. I kept calling him and walking quickly through each room. Perspiration broke out on my neck as it suddenly hit me. Wayne was not in the house!

This was my worst nightmare. Our house was surrounded by wilderness. A wildcat frequently raided our
henhouse and would view a small child as perfect prey.
Rattlesnakes, copperheads and cottonmouths slithered
through the thickets. If that was not enough danger, a
fishpond nestled in the pasture just below the house.

I ran to the front door. It was still latched with a hook
and eye far above my son's reach. The back door was the
same. I stood in stunned amazement for a moment, until I
remembered Wayne's open window. Fear rose in my heart
as I pictured my toddler trying to climb out the window.
The drop to the ground would have been more than five
feet. Surely he would have hit the ground hard enough to
make him cry. Why wouldn't I have heard him?

Running out the door, I yelled for Wayne. Thankfully,
he wasn't lying beneath his window. But where was he?
Sonny was lying in the middle of our yard, with his back
toward me. As I looked at Sonny, he swung his head up
and down, but never made an effort to get up. But Sonny
was often lazy in the midday summer sun. Still each time
I yelled for Wayne, Sonny swung his head up and down,
more vigorously than before. I made a mental note that
once I found Wayne, I'd have to put fly wipe on Sonny's
face. The flies must really be bothering him.

Yelling at the top of my lungs and beginning to panic, I
raced to the fishpond. No Wayne. I ran to the barn, but
again I didn't find him. He had to be in the woods. I could
travel faster and further if I rode Sonny. I raced across the
yard to Sonny and dashed around his rump.

There, stretched to the four winds across Sonny's four
legs, lay Wayne, sound asleep. His head rested on Sonny's
front legs and one foot was propped on the horse's hip,
the other on one of Sonny's back legs. Sonny lifted his
head up and down once more before placing his muzzle
across Wayne's chest. Now I understood what all that

head bobbing was about. Sonny couldn't stand up without sending the child tumbling, and if he nickered, he'd wake the boy. Sonny had been doing everything he could to let me know Wayne was safely sleeping in his embrace.

I carefully picked Wayne up, carried him to his bedroom and eased him into bed. Sonny had already poked his head through the window by the time I got to the bedroom door. He whickered, and Wayne roused. I backed up so I could watch without being seen. Wayne went to the window and grasped Sonny's mane. Sonny lifted his head, and Wayne wrapped his arms around Sonny's neck. He was carried out through the window and slowly lowered onto the ground. I wouldn't have believed it if I hadn't seen it. Another mystery solved.

When my husband came home, we discussed how we could stop another "window escape." We replaced the screen and nailed boards across the window at intervals that were too close for Wayne's head to fit through. The boy pouted, and the horse whinnied on the other side for a few days—until Sonny managed to get his teeth between the boards and rip off the new screen. His head still wouldn't fit, but now he could at least get his nose between the boards.

With Wayne now safe in his room, I enjoyed walking by and seeing Sonny's black muzzle thrust through the slats. And when my husband came home from work, often his first view of the house showed a huge, black horse pressed against the white boards with the lower part of his face disappearing inside the window.

Even when the cold weather forced me to close the window, Sonny remained outside with his face pressed against the glass, the comfort of a stable forsaken to be near his boy.

Alicia Karen Elkins

Greyfriars Bobby

In death they were not parted.

Sometime in the mid-1850s, a Skye terrier came to live on a farm in the hills outside of Edinburgh, Scotland. Named Bobby, the little dog attached himself to Auld Jock, the farmer's shepherd.

Auld Jock was a fixture in those Scottish hills, and soon he and Bobby became inseparable, tending the farmer's sheep and traveling once a week to market in the capital. Market day always featured a special lunch at the Greyfriars dining rooms. When the Edinburgh Castle gun sounded at 1:00 P.M., Jock and Bobby left whatever they were doing and headed for the dining room where the man and his dog shared their meal . . . sometimes over the protests of the manager.

Within a couple of years after meeting Bobby, Jock's age began to weigh on him, and he contracted tuberculosis. He headed into retirement, taking small quarters in Edinburgh. Forced to leave Bobby at the farm, Jock sadly bid his companion good-bye and moved to the capital alone.

However, the next day, when Jock showed up at the Greyfriars dining rooms at the sound of the one o'clock gun, he was astonished to see Bobby rushing in to join him. Bobby had escaped from the farm and run all the way down from the hills to make sure he kept up their market-day custom. Reunited, the two friends enjoyed their lunch, then returned to Jock's rooms where the old man made plans to return the little terrier to the farm the next day.

It was never to be. Before he could return Bobby, Jock's tuberculosis overtook him, and he died. Two days later neighbors found Bobby guarding the body, at first not allowing anyone to come near. Jock's few friends arranged a simple funeral.

As the mourner's procession moved through the streets of Edinburgh, a small, distraught dog trailed behind them, following the casket containing his friend to Greyfriars Cemetery. The cemetery used for the royalty of Scotland was the final resting place for Auld Jock.

When the funeral service ended and the mourners departed, Bobby remained, lying on the grave, forlorn, a lone dog mourning his adored master. However, such revered ground wasn't for the convenience of dogs. James Brown, the sexton, spotted Bobby lying on the newly made mound and chased him from the hallowed ground.

But the next morning, when Brown started doing his chores, he again spotted a sleeping dog on top of the most recent grave. Bobby must have sneaked back to the grave as soon as the sky had turned dark and spent the night there.

Brown chased him from the cemetery again, but that night Bobby returned and lay down once more on his master's grave. The next morning was cold and wet and when the sexton saw the faithful animal lying shivering on the grave, he took pity on him. He gave him some food, and though it meant breaking the cemetery's rules, Brown allowed Bobby to stay near the grave. He even taught Bobby to hide on Sundays, when the churchyard had its largest number of visitors. To the church's high-ranking patrons, having a dog in the cemetery would have been next to blasphemy.

For a couple of weeks Bobby kept lonely vigil, without a break, ignoring even his own needs. Then one day, at the sound of the castle gun, he showed up at the Greyfriars dining rooms. The innkeeper recognized him as Auld Jock's dog and fed him. From that day forward, Bobby arrived at the inn every day at one o'clock to be fed.

Once he'd gained the sexton's friendship and found a way to get regular meals, Bobby lived by the grave of the shepherd unhindered for nine years, until 1867, when the city began to round up all unlicensed dogs. Dogcatchers nabbed Bobby and took him to Edinburgh's version of the pound.

When the terrier failed to answer the one o'clock gun one day, the innkeeper guessed what had happened. He rescued Bobby from being destroyed by telling the story of the faithful little dog to the city's Burgher Court. The innkeeper's plea brought Bobby instant fame, and none other than the Lord Provost of Edinburgh paid for the dog's license. He even ordered a collar made with an inscription that read, "Greyfriars Bobby. From Lord Provost. 1867. Licensed."

Sporting his new collar, Bobby had the run of the city. Still, he held to his routine, guarding his master's grave and dropping by for lunch at the Greyfriars every day at one. Bobby's fame and popularity spread until he no longer had to hide from visitors—in fact, many visitors came to the cemetery just to see him. More than one artist painted the dog's portrait as he lay near his master's simple grave.

In 1872, after maintaining his vigil over Auld Jock's

grave for fourteen years, Greyfriars Bobby, now old and feeble, died. The entire city mourned his death. In secret, the sexton dug Bobby a small grave near Jock's then marked it with only a rosebush. If the church wouldn't let dogs visit the cemetery, how could it allow a dog to be buried there?

Upon learning about the inspiring little dog, a Scottish noblewoman, Baroness Burdett-Coutts, commissioned a work to honor Bobby, which would stand on Candle-maker Row, outside the churchyard gates. A year after Bobby's death, city officials unveiled the monument: a solid granite column, with water from bubbling fountains that poured into two basins; and on top, a bronze likeness of Bobby which faced longingly toward the gates of the cemetery.

At last, in the early 1930s, the church allowed American donors to erect a small stone in the Greyfriars Cemetery marking the grave of the faithful little dog. Today, when you walk inside the gates of the old cemetery, the first headstone you see pays tribute to the endurance of love beyond death. It reads:

> Greyfriars Bobby.
> Died 14th Jan 1872.
> Aged 16 years.
> Let his loyalty & devotion
> be a lesson to us all.

Tim Jones

A Friend in Need

Brownie and Spotty were neighbor dogs who met every day to play together. Like pairs of dogs you can find in most any neighborhood, these two loved each other and played together so often that they had worn a path through the grass of the field between their respective houses.

One evening, Brownie's family noticed that Brownie hadn't returned home. They went looking for him with no success. Brownie didn't show up the next day, and, despite their efforts to find him, by the next week he was still missing.

Curiously, Spotty showed up at Brownie's house alone, barking, whining and generally pestering Brownie's human family. Busy with their own lives, they just ignored the nervous little neighbor dog.

Finally, one morning Spotty refused to take "no" for an answer. Ted, Brownie's owner, was steadily harassed by the furious, adamant little dog. Spotty followed Ted about, barking insistently, then darting toward a nearby empty lot and back, as if to say, "Follow me! It's urgent!"

Eventually, Ted followed the frantic Spotty across the empty lot as Spotty paused to race back and bark encouragingly. The little dog led the man under a fence, past clumps of trees, to a desolate spot a half mile from the house. There Ted found his beloved Brownie alive, one of his hind legs crushed in a steel leghold trap. Horrified, Ted now wished he'd taken Spotty's earlier appeals seriously. Then Ted noticed something quite remarkable.

Spotty had done more than simply lead Brownie's human to his trapped friend. In a circle around the injured dog, Ted found an array of dog food and table scraps— which were later identified as the remains of every meal Spotty had been fed that week!

Spotty had been visiting Brownie regularly, in a single-minded quest to keep his friend alive by sacrificing his own comfort. Spotty had evidently stayed with Brownie to protect him from predators, snuggling with him at night to keep him warm and nuzzling him to keep his spirits up.

Brownie's leg was treated by a veterinarian and he recovered. For many years thereafter, the two families watched the faithful friends frolicking and chasing each other down that well-worn path between their houses.

Stephanie Laland

Lucy

The honeymoon was definitely over. Although Larry and I had been married less than a year, we were headed for disaster. My expectations of marriage were high—probably too high. My parents' relationship had been happy, loving, full of laughter and mutual respect. Larry didn't come to the marriage with the same kind of dreams, and he felt pressured by my needs. Our home was not a happy one, with tensions, resentment and hurt feelings seething just below the surface. We just couldn't communicate.

During this rocky time, I had the idea to get a dog. Larry and I talked about it, and he said a dog would be fine, as long as it wasn't a "yappy little thing." He had grown up with German shepherds and liked them. I called the local pound and asked if they had a German shepherd who needed a home. It just so happened that they had a white German shepherd mix, so I went right over to see the dog.

At the pound, I made my way to the white dog's cage. She was part shepherd all right, but the other part must have been Mexican jumping bean. She moved like she had springs on the bottoms of her four paws, continuously jumping five feet in the air and barking enthusiastically—just the way a kid waves his arms and yells, "Pick me! Pick me! Me! Me! Me!" when captains are choosing their teams. I took her out of the run and she tore around the room, stopping only to jump up on me and try to lick my face as she streaked by. I was impressed by her vibrant personality.

I brought Larry to see her a few hours later, and he liked her well enough for us to walk out with her. She strained on her leash, obviously eager to leave the pound behind.

We named her Lucy, and she and I became best friends. I loved getting up in the early morning and walking her when the streets were quiet. A long walk in the park every afternoon became another wonderful part of our daily routine. She liked to be wherever I was, watching me or snoozing in the sun as I went about my housework and gardening. I took her in the car when I went into town to do errands, and she sat in the backseat, her nose stuck out of the window to sniff the wind. I found her company entertaining and comforting. Larry seemed to like her, too.

As the weeks went by, I felt happier and more settled. I have to admit that I talked to Lucy when we were alone together during the day. I even made up silly songs and sang them to her when we were out driving. She seemed to like the sound of my voice, and she wagged her tail and always looked right at me when I told her things. I relished my position at the center of her universe.

One evening, I was showing Larry a silly game that Lucy and I played—I would stand in front of Lucy and poke her with my right hand a few times, then when she was expecting a poke from the right, I'd poke her from the left. Then a poke from the top, and then from the bottom. She seemed to love trying to figure out where my hand would come from next. We were playing this game when Larry came up behind me and started playing, too. I leaned back into the warm bulk of Larry's chest, and his arms closed around me. We stood like that for a moment, before I turned around and held him tight. We hadn't done that for a long time.

Things began to fall into place after that. All that canine companionship had enabled me to stop demanding love and attention from Larry—and as I felt happier, I was able to be more loving and certainly more fun to be around. Our wounds began to heal, and our marriage blossomed.

We've been married for over ten years now. When people ask me the secret of our happy partnership, I always tell them, "It's simple. If you want dog-like devotion . . . get a *dog!*"

Carol Kline

Weep Not

The God of the whole gave a living soul
To furred and to feathered thing.
And I am my brother's keeper.
And I will fight his fight;
And speak for the beast and bird
Till the world shall set things right.

Ella Wheeler Wilcox

If you saw her at all, you'd see her in a cemetery late at night. She'd be clambering about one of those huge cemeteries in Brooklyn and Queens, the ones you can see from certain expressways; graveyards with comforting names like Evergreen, Mount Neboh and Cypress Hills.

She was there on the hottest, stickiest summer night when New Yorkers without air conditioners couldn't sleep, and she was there when the temperature was below zero and the snow was hip-deep and nobody was awake. Amid the chalk-white and gray polished marble sentries guarding the dead of a great city, Gloria Stradtner looked only for life.

Mrs. Stradtner looked for stray animals: the thousands

of dogs and cats abandoned every year by people who, having tired of their pets, thought not of bringing them to an animal shelter but of leaving them in a cemetery. Humans may think of cemeteries as woodland-like sanctuaries. But for animals, they are only places to starve to death in the wild.

But Gloria—as everyone called her—was determined that this was not to be. Not for her strays.

And so for fifty years or maybe more (nobody can remember when she did not make the rounds of the graveyards at night), she would go forth, lugging large bags of dog food and cat food and big and small traps of the type that cannot hurt animals. She would bait these traps and go back to her car and wait. In an hour or so, she would return to her traps. Sometimes, she would entrap a dozen animals or more in a single night, her prisoners of love. And then she would feed them.

Gloria, who was a widow, never had much money, and so to supplement the dog and cat food she bought with her Social Security money, she would take jobs working in catering halls, even when she was getting on in years, so she could scoop up the scraps and bring them to her strays in the graveyards. When she was younger, back in the 1950s, she worked as a clerk and data entry specialist for IBM. But later she did not mind doing menial work in a catering hall. Not if it meant she could feed the animals.

And after she fed them, she would spend the next day making the rounds of veterinarians, imploring their help to neuter the dogs and cats (they usually charged her reduced fees, which she paid with the money from her modest Social Security check). And then she would visit the shelters, asking them to please take and care for the dogs and cats that New Yorkers did not want.

With her puppies and kittens in tow, she sometimes visited animal sanctuaries outside New York City, in Long

Island, upstate and in Connecticut and New Jersey, too. Nobody could refuse her. Over the years, she saved thousands of animals.

Sometimes, her friends would go with her on her night visits. And the cemetery workers helped, too. In one cemetery, they built little igloos in the bitterest part of the winter, hoping that Gloria's strays would use them to keep warm.

Friends told her more than once that cemeteries are not the safest places to be after dark. But she scoffed at such advice.

Once somebody stole her car, which was parked on a Brooklyn street near her home. She called her close friends, Michael and his wife Anne Marie, and told them she didn't care about the car. She was angry because there was one hundred pounds of dog food in the trunk.

One summer, there was a dog she was worried about. She called the dog Peekaboo because it peeked around gravestones at her. Peekaboo kept having litters. In one delivery, she had ten pups. Gloria was determined that Peekaboo be spayed. But Peekaboo was elusive. She would come when Gloria called her name, but no closer than ten feet. The wild Peekaboo trusted nobody; life in a cemetery does that to a dog.

Then one day Michael spoke to Gloria on the telephone, and he noticed that her speech was slurred. He knew she had not been drinking. She never drank and had not smoked for twenty years.

The doctor said she had cancer. It had started in her lungs and spread to her brain. She was admitted to a hospital and died six weeks later. She was seventy-two years old.

Two days before she died, she called Michael to say that she wanted to make sure that Peekaboo had been spayed (she was) and that her own two dogs, Lance and Ivy, would be taken care of after she died (he promised her they would be).

A poem she was believed to have written was read at her funeral. It was entitled "Weep Not" and began this way:

> Do not weep for me when I am gone
> For I have friends in the great beyond.
> All the little ones I used to feed
> Will come to me in my time of need.
> They will purr and bark in great delight,
> And I will hold and hug them tight.
> Oh what a great day that will be
> When my furry friends all welcome me.
>
> *Richard Severo*

Love Makes Us Whole

We got him with the other animals when we purchased the farm. Not that we wanted the black, shaggy mongrel. We had our hearts set on a collie—a pup we could train for the farm and as a companion for five-year-old Tim. But when the former owners informed us he was part of the deal, we resigned ourselves to keeping him. Temporarily, we thought, just until we can find him another home.

But the big dog apparently considered the farm his permanent responsibility. Each dawn, he inspected the animals and the farm buildings. Then he made a complete circuit of the entire eighty acres. That finished, he bounded across the sloping fields to slip beneath the fence for a visit with old Mr. Jolliff, who lived near a brook at the farm's edge.

The dog—we learned from Mr. Jolliff that his name was Inky—was pensive and aloof those first weeks. Grieving for his former masters, Inky asked no affection; busy settling in, we offered none. Except Tim, who sat by the hour on the back steps, talking softly to the unresponsive animal. Then, one morning, Inky crept close and laid his head in the boy's lap. And before we knew it, he had become Tim's second shadow.

All that summer the boy and the dog romped through fields and roamed the woods, discovering fox dens and groundhog burrows. Each day, they brought back treasures to share.

"Mom, we're home!" Tim would shout, holding the screen door wide for Inky. "Come see what we've got!" He'd dig deep in his jeans and spread the contents on the kitchen table: a pheasant's feather; wilted buttercups with petals like wet paint; stones from the brook that magically regained their colors when he licked them.

September arrived all too soon, bringing with it school for Tim and Carl, my schoolteacher husband, and lonely days for Inky and me. Previously, I'd paid little attention to the dog. Now he went with me to the mailbox, to the chicken coop, and down the lane when I visited Mr. Jolliff.

"Why didn't they want to take Inky?" I asked Mr. Jolliff one afternoon.

"And shut him up in a city apartment?" Mr. Jolliff replied. "Inky's a farm dog; he'd die in the city. Besides, you're lucky to have him."

Lucky? I thought ruefully of holes dug in the lawn, of freshly washed sheets ripped from the clothesline. I thought, too, of litter dumped on the back porch: old bones, discarded boots, long-dead rodents.

Still, I had to admit that Inky was a good farm dog. We learned this in early spring when his insistent barking alerted us to a ewe, about to lamb, lying on her broad back in a furrow, unable to rise. Without Inky's warning, she'd have died. And he had an uncanny way of knowing when roving dogs threatened the flock, or when sheep went astray.

Inky's deepest affection was reserved for Tim. Each afternoon when the school bus lumbered down the road, Inky ran joyously to meet it. For Inky—and for Tim—this was the high point of the day.

One mid-October day when I had been in town, Tim rode home with me after school. He was instantly alarmed when Inky wasn't waiting for us by the driveway.

"Don't worry, Tim," I said. "Inky always expects you on the bus, and we're early. Maybe he's back by the woods."

Tim ran down the lane, calling and calling. While I waited for him to return, I looked around the yard. Its emptiness was eerie.

Suddenly I, too, was alarmed. With Tim close behind me, I ran down to the barn. We pushed the heavy doors apart and searched the dim coolness. Nothing. Then, as we were about to leave, a faint whimper came from the far corner of a horse stall. There we found him, swaying slightly on three legs, his pain-dulled eyes pleading for help. Even in the half-light I saw that one back leg hung limp, the bone partially severed. With a little moan, Tim ran to Inky and buried his face in the dog's neck.

By the time the vet arrived, Carl was home. We placed the dog on his blanket and gently lifted him into the pet ambulance. Inky whimpered, and Tim started to cry.

"Don't worry, son," the vet said. "He's got a good chance." But his eyes told a different story.

At Tim's bedtime, I took him upstairs and heard his prayers. He finished and looked up. "Will Inky be home tomorrow?"

"Not tomorrow, Tim. He's hurt pretty bad."

"You tell me that doctors make people well. Doesn't that mean dogs, too?"

I looked out across the fields flooded with amber light. How do you tell a little boy that his dog must either die or be crippled? "Yes, Tim," I said at last. "I guess that means dogs, too." I tucked in his blanket and went downstairs.

I tossed a sweater over my shoulders and told Carl, "I'm going down to Mr. Jolliff's. Maybe he'll know what happened."

I found the old man sitting at his kitchen table in the fading light. He drew up another chair and poured coffee.

Somehow I couldn't talk about the dog. Instead, I asked, "Do you know if anyone was cutting weeds around here today?"

"Seems to me I heard a tractor down along the brook this morning," Mr. Jolliff replied. "Why?" He looked at me. "Did something happen?"

"Yes," I said, and the words were tight in my throat. "Inky's back leg's nearly cut off. The vet came for him. . . ." I wanted to say more, but couldn't. "It's growing dark," I finally murmured. "I'd better head home."

Mr. Jolliff followed me into the yard. "About Inky," he said hesitantly, "if he lives, I'd give him a chance. He'll still have you folks and Tim, the farm and the animals. Everything he loves. Life's pretty precious . . . especially where there's love."

"Yes," I said, "but if he loses a leg, will love make up for being crippled?"

He said something I didn't catch. But when I turned to him, he'd removed his glasses and was rubbing the back of his stiff old hand across his eyes.

By the time I reached our yard, the sun was gone. I walked down by the barn and stood with my arms on the top fence rail. Then I dropped my head to my arms and let the tears come.

I cried because Inky had been so gentle with the animals, and because he loved Tim so much, and Tim loved him. But mostly I cried because I hadn't really wanted him; not until now, when this terrible thing had happened.

Inky's paw couldn't be saved. Too vividly, I recalled how Inky had raced across fields and meadows, swift and free as a cloud shadow. I listened skeptically as the vet tried to reassure us: "He's young and strong. He'll get along on three legs."

Tim took the news with surprising calmness. "It's all right," he said. "Just so Inky comes home."

"But those long jaunts the two of you take may tire him now," I cautioned.

"He's always waited for me. I'll wait for him. Besides, we're never in much of a *hurry*."

The vet called a few days later. "You'd better come for your dog. He's homesick." I went immediately and was shocked at the change in Inky. The light was gone from his eyes. His tail hung limp and tattered, and the stump of his leg was swathed in a stained bandage. He hobbled over and pressed wearily against my leg. A shudder went through the hot, thin body and he sighed—a long, deep sigh filled with all the misery and loneliness of the past few days.

At the farm, I helped Inky from the car. He looked first to the sheep, grazing in the pasture; then, beyond the fields of green winter wheat, to the autumn woods where the horses, dappled with sunlight, moved among the trees. My heart ached as I realized how great must have been his longing for this place. At last, he limped to the barn and slipped between the heavy doors.

While his wound healed, Inky stayed in the barn, coming out only in the evenings. Throughout those days a sick feeling never left me. *You are a coward to let him live in this condition,* I told myself. But in my heart I wasn't sure.

About a week after bringing Inky home, I was in the yard raking leaves. When I'd finished under the maple, I sat on the steps to rest. It was a perfect Indian summer day; our country road was a tunnel of gold, and sumac ran like a low flame along the south pasture.

Then, with a flurry of leaves, Inky was beside me. I knelt and stroked the fur so smooth and shiny again. He moved, and I was achingly aware of the useless limb. "I'm so sorry, Inky," I said, putting my arm around his neck and pressing my head against his.

Sitting awkwardly, he placed his paw on my knee and looked up at me with soft, intelligent eyes. Then he pricked his ears and turned to listen. In an instant, he was off to meet the school bus. He ran with an ungainly, one-sided lope—but he ran with joy.

Tim jumped from the high step and caught the dog in his arms, "Oh, Inky! Inky!" he cried. Inky licked Tim's face and twisted and squirmed with delight. They remained there for a time, oblivious to anything but the ecstasy of being together again.

Watching them, I knew I'd been right to let the dog live. What was it Mr. Jolliff had said?

"Life's pretty precious . . . especially where there's love."

Aletha Jane Lindstrom

2

THE MAGIC
OF THE BOND

We are shaped and fashioned by what we love.

Goethe

The Fishermen

Peppy was an old dog put together with a few genes of this and that. His body was a mass of gray curls that still had traces of the black that once covered him from head to toe. A lot like my own hair. But it was his eyes that could melt your soul. Dark-brown discs were clouded milky white. Pep was blind and a stroke had rendered his legs useless. The poor dog had to be carried everywhere. He was 15, 105 in human years, and I was nearing 80. We could commiserate.

We met for the first time in an elevator that took us down from the thirty-second floor. Peppy's master, Nick, held the old dog in his arms. They were my new neighbors and had come to Florida from the north. I said a few words to break the awkward silence, and Peppy immediately lifted his drooping head at the sound of my voice. His nose sniffed in every direction searching for this new stranger in his midst. Reaching out his snow-white muzzle and shaggy white head, he licked my fingertips with a warm tongue. I stroked his head. His tail wagged a little faster, and his backside moved to the same tempo. By the time we reached the lobby, I knew I had a friend.

With Nick's enthusiastic approval, I started taking care

of Peppy while Nick was off at work. I'd spend hours telling him about my life. He would close his sightless eyes and listen to everything I had to say. His curly tail would wave slowly, and his nose would punch the air catching the different tones of my voice.

After a while, Nick rigged up a baby carriage with a platform built on its frame. How wonderful—Pep now had a set of wheels. I even began taking Peppy to my favorite fishing spot. Peppy loved being wheeled along on the quay. The wind pushed back his floppy ears, and he lifted his nose to drink in the many fascinating, fishy smells.

It wasn't long before another old critter joined our party. It was a pelican that usually sat nearby and waited for a meal every time I threw over the line. I knew what an effort it was for him to fly. He was too old and worn out to join his wingmen, diving from high altitudes and skimming fish from the edge of the sea. The other pelicans flew off in perfect formation, but the old one just sat there and watched. He survived by gliding a few feet off the dock and snaring baitfish in his huge mouth. Between that and my handouts, he just barely survived.

Peppy and the pelican hit it off from the first time they met. They sat close to each other and developed a special kind of rapport. What a picture we must have made, Pep on his platform carriage, the tattered bird dozing and me, still casting in the twilight of my own ancient life.

One day I dropped a baited hook in the water and waited as the line swayed gently in search of a fish. Suddenly Peppy whimpered, not loud, more like a purr. He could see nothing, but his head stretched over the platform till he was facing directly into the sea. His tail beat faster, and his ears stood erect. Somehow the old dog was trying to help me catch a fish. His motions and whimpering alerted the pelican. The old bird stood up and also peered into the water. His yellow eyes bulged, and he stared at my line. The two clairvoyants were telling me something was about to happen. Sure enough, it did! The line became taut! Wham! We had a hit! The pole bent in half, and I strained with all I had to bring something up to the planks. Peppy was half-crazy with excitement; he even pulled himself up on his haunches to get closer to the struggle. And the pelican waddled over to keep an eye on the end of my pole.

With a lot of grunting, I finally brought up a big, beautiful yellowtail snapper and laid it at Peppy's feet. Peppy sniffed at the fish madly, then rested on his blanket and seemed to enjoy the sound of the pelican eating his freshly caught lunch.

These days I'm spending more time at the quay than ever and catching loads of fish. My two pals never disappoint me. Alerted by a wagging tail, a whimper and a flutter of wings, I'm always ready when the magic begins. Everyone knows about bird dogs, but who's ever heard of a fish dog? Or a fish bird? Who'd ever believe I have pets like this?

These are wonderful days for old Peppy. Instead of moping indoors, alone all day, he's out in the sunshine with a whole new mission in life. Just last week, Peppy celebrated his sixteenth birthday with some of the most exciting catches of his new career.

And the pelican? All this activity's had an effect on him, too. As dusk came to the quay not long ago, I watched as he unfurled his trailing feathers and actually lifted himself off the ground. He pumped his long, weathered wings, and slowly made it to a roost to sleep for the night.

We're a threesome of old fishermen. A sightless dog, a flightless bird and an old man who's having the time of his life.

Mike Lipstock

Sister Seraphim's Deal with God

Ye shall not possess any beast, my dear sisters, except only a cat.

Ancrene Riwle ("Nun's Rule," c. 1200)

Mother Superior wrung her hands. "Sister Seraphim, you know full good and well that a convent is not a refuge for every stray cat."

"Yes, Mother."

"One mouser per convent is quite enough."

"Yes, Mother." The diminutive Russian Orthodox nun bowed her head, more to conceal a grin than to convey contrition.

At that moment, a voice in the hallway murmured, "Oh! The sweet precious babies. Please Sister Seraphim, the mama must have another saucer of milk."

The diminutive Russian Orthodox nun slipped unnoticed out of the room.

Mother Superior shook her finger at empty air. "And just last week we found the kitchen coffer empty because you took the money to purchase two ragged kitties from little boys, who were unable to care for them." Mother added,

"And Sister, how many times must I remind you, you are not allowed to raid the refrigerator for meat for the cats."

Sister Seraphim returned to the lecture scene. "Yes Mother, but when I was but a child, I made a deal with God."

"Sister Seraphim," Mother said with long-suffering patience, "We do not make deals with God!"

"I do," Sister said serenely. "I vowed early in life to take care of all living creatures who came my way so long as God provided the means."

Mother Superior sighed as she watched the sisters file into Sister Seraphim's room to coo and pet the newest addition to Sister Seraphim's collection of waifs—Grisette and her three newborn white balls of fluff.

For Sister Seraphim, cats had spirits and every one had to have a name. She rescued Shadrach, Meshach and Abednego (named after the men in the Old Testament who survived the fiery furnace) from the burning heat of the summer sun. The duo hiding behind the nunnery received the Biblical names of Luke and Eli. Mary Magdalene was christened after she waited at a well for Sister.

And then there was Pandora, the born troublemaker. Pandora believed in the virtue of awakening Christian nuns at the crack of dawn. At first she tried to pry Sister's eyes open with her paw. Soon the mere presence of Pandora's paw on Sister Seraphim's face was enough to roust the sister out of bed. But that wasn't the worst of Pandora, as Sister Seraphim found out one Sunday after services, when Mother Superior called her over.

Mother Superior stood with her arms folded. "That cat is impossible. Come see what she has done to the convent bathroom."

Sister Seraphim's eyes widened with horror at the destruction. The haughty Pandora was sitting on the window sill, licking her dainty paws.

Sister asked sternly, "What have you to say for yourself?" But Pandora's attitude only said, "See how I have excelled at bathroom transgressions. Pulled down all the curtains and towels. Chewed on the toothbrush bristles. Sharpened my claws on the toilet paper and then shredded it into confetti. One good swipe broke all the pretty bottles and knocked over tin cans. Then I mixed up the powder, vitamins, and cough syrup and rolled in the mess."

Mother Superior continued, "Why just this morning after being ousted from the chapel, again, Pandora actually had the impudence to flick her tail at His Most Holy Reverence the Bishop."

Suppressing a giggle, Sister Seraphim admitted, "Yes, Pandora is incorrigible, but if I don't love her, who will?"

Mother Superior looked at her sternly. She was not going to make any concessions. "Other arrangements will have to be made. For all the cats."

Sister Seraphim's round face grew troubled. She knew she had to obey Mother's instructions, but what would happen to her cats?

Over the next few weeks, after much worry and many phone calls and visits to local families, Sister Seraphim managed to find homes for all the cats. She vowed to start afresh with a slate clean of animals and an uncomplicated life. But it wasn't long before a couple of stray cats appeared, obviously in need of her help. Sister Seraphim fed them. What else could she do? And of course it wasn't long before word spread along the feline grapevine, and more unwanted cats sought succor from the angelic sister.

Mother Superior appeared to turn a blind eye at first, but inevitably, the day came when "other arrangements" had to be made.

And so the years passed. As she grew older, Sister Seraphim began to suffer from respiratory problems and arthritis. The time came when her order arranged for her to move to Arizona, hoping that the dry climate might improve her health.

Of course, Sister Seraphim's compassion for homeless cats didn't lessen at all in her new location. Shortly after arriving in Tucson, she decided to take matters into her own hands. The elderly nun persuaded a local real estate agent to donate a house and land. And there she founded the Hermitage, a no-kill cat shelter. At the Hermitage, Sister Seraphim and her cats found a refuge where, for the rest of her days, she no longer had to make "other arrangements."

And when Sister Seraphim finally met God, they had both kept their end of the bargain.

Jane Eppinga

Heart of a Champion

Though it's been years since his racing career ended, Niatross is still a powerful horse. Taller than most men, he weighs half a ton, with a broad chest and chiseled muscles that ripple under a rich bronze coat.

A racing legend, the champion Standardbred racehorse won thirty-seven of thirty-nine races in 1979–80 and over a million dollars. No horse could pass him once he got the lead.

In 1996, when he was nineteen years old, Niatross made a twenty-city tour across North America. For sixteen years, Niatross had done little more than romp in his paddock and munch hay and oats. Now he'd have a rock star's schedule, with press conferences and photographers in every city, a strange stall to sleep in and thousands of fans wanting to pet and fuss over him. As his tour manager, I traveled with him.

Niatross greeted fans from Maine to Illinois, in big cities and county fairs, in scorching heat and chilly winds. Niatross endured it all with grace and almost eerie intelligence. He was always able to sense what was expected of him and do it.

One night in Buffalo, New York, Niatross pawed and

stomped his feet as he waited for his cue to pace down the racetrack for a photo session. The big horse, in his impatience, reared up on his hind legs, pulling his handler (a six-foot, six-inch man) off his feet, before lunging on to the track. But the outburst was over quickly and soon he stood to be photographed, once again the obliging star.

After his track appearance, Chris, his handler, unharnessed Niatross and brushed his lustrous coat. As the two rounded the corner from the barn to the grandstand where a crowd of fans waited, Niatross rolled his eyes and stopped in his tracks, as if to say, "Oh, no. I have to do this again?" But with a gentle tug on the lead rope, Niatross moved ahead to take his place of honor.

For two hours, he was petted, stroked, prodded and swooned over. I was silently thanking Niatross for another night of patience with us when out of the corner of my eye, I saw a moving, buzzing blur zipping across the pavement toward Niatross. As it drew closer, I could see that the blur was a child in an electric wheelchair. The child had his chair going full throttle and before I could caution him not to scare Niatross, he came to an abrupt halt under the horse's nose, mere inches from his powerful front legs.

Clearly startled, but maintaining his poise, Niatross widened his eyes and craned his neck to peer down at the tiny blond boy, who was around five years old and looked like a doll in the heavy, motorized chair. I said hello to the child, who perhaps because of his handicap, was unable to speak. The fingers of his right hand were clutched around a button that propelled his chair; the fingers on the left hand were frozen around a Niatross poster. He looked at me intently, his eyes burning a hole through my face.

"Would you like Niatross to sign your poster?" I asked. With great solemnity, he nodded his head yes. I pulled the poster from his fingers, tapped Niatross's foot to get him to lift it, placed the poster beneath it and traced his hoof.

"There," I said, slipping the poster back between his fingers, "Niatross signed his name for you." The child said nothing, but continued his fixed gaze at me.

"Do you want to give Niatross a pat?" I asked. Again, he solemnly moved his head up and down. Yes.

A mild panic came over me. *How could we do this?* The boy couldn't extend a hand or unclench his fingers, his arms were frozen at his side. How could he reach up to pat a horse? I turned to Chris, not knowing what to do, but knowing we couldn't disappoint this child.

"Chris?" I said, hoping he'd have an idea. Without hesitation, Chris placed his hand a few inches beneath Niatross's soft muzzle. Niatross lowered his velvety nose into Chris' hand. Slowly, cautiously, Chris moved his hand, with Niatross following, lower and lower, past the boy's head, past his tiny shoulders. Chris pulled his hand away and Niatross, closing his eyes, rested his head in the boy's lap.

The boy's intent expression melted into a faint, tranquil smile. The tension gone from his frail body, he laid his head alongside Niatross's powerful head, the same head that jerked a man off his feet just hours before. The two were secure in the only kind of embrace a horse and a wheelchair-bound child could have. Boy and horse looked like old friends, exchanging a wordless greeting understood only by them.

Slowly, steadily, Niatross lifted up his head to look down at his new friend. With a flick of his finger, the child spun the wheelchair around. Still smiling and sitting a little taller now, he disappeared as quickly as he'd appeared, into the chilly night.

Ellen Harvey

A Duchess in the Desert

In January 1996 when I visited Qatar, on the Arabian Peninsula, the emir invited me to return in March for their annual "Festival of the Horse"—and, most intriguingly, to ride in the International Qatar Horse Marathon, popularly known as "Desert Storm."

The race, I knew, was one of the most grueling in the world. It asked everything from rider and horse alike to go twenty-six miles over sand. I was reasonably fit at the time, but I wasn't riding fit. Could I withstand hours of competition in hundred-degree heat?

Still, I was tempted by the emir's proposal. If I rode, an oil company would sponsor me and they would donate a significant sum to Children in Crisis. I decided to do it.

As soon as I declared I would race, the press pegged me as a mad and frivolous publicity hound. The betting was that I would pack up a quarter of the way through, pose for the cameras, and thumb a ride to the nearest oasis. The *Daily Express* even ran the headline, FERGIE RIDING FOR A FALL.

But I had given my word, and the more that I heard I couldn't do it, the more intent I became.

In England I went on a fiercely healthy diet, pushed my

workouts to seven days a week. By the time I returned to
Qatar, the race had taken on larger significance. Now it
was a question of integrity, of my ability to stay the
course and be the serious person I claimed. I could not
expect to win the race, but I knew that I had to finish.
Only then could I show my doubters—including the
toughest one, myself—that I was for real.

When we took a look at the horse they'd assigned me,
my equine consultant, Robert Splaine, could tell straight
away that he wasn't fit enough to last. Then our luck
turned; we met another rider, who happened to have
available a seven-year-old chestnut gelding named Gal.

Gal was an Akhal-Teke, a Russian breed once ridden by
Alexander the Great. With their lanky bodies and thin
skin, Akhal-Tekes are bred to thrive in the desert, and
they are famous for endurance. "Just remember," his
owner told me, "my Gal loves to be spoken to. Just talk to
him and he will help you."

We lined up the next morning across a broad expanse of
light sand: forty-six ready steeds and their riders, almost
all of them men. Behind the horses were twice as many
cars and jeeps and ambulances—including one open-
topped car filled with British press, their huge lenses
bristling like monstrous antennae, and every man jack of
them aching to immortalize my failure.

Minutes before we were off, a bank of dark clouds rolled
in, then burst, drenching everyone to the skin. At the
starting gun there was chaos, and it was all I could do to
keep my wits about me. Horses reared and motors roared
and everyone charged off in what seemed like a dozen different directions. It was then that I discovered that I had
saddled a racehorse. Gal took the bit and was gone, in a
flat-out gallop, as if he were sprinting six furlongs. He just
wanted to win, and he didn't know the finish line was
twenty-six miles off.

Once I had been like Gal, I thought, *always pushing past my limits until I flamed out.* Now I knew better: Slowing down wins the race.

Finally I regained control, and we settled into a gentle trot. I'd been prepared for heat, but not the damp of a fluke storm. The rain added weight for my horse, and distance to the course, since we'd have to skirt several bogs where the water had pooled. And it churned up the sand and stones till the footing was heavy and treacherous. I was dripping wet and scared. The rain had changed all my equations.

In advance of each water station, where open containers were handed out, Robert would lean out the window of the jeep and shout, "Water!" When it was time to douse Gal's neck and shoulders, he called out, "Horse!"

About halfway through we reached the vet station, where the riders had to dismount and walk their horses in to be checked for soreness or rapid heart rate. Gal was in great shape, but my own legs barely functioned after rubbing so hard on the saddle.

The going was lonely. The wet desert stretched out before us, flat and monotonous. The universe was brown. Would it never end? Three miles from the end, Gal slowed from a trot to a walk, then a slower one. Each step was more labored than the last . . . and then Gal stopped. *I don't want to go on,* my horse was telling me. *I am tired.*

I was used up myself, but the thought of quitting repelled me. I *had* to pass the line.

But neither could I be cruel to my horse; I could not, would not, force him. As the car idled alongside I asked Robert what to do.

Under the rules, Robert could not leave the car, but he trained his keen eyes on Gal for a long moment. Then he said, "From what I can see, with the distance you have left, you're fine."

Thus assured, I appealed to my horse as a friend, "Gal, you have got to trust me here. I know that home is the other way, and it looks like we are going into the middle of the desert. But you have got to trust that there is something out there—you have to believe enough in me to know that I will get you through it."

By that point I was crying, and I said, "Because if you don't believe in me now, we are going to fail, and we *can't* fail. Because then they will say, 'There she goes again, just being her usual stupid, crazy self.'"

Gal stayed stock still, and my heart dropped. I knew that Gal and I would go as far as our joint spirit carried us, but we'd need to tap into our deepest reserves; we'd need to make our leap of faith. I tried one last time: "Will you go on? When the whole world has given up on me, will you go *on*?" And then I heard the saddle creak, and I felt those weary limbs heave into motion. Gal trusted and believed in me when all logic stood against it. My horse took a gamble and walked on.

That kindness killed me; that heart and courage laid me out. There was so much potential on this earth, so much greatness in its creatures—how could I ever feel hopeless again?

A mile or so from the finish, Gal rounded a bend and spied the grandstand. He got excited then, because he knew I had not lied to him. A half-mile out, he broke into a confident canter. That was the way he went across the line, cantering freely, as fresh as a romping colt.

After I peeled myself off the saddle, I made sure Gal drank first, then I took my turn. I wanted to take care of that horse forever.

Sarah, Duchess of York

Boris in New York

It was nearly midnight on a rainy Christmas Eve. Barbara Listenik walked the cold dark streets of Queens, New York, alone. "Excuse me," she said to a stranger in front of an all-night market. Showing the man a photograph, she asked, "Have you seen my lost dog?"

Only hours ago, Barbara had been on her way to La Guardia Airport to pick up her four-year-old boxer-mix dog, Boris. Barbara had moved to New York one week previously, hoping to further her art career, while Boris stayed behind with a friend in Florida. New York was such a big place; Barbara found it overwhelming and sometimes lonely. And now that she was settled into her new apartment in Brooklyn, Barbara couldn't wait to see her best four-legged buddy. *It's the perfect Christmas gift to myself,* she thought as she waited in line at the airline baggage counter.

But then an airline employee took Barbara aside to tell her there'd been an accident. During offloading, Boris's carrier had opened, and he had escaped. Several baggage handlers and airport police had chased the frightened dog across busy runways and through a terminal jam-packed with holiday travelers. But Boris had eluded them all, and now he was running loose somewhere in neighboring Queens.

For several hours Barbara and the baggage handlers and police canvassed nearby neighborhoods searching for Boris. Then Barbara returned to her apartment for a photo of him. She then spent Christmas Eve showing the photo to strangers and calling Boris's name until her voice grew hoarse and she felt nearly frozen from the icy rain.

Christmas morning, Barbara resumed her search. Thinking of how frightened her dog must be, she found herself crying as she ventured into yet another bleak alleyway. Boris had never known cold weather or the big city with all its unfamiliar smells and loud noises. And there were so many cars and trucks to avoid. What was worse, Boris had no collar or ID tags on. For safety reasons, the airline insisted that animals not wear their collars during transport. It seemed hopeless—she was just one person trying to find one small dog in an enormous city. She trudged through the streets, calling the dog's name over and over, until she was exhausted.

Bright and early the next morning, Barbara began telephoning area shelters. Boris wasn't in any of them. But he had not been reported dead, either, which Barbara considered a good sign.

Soon Barbara was back in Queens posting fliers to utility poles and inside markets and laundromats. She asked everyone she met if they'd seen Boris. No one had. But then toward evening one man told her, "An off-duty transit cop was just here asking about that same dog."

Barbara was surprised and touched. *Well, Boris, there's at least one person in this big, cold city who cares if we're reunited.*

What Barbara didn't realize was that there were many others who cared. Many hundreds of others, as it turned out. For as word of Boris's plight spread, people began telephoning Barbara with messages of support and more than three thousand dollars was contributed to a reward fund established by a local newspaper. Well-wishers from as far away as New Jersey turned up in droves to join the search.

Meanwhile, an animal welfare society began organizing search parties. Every weekend more than a hundred volunteers fanned out through the neighborhoods bordering the airport. Barbara marveled at this show of support as she thanked her new friends for their help and their words of encouragement.

But after seven weeks Barbara began to lose hope. *Maybe it's time for me to get on with the rest of my life,* she considered as she traveled home to Brooklyn late one night.

There, Barbara discovered fifteen messages on her machine. Only she was too depressed to listen to them. She was afraid they would be more false leads. So far Barbara had looked at over a hundred strays that turned out not to be Boris. Each time she'd felt a little bit of herself dying deep inside.

When the telephone abruptly rang, Barbara picked it up without thinking. It was one of the volunteers searching for Boris. "I think we found him!" the woman said.

A young college student named Johnny had been on his way to a family function when he spotted one of Barbara's fliers at a cab stand. "This looks like the dog we've been feeding behind the empty barber shop next door," he told his wife. Johnny telephoned one of the volunteers, who traveled to Queens to see for herself. She'd been trying all night to reach Barbara with the good news.

Barbara suspected it would turn out to be another dead end, but she hurried anyway to the address that was only two miles from the airport. Sure enough, her heart sank when she was escorted into the tiny house to see the dog. This stray was bone thin, and his coat was solid gray.

"Boris is fawn and white," she murmured, crestfallen. "I'm sorry—that's not my dog."

Tentatively, the pup approached Barbara. He sniffed once, then began wagging his tail. Their eyes met.

"Boris? Is that you?" Barbara gasped. He had lost fifteen pounds, and grime and road tar had turned his coat completely gray. But there was no mistaking those loving brown eyes.

"Boris! It *is* you!" Barbara exclaimed. An instant later her knees gave out, and she collapsed onto the floor. "Oh Boris," she said, laughing and crying as her faithful companion began licking the tears from her cheeks.

Before they left, Boris padded over to Johnny and offered up his paw. "If he wasn't your dog, I was planning to keep him for myself, he's so sweet," Johnny said as he took the proffered paw.

At home Barbara gave Boris a much-needed bath. Now that they were together once again, she finally lit the holiday lights and celebrated Christmas. She then stayed up all night feeding him dog biscuits and gourmet pet food. She was too excited to sleep; she kept trying to absorb the fact that Boris was really there with her.

These days Barbara and Boris enjoy spending time with the many kind people Barbara met while Boris was M.I.A. Flying Boris to New York had been her big Christmas present to herself, but Boris's present to her had been even bigger. He'd given her a whole city of friends.

Bill Holton

The White Dog

"We can't leave her here," I said, turning a resolute face to my husband, "We just can't."

The white dog was in a small fenced area in someone's backyard. She had a rough wooden shelter and food and water, but she was obviously never walked—large piles of excrement covered the dirt floor of her enclosure. She pressed herself eagerly against the fence as I petted what I could reach of her.

The backyard was visible from the parking lot of the school, where my husband Larry and I had parked our car and gotten out, intending to go to a game in the gymnasium. Seeing us, the dog had started barking. Always interested in dogs, I walked to the edge of her yard. She was a creamy-white color and looked to be a white shepherd/golden-retriever mix. She had the kind face of a golden retriever and a set of cockeyed ears, one upright, the other flopping gently over at the tip. My own dog Lucy was a white shepherd-mix, too, and I was struck by the resemblance.

I walked over to her pen to get a closer look. As I approached her, she lowered her head and started to do a rear-wiggling dance of happiness. I put my hand up to the fence for her to sniff, and she whimpered with pleasure. As I petted her awkwardly through the chain-link, she leaned heavily into the fence and sighed blissfully. The moment I took my hand away, she began to bark, stopping only when she felt my fingers on her touch-starved body once more. Her coat was muddy; the food and water bowls were grimy.

That's when I told my husband I couldn't walk away from this dog.

"She's okay," he said, slightly exasperated. He knew I often became less than rational when it came to animals. "Look, she seems healthy, and she's got food and water."

"But look at this pen she's in—it's filthy!" I argued. "And she seems so lonely."

"Maybe they've been away or been ill," he said.

"Maybe, but it can't hurt to find out what her story is."

Larry shrugged. He knew me well enough to know when it was useless to argue any more.

I wasn't sure what I was going to say, but I walked around the house and marched up the steps to the front door. I knocked immediately, not giving myself time to reconsider my plan. What *was* I going to say?

While I waited for a response, I looked around. There was a rusty car up on blocks in the front yard, and the front porch was crammed with bulging garbage bags. Some were ripped, so that trash was strewn across the dirty floorboards.

A teenaged girl came to the door and eyed me suspiciously, "What do you want?"

"I'd like to talk to the owner of the dog in back," I said brightly.

"That's my brother's dog," she said, and a slack-faced young man of around twenty appeared beside her. He stared at me blankly.

"Hi. It looks like you must be very busy—and have no

time to walk your dog," I smiled, hoping my voice wasn't as condemning as I felt.

"I never walk her." He spoke in a flat tone, neither defensive nor ashamed.

"Oh," I said. There was an awkward silence while my mind raced, and I tried to think of something more to say.

"Well, I noticed her right away and I thought, what a beautiful dog, she's so white. You see, I have a dog at home that looks just like her, and I thought it would be nice to have a matched pair, so I was wondering if I could buy her from you—"

The girl interrupted me, "How much will you give us for her?"

"Twenty dollars."

"We'll take it," she said, without a moment of hesitation. Her brother nodded in agreement.

Dizzy with relief, I fished a twenty out of my purse and handed it over. I hadn't expected it to be this easy.

As I turned to go, the brother called after me, "Her name is White Fang."

Not any more, I thought. I could think of no name that suited the white dog less.

Larry and I went to the game, but I spent the whole time thinking about the dog. I was eager to get her out of that awful cage and to give her a large dose of the attention she craved. I intended to find her a new home that provided a life that was full of comfort, fun and especially love.

When the game was over, I hurried over to the dog's pen. She was as happy to see me as before. I fumbled with the latch to the gate, my excitement making me clumsy. Finally I yanked the gate wide, expecting her to bolt. My husband was waiting with a leash to catch her as soon as she left the enclosure.

To our surprise, she didn't move. She stood motionless in front of the now-open space in the fence. It seemed as if she didn't fully register what was happening. Then her brow furrowed slightly, and an expression of mild bewilderment crossed her face. She took two steps forward, then stood still again, half in and half out of the pen. She looked up at me and when I smiled at her, her tail, held low, wagged once or twice uncertainly.

"C'mon, girl," I said. "Let's get outta here."

She took another step, and this time there was no mistaking the look of confusion in her eyes. But with each step away from the pen and toward our car, her confusion faded. Not once did she look back at the filthy prison that had been her home for so long.

With her tail sweeping madly from side to side, she trembled with anticipation and joy as she jumped in to the back seat of our car. She poked her nose over the seat rest and started snuffling the side of my face, punctuating her affection with little woofs of excitement.

When my husband got in and started the car, the dog transferred her snuffling to the back of his head. She seemed very pleased to be with us. I think we both knew, even then, that the white dog was going to be ours for a long time.

What we didn't realize then was that we had probably saved the dog's life. A few months later, the police had to break into that same house when the neighbors alerted them to continued barking coming from inside. The people living there had gone on vacation for two weeks, leaving numerous cats and dogs inside with inadequate food and water. Many of the neglected animals had to be euthanized. The white dog could so easily have been one of them.

That is how White Fang became our Hannah. The first time she went indoors, I saw that same mildly bewildered look on her face that I'd seen when she left her pen. It appeared again going up her first flight of stairs, and the first time we rubbed her belly. On her first walk in the park, she seemed overwhelmed by the sights and smells around her. She didn't strain on the leash, but walked steadily in front of me, swinging her head from side to side, her nose twitching.

When she first laid down on her fleece-covered dog bed in a sun-drenched spot in the living room, she looked as if she couldn't quite believe anything could really be so comfortable. No more awful pen, it had been left behind like a bad dream. Hannah gave a long contented sigh as she rested her head on her paws, closed her eyes and settled into sleep.

Carol Kline

The Princess and the Toad

Some years ago, our family expanded to include a one-year-old Siberian husky named Princess Misha. Like all Siberian huskies, Misha had an innate love of the outdoors, and of course, the cooler the better. She would lie curled up in a ball on top of a snowdrift on the coldest of winter days with her tail flicked over her only vulnerable spot—her nose. When fresh snow fell, she would lay so still that she soon disappeared under a blanket of snow and became a part of the landscape. Every so often, she stood up, shook off, turned in a few circles, and then laid back down to keep watch over her domain.

On warm summer days, she found the coolest corner in the house and spent her days napping. Then after her nightly walk, she'd spend the rest of the evening stretched out on the cool cement of the front patio. All through the hot summers and into the fall, this was her nightly ritual.

One summer evening, as we sat out on the front patio relishing a late-evening breeze, we saw a small toad hop out of the grass, then down the sidewalk to a few feet away from where Misha was lying. Suddenly Misha stood up, walked over to the toad, picked it up in her mouth and then walked back to her resting place and lay back down.

She then put her chin down on the walk, opened her mouth and let the toad hop out while we watched in astonishment. The toad sat there in front of Misha's eyes, the two seeming to stare at one another for some time. Then the toad hopped down the walk and back into the grass.

On other nights that summer, we noticed this same ritual. We commented on the fact that Misha seemed to have a fondness for toads. We worried because some toads can be poisonous, but since she never experienced any ill effect and never hurt them, we didn't interfere. If she spotted a toad in the street on one of her walks, she would actually run over to it and nudge it with her nose till it had safely hopped off the street and back on to the grass, out of harm's way.

The following summer was the same. Misha enjoyed cooling off by lying out on the front patio after nightfall. Many times, we noticed a toad within inches of her face. At other times, we watched as she walked into the grass and came back to her resting spot with a toad in her mouth, only to release it. The toads always stayed near her for some time before hopping off into the night. The only difference from the previous summer was that she spent more nights in this manner, and the toads were bigger. A toad always seemed to be close at hand.

One night early in the third summer, after letting Misha out, we watched as a large toad hopped out of the grass and over to her, stopping inches in front of her. Misha gently laid her head down so that her nose almost touched the toad. That was when it finally dawned on us—perhaps there was just one toad! Could Misha have shared the past three summers with the same toad? We called a local wildlife expert who told us that toads can live three to six years, so it was entirely possible. Somehow these two unlikely companions had formed a bond. At first it seemed so strange to us. But then we realized we were very different from Misha too, but the love between us seemed completely natural. If she could love us, we marveled, why not a toad?

Misha had a minor operation that summer, and we kept her indoors for a while afterwards to recuperate. Each night she went to the front door and asked to be let out, but we didn't let her. Instead, leash in hand, we took her for short walks. One evening a few days later, I went to the front door to turn on the porch light for guests we were expecting. When the light came on illuminating the front stoop, there, to my utter amazement, sat Toad (as we came to call him), staring up at me through the screen door! He had hopped up the three steps from the patio, and we supposed he was looking for Misha. Such devotion could not be denied. We let Misha out to be with her pal. She immediately picked the toad up in her mouth and took it down the steps where she and Toad stayed nose to nose until we brought her in for the night. After that, if Misha didn't come out soon enough, Toad frequently came to the door to get her. We made sure that the porch light was turned on before dark and posted a big sign on the porch, "Please don't step on the toad!"

We often laughed about the incongruous friendship—they did made a comical sight, gazing into each other's eyes. But their devotion sometimes made me wonder if I should regard them so lightly. Maybe it was more than just friendship. Maybe in her stalwart toad, Princess Misha had found her Prince Charming.

Joan Sutula

Sheba

I first met Sheba in 1956. I was a third-grade student at the Round Meadow Elementary School. She was a seven-week-old kitten in a pet-shop window. She caught my eye immediately. I had always wanted a kitten, or at least that's what I told myself when I saw her there on display.

At first, she didn't even notice me standing there. I tried tapping on the glass, but her concentration remained elsewhere as she gave full attention to the task at hand. A thousand generations of hunting and stalking instinct were brought to bear as she successfully brought down her quarry—her sister's tail.

I tapped again. She stared at me for a moment, and the bond was made. Following a brief discussion through the glass we concluded that we were made for each other. I vowed to return later in the day to take her home with me.

Unfortunately, I soon found that the road to kitten ownership was not without obstacles. Mom and Dad didn't think much of my plans. It seemed that they knew quite a lot about the subject of acquiring pets. "Who ever heard of paying money for a cat? A kitten is something that you can get for free at any barn. Besides, we're dog people."

I wasn't sure what that meant but, even at eight years old, I could see that the only true stumbling stone here was the finances. You see, Sheba came with a stiff price tag, two dollars and fifty cents. "A lot of money for something that you can get for free anywhere."

Getting my own way this time was not going to be easy. However, I felt up to the challenge at hand and, after a day of typical little kid whining and a chunk of "birthday money" that came from Uncle Lou, Sheba was mine.

I was an instant hit with her, and the feeling was mutual. She slept on my bed every night. We had long and meaningful conversations when no one else was around. In fact, it was Sheba who was largely responsible for my deciding somewhat early in life to pursue a career as a veterinarian.

Through junior high, high school, college and veterinary school, she remained a close feline friend. Many important decisions regarding my career as well as my personal life were influenced by conversations, whether real or imagined, with Sheba.

Though she lived with Mom and Dad while I was busy getting married, raising a family and practicing the profession that she influenced me to join, she remained a close friend and seemed to enjoy visits from me, my wife and kids.

Undoubtedly, it was her influence once again that got me thinking about opening a veterinary hospital for cats only. She seemed to love the idea when we "talked" about it, and I knew from past experience that her judgment was flawless, so I set off down a new career path. In June of 1978, my new hospital, The Allentown Clinic for Cats, opened its doors.

Sheba was twenty-two years old on opening day when Mom and Dad brought her to see me and the beautiful new hospital that she had inspired. They hadn't warned me in advance that there was a second reason for the visit.

Sheba looked horrible. Apparently she had become quite ill that week. I did a thorough exam and was forced to a bitter conclusion. You see, I had been in practice long enough to know when a situation was hopeless.

It seemed fitting that in the new hospital, Sheba was the first cat whose suffering we could ease. We had the last of our long conversations as she fell gently asleep in my arms.

Michael A. Obenski, V.M.D.

Ranch of Dreams

After reading the book *Black Beauty* as a child, I dreamed that I would someday have a place—a ranch—where animals would not be abused, but like Black Beauty, would live their lives roaming proud and free.

Yet even in my dreams, I thought more about what the Black Beauty Ranch would *not* be rather than about what it would be. It would not be a place where animals were primarily to be looked *at*; rather it would be a place where they were primarily to be looked *after*. And it would not be a place where animals did what people wanted them to do. Instead, the animals would do whatever they wanted to do, because finally, it would not be a people's place at all but an animals' place—a place that the animals felt, from the day they arrived, belonged to them and would always belong to them as long as they lived.

I even dreamed about the sign that would be on the gate at the ranch. It would have on it the words from the last lines of *Black Beauty:* "I have nothing to fear and here my story ends. My troubles are all over and I am at home."

Today Black Beauty Ranch is all that I had dreamed of and more than I could have imagined. The Ranch, over a thousand acres located in Texas, is home to almost six hundred animals, including buffalo, horses, chimpanzees, deer, cats and elephants, to name a few. Rescued from cruel situations or retired after years of service, all the animals have the best care we can provide and the most freedom possible. The animals in our sanctuary live in that extraordinary gray area that lies between petdom and wilddom as the following story illustrates.

At the time we first acquired the Ranch, it was to be primarily a home for—of all animals—burros. We rescued the burros from the Grand Canyon and later Death Valley. In both places, they were scheduled to be shot and killed by the National Park Service. After extensive research on the safest and most effective way of getting the burros out of the canyon, we hired highly skilled ropers to catch the burros and then we airlifted them out by helicopter. Altogether, the Grand Canyon rescue took two years and involved saving 577 burros. To my knowledge, not a single burro, horse or rider was badly injured.

Some of the burros we rescued ended up staying on at Black Beauty Ranch. Before the rescue, no one had had much experience with burros, but we found that they were completely charming—intelligent, curious, playful and even humorous. They quickly became our favorite animals and even the groups of people who come to tour the Ranch today, who at first show little interest in seeing the burros, become first respectful, then affectionate, and finally begin to love them just the way we do.

From the beginning though, we had one *favorite* favorite and that was Friendly. Friendly had come up in a sling under the helicopter in the very first batch of burros we rescued in the Grand Canyon. I was in the corral when she was lifted up and over the rim and delicately dropped to the ground. I was also one of the crew that untied her. As sudden and uncomfortable and even crazy as her rescue had been, she seemed to realize that no one had really hurt her, and therefore we were not all bad. That was why, then and there, in those first moments at the corral when she stood and looked at us and had not trotted away, and then let us come closer and then even came closer herself, I had given her a name.

One evening, I went looking for Friendly in the corral to show some people just how friendly she really was. I kept walking up to burro after burro, but I couldn't find her. I heard the cowboys sitting on the corral rail laughing at me, but as they often laughed at me, at first I thought nothing of it. But when finally their laughing veered on the uproarious side, I swung around to stare at them and there was Friendly—the whole time she had been plodding along behind me, looking for me as hard as I had been looking for her.

After Friendly finally arrived at the Ranch, we soon discovered she was pregnant, and in good time she gave birth to a burro we called Friendly Two. Soon after Two was born, I went to see the new mother. She spotted me and trotted over with her baby from a distant pasture. Almost always when I see Friendly she has a customary greeting—she pushes her head into my stomach. This time she had started to put her head there all right, but suddenly she stopped, moved back, and instead—with some pride—pushed her baby toward me. Immediately I started hugging and gushing over the baby until suddenly, she pushed her baby away, and pushed her own head hard back into my stomach. It was as if she was saying, in no uncertain fashion, that she wanted to show me her baby all right and even wanted me to hug her, but "enough was enough!"

Burros are such faithful friends. To this day Friendly One, now over twenty years old, and sometimes Friendly Two, will, when I am visiting the Ranch, clump over to the veranda at the main house at four o'clock for tea, tidbits and gossip.

One visitor to the Ranch told me recently, "I have never in my life seen so many happy animals."

No comment has meant more to me than that.

Cleveland Amory

Prince Charming

Every dog is a lion at home.

Italian Saying

"Hey, Mom, I can read this!" Lorne, our seven-year-old son, shoved the newspaper toward me.

With a grubby little finger under each word, he began: "For free . . ."

He paused, so I filled in: "Rescued, abused spaniel-type . . ."

". . . male dog," Lorne continued. "Can't keep. Needs good home."

"We already have a dog," I said, patting my little Maltese.

"But he's wimpy," protested five-year-old Lee.

"Let's just go see what he looks like," begged the boys.

Twenty minutes later, we were knocking on a door in an apartment building with a large "No Pets" sign. A college student answered and told how he'd stopped to get gas when he saw a man yelling and mistreating this dog. When the student asked if he could have the unwanted animal, the man had roughly lifted the trembling dog into the student's car and left. As I reached out to pet this cowering, pitiful dog, I felt sores from his massive tick infestation. His ribs stuck out from a dull matted liver-and-white coat, and his huge brown eyes looked at me shyly over a freckled nose. He wagged his tail halfheartedly. Talk about wimpy! One look in those sad eyes, though, and I was hooked.

I bundled him and our four delighted children into the car and hurried to the vet's office, where we determined he was an English springer spaniel, about two years old. X-rays confirmed several broken ribs; a respiratory infection coupled with severe malnutrition, plus a skin infection, requiring several medications. As I explained to my husband that evening, our free dog was rather expensive.

Somehow, I knew he was going to be worth it.

That evening, I listened as the children held a forum on naming our new pet. Laurie, our nine-year-old, led the discussion. "He's lived such a sad life, he needs a really good name," she said. They tossed around several names, when three-year-old Leslie lisped: "How about Printh Charming? He'th alwayth the good guy."

Thus we found our Prince Charming, admittedly a little ragged. We had our work cut out for us if we were going to transform this pauper of a creature into a dog worthy of his title. Like mother hens, we hovered over him, pouring medicines down his throat and watching his battered body slowly heal. As his sores disappeared, Prince put on weight, and his coat turned glossy.

Even better, he began to relax in our presence and show tentative signs of trust.

Bolstered by his new sense of security, Prince began taking daily jaunts over our four acres, exploring the fields and bringing me back souvenirs from his forays—gnarly sticks or a chunky rock. And then, Prince discovered the barn. That's where he found his place in this world.

Prince proclaimed himself a nanny. With amusement, we watched as Prince warmed himself to the creatures of the barn—the sheep and goats—but we didn't realize he was about to become an official midwife. At all the deliveries of each new creature, Prince was first on the spot, comforting the laboring mother and standing watch over the newborn lamb or kid. Prince nuzzled and licked the newborns as if they were his own, and when a newborn took its first wobbly steps, Prince ran around excitedly. What did the real mothers think about all this? They seemed to sense Prince's calling, and they were unthreatened.

Prince's gifts to us, naturally, started to take on a very maternal bent. One morning, he proudly deposited a new kitten on my stoop. "Thanks, Mr. Charming," I said as I opened the door, "but please take this back." A scowling mother cat from next door appeared a few minutes later to retrieve her offspring. Undaunted, Prince found me a new present: the neighbor's pet duck. It became a daily ritual. Prince plopped the duck down, the duck gave me a "here-we-go-again" look, and the three of us waddled and trudged back across the field to my neighbor's pond. "Oh, well," I told myself. "It's good exercise." And it was awfully endearing.

I suppose that's why, one morning, I was so surprised to hear Prince emit a long, low, menacing growl. I was watering flowers near the house, Prince by my side, when he made the noise, and I stood up to see a large, disgruntled rottweiler advancing on us. Frightened, I reached for the faucet, hoping to turn a blast of water on the rottweiler with my hose. Prince, feeling my fear, positioned his small body in front of me—did we ever call him wimpy?— meeting the dog halfway as it lunged for me. The combination of the hose and Prince gave the rottweiler pause, and he turned and ran off. Prince had taken a gash on the neck, but he recovered with only a small scar to remind us of his valor.

We still talk about that shining moment of Prince's bravery, the pinnacle of any dog's life, but more than that, we marvel at his selfless love and nanny instincts. Where did a dog who had been shown nothing but abuse learn to treat other creatures with such tenderness and kindness?

We'd like to think it was our doing, but I have a feeling that our beloved dog was never the pauper we took him to be. Underneath that ratty disguise he had always been the good guy.

Sharon Landeen

"I listened to some of your motivation tapes while you were at work and I've decided to become a Great Dane."

Fifteen Minutes of Fame

If your dog thinks you're the greatest person in the world, don't seek a second opinion.

Jim Fiebig

I dashed out an exit at O'Hare International Airport in Chicago and ran towards a waiting cab. I was greeted by a cab driver with a three-day-old beard, an old baseball cap and arms the size of tree trunks.

As he tossed my bags into the trunk, he spotted my luggage tags and said, "What kind of doctor are you?"

"A veterinarian," I said. Instantly, his grizzled face broke into a smile. This happens to veterinarians all the time, as people love to talk about their pets.

The doors slammed, he put the car into gear and hit me with this opening salvo, "My wife claims I love my toy poodle Missy more than I love her. Just once, she wants me to be as excited to see her as I am Missy. But Doc, it ain't gonna happen. Ya see, when I get home from a long day in the cab, dead tired, I open the door and there are the two of them looking at me, Ma and Missy. Ma has a scowl on her face and is ready to tear into me. Missy, on the other hand, is shaking all over, she's that happy—her face is grinning so wide, she could eat a banana sideways. Now who do you think I'm going to run to?"

I nodded my head in agreement because I understood his point only too well. He loved his wife, but he simply wanted permission to savor his fifteen minutes of fame.

Everybody gets fifteen minutes of fame once in his lifetime. We pet owners get our fifteen minutes every time we come home—or even return from the next room.

A few days after I saw the cab driver in Chicago, I returned home. I was tired from my travels and looking forward to seeing my family.

Pulling into the driveway, I peered through the windshield, straining to catch my first glimpse of my loved ones. My two children, Mikkel and Lex, are very close to good ol' dad, but I didn't see their faces pressed against the window looking for me. Nor did my beloved wife, Teresa, come running in super slow motion across the yard, arms open wide ready to embrace me.

But I didn't despair. I knew I was still wanted, a Hollywood heartthrob, hometown hero to my two dogs: Scooter, a wirehaired fox terrier, and, Sirloin, a black Labrador retriever!

As soon as I exited the pickup, Sirloin and Scooter charged to meet me. Their love-filled eyes danced with excitement, and their tail turbochargers whipped them into a delighted frenzy of fur.

Was this affection-connection routine, or ho-hum for me? Was I cool, calm and collected?

Heck no. I turned into a blithering idiot as I got out of my truck and rushed to meet the hairy-princess, Scooter, and Sirloin, the fur-king.

There I stood, all the false layers stripped away, masks removed and performances cancelled. It was my true self. Extra pounds, bad-hair day, angry people, travel strains, no matter. Scooter and Sirloin came to the emotional rescue and allowed me to drink in the sheer love and joy of the moment. I was drunk with contentment.

I was glad this took place in the privacy of my own home. What happened next might have spoiled my polished professional image. I immediately smiled, and raised my voice an octave or two, exclaiming, "Sirloin, yuz is daaaaddy's boy, aren't ya?" And, "Scooter, have you been a good girl today? Yeah you have, you've been a goooood girl!!"

They responded by turning inside out with delight, pressing themselves against my legs and talking to me. I felt as if I could tap directly into their wellspring of positive, healing energy. Gee, it was great to be home!

I bounded up the steps to find the rest of the family, heart open, stress gone and spirits restored by my fifteen minutes of fame.

Marty Becker, D.V.M.

A Gift Exchange

My favorite Christmas custom is placing reminders of special people or events on my tree. It's only a tiny artificial tree, but it's loaded with mementos. Many were never intended to be ornaments: intricately whorled cross sections of pink seashells from Florida; several small, hand-carved olivewood crosses from my trip to the Holy Land. A few traditional ornaments, such as a deep blue, hand-blown ball well over a century old, given to me by an "adopted aunt," bring to mind people I love. Two antique stars are family heirlooms. But the ornament I save to put on last, most honored at the very top, came to me in a most unusual way.

It started late one autumn, a chilly evening in 1980, when I got home from work. I happened to glance up at the crooked old apple tree next to the apartment garage, and a squirrel caught my eye. His patchy coat looked unhealthy, and his tail downright bedraggled. He looked hungry as well as sick. I watched as he climbed the tree, but he couldn't climb very fast. I felt sorry for him. He looked as forlorn as an old bachelor with no one to love or look after him.

I went inside and found an old sack of pecans. Then I placed one on the open cement porch, went back inside, and peeked between the red-and-white-checked door curtains. "Come on down, Old Batch," I thought.

But the squirrel stayed in the tree. I was too tired and hungry to keep vigil so I fixed supper and forgot about the nut. Next morning it was gone, and I put another in its place before leaving for work. That evening it was gone too, so I put out a couple more. This became a daily ritual even though I seldom saw Old Batch.

About a week later, I was surprised to be welcomed home by the cautious old squirrel, who approached to within three feet of me on the sidewalk, obviously ready to back off if I made even one wrong move. I spoke softly, and slowly climbed the steps: "I'm glad you can use the nuts," I said. "Let me get another one."

When I returned with it, I stooped to place it in the accustomed spot. Then I went inside, gently closing the glass storm door. Old Batch could see me, but he must have known I could not get near him. I waited excitedly, hoping to watch him eat this time.

Sure enough, the aging squirrel hopped up my steps. But Old Batch ignored my nut. Instead, he inched his way to the brick planter next to the porch, hopped in, rummaged around and quickly pulled out a whitened fragment of bone from his hiding place beneath the dead leaves. Holding it in his paws, he seemed to be using it as a tool, as if he was sharpening his teeth. His bright eyes watched me all the while. Then he dropped the bone and picked up the nut. He held it near his mouth but made no attempt to crack it with his teeth. Dropping the nut, he hopped down my steps one by one, turned and cocked his head, and waited on the sidewalk. His silent message came through loud and clear: this old squirrel was too decrepit to crack hard old shells without breaking his teeth! He must still be hungry.

I found my nutcracker, cracked three nuts and slowly opened the door. I placed the meal on the porch and retreated. Back in a flash, Old Batch ate two nuts, nibbling away as he held each one in his tiny paws. He took the third nut with him. From then on, I put out only cracked nuts, several at a time. I continued to put cracked pecans out till mid-January, when the nuts went untouched. I never saw Old Batch again. But he left behind vivid memories and something else.

The day after I began cracking the pecans, in exactly the spot where I had left them, I found a glittering, many-faceted amber glass bead, about half an inch long. I wondered where the mysterious gem had come from. Maybe Old Batch had scavenged it from a trash sack, or picked it up after someone dropped it in the alley. Had he held it in his tiny paws, turning his treasure around as the sun sparkled on it? I like to believe that he left it just for me, as his only way of thanking me for understanding his need.

I was so moved that I sent the bead to a Florida cousin, a jeweler who created a metal holder for my trinket. I carefully sewed it in the center of a miniature white star made of starched hand-crocheted lace. And at Christmas time the squirrel's sparkly gift is always the topmost ornament on my memory tree.

For me it is a beautiful reminder that I must never take for granted all the incomprehensible wonders of nature or forget that even the apparently voiceless can communicate very clearly if we pay attention when they feel moved to say "God bless you."

Mary Bucher Fisher

Chitra's Calling

*Teaching a child not to step on a caterpillar is
as valuable to the child as it is to the caterpillar.*

Bradley Miller

Chitra Besbroda didn't plan to be a hero, but she is. And as often happens, Chitra's heroism began with one small act of kindness.

Many years ago, shortly after arriving in the United States from her native Sri Lanka, Chitra was walking home from her job as a clinical social worker. Her path took her through the streets of Harlem. As Chitra passed by one of the area's many dilapidated buildings, she heard a strange sound from inside. She paused for a moment, and was about to continue her journey, when again she heard an almost imperceptible high-pitched whine. Walking over to the weathered door, Chitra peered through its small keyhole. Peering back was a large dog with sad, brown eyes. From what Chitra could see, the dog looked like a German shepherd crossed with who-knew-what else. She guessed he had been left to guard the building from intruders. But if so, the dog wasn't doing his job, because Chitra could see that he was wagging his tail as she spoke softly to him.

As a Buddhist-born woman, Chitra had been raised to respect all forms of life equally. It didn't seem right for such a friendly dog to be expected to stay by himself day and night behind locked doors. Gazing through the keyhole into the dog's mournful eyes, Chitra vowed to help him gain his freedom.

This decision set Chitra on an arduous journey. For a few weeks she visited the dog, whom she called Teddy, on her way to and from work, carrying a small bag of dog food. The door was always locked, so to feed her lonely charge she sat by the door, poking the small morsels of food through the keyhole—piece by piece. Soon, Teddy learned to hold his tongue under the hole to catch the food. Chitra's only reward for her efforts was his occasional high-pitched whine. It was enough.

Eventually, after asking around the neighborhood, Chitra learned the name of the man who owned the building and Teddy. Cautiously she approached the owner and introduced herself, being careful not to anger him or make him feel guilty about Teddy. After a couple of weeks, she convinced the man to let her take Teddy home with her for the weekend. After all, she told him, she had a nice place downtown where Teddy would be well-cared for, and it would save him the expense of feeding the dog, at least for a couple of days each week. The man agreed after Chitra promised to bring his dog back early on Monday. Thus began Teddy's weekend excursions downtown, where Chitra pampered him like a child.

Bringing him back to his desolate place behind the shabby door each Monday became harder and harder. One weekend, Chitra picked Teddy up from the ramshackle building that had been his prison for so long and never returned.

For weeks Chitra suffered verbal abuse and threats of physical violence from Teddy's owner, but she refused to return the dog to him, knowing how unhappy Teddy would be imprisoned again. Instead, she pleaded with the man to have compassion and to let her keep Teddy. Finally, he relented. Chitra was overjoyed but quickly realized it would be impossible to keep such a large, rambunctious shepherd in her small downtown apartment full-time. Even though she knew she could not be Teddy's owner, she prayed for someone to appear who could give Teddy a good life.

One day she was told of a kind, soft-spoken Spaniard who worked at the United Nations who wanted a dog. Chitra called him, instantly liked him and felt in her heart he'd make a good owner for Teddy. But even so, she conducted a thorough background check and insisted on meeting the man before she'd decide whether to relinquish Teddy to him.

There were a number of delays, but finally, the day arrived when Chitra and Teddy would meet the man with the gentle voice. Chitra's heartstrings were taut with conflicting emotions. She longed for Teddy to find the perfect home where he could live out the rest of his life in luxury, but at the same time her heart ached at the thought of losing him. With a simple prayer, she promised to do whatever was right and trusted that she'd know what that was once she met the man face-to-face.

The three met in a park not far from Chitra's apartment. The meeting did not start well. The Spaniard appeared nervous and ill at ease. *Was he hiding something that I should know?* wondered Chitra. Teddy also seemed a bit concerned, partially hiding behind Chitra's legs. After a few minutes of chitchat, Chitra wasn't sure about this man and, remembering her prayer, thought she should call the whole thing off.

Then the man's attention switched to Teddy. He bent down and coaxed Teddy to him. Slowly the dog crept closer to the man, whining softly. As he did so, the man reached into the pocket of his trench coat and brought out a few small nuggets of dog food. Seeing and smelling the food, Teddy scurried closer. As the man held out a nugget between his fingers, Teddy gently reached out with his tongue for it, as he had done at the keyhole hundreds of times before.

Chitra looked across at the man's face and saw that it had broken into a smile of pure pleasure at how Teddy had accepted his offering. Chitra knew that look. It was the look of a true dog lover. As Chitra gazed at the kind man and the big dog, she knew she had fulfilled her vow. Teddy was finally free.

But it wasn't long before she realized there were "Teddys" everywhere. All around Harlem, she noticed other dogs being used as "living burglar alarms." She could not turn her back on them either.

For over twenty-five years, Chitra has continued her crusade to save the "junkyard dogs and cats" of Harlem. In the process, she has helped rescue over three thousand animals, many of them starved and physically abused. Eventually Chitra founded Sentient Creatures, Inc., a charity dedicated to helping pets and people live harmoniously together.

The need of the animals called her so strongly, Chitra couldn't help but answer. Teddy, her first rescue, had left indelible paw prints upon Chitra's soul.

W. Bradford Swift, D.V.M.

3

PETS AS HEALERS

A faithful friend is the medicine of life.

Old Proverb

"Eat some grass."

Reprinted by permission of Charles Barsotti.

The Therapy Team

My sister found Jake roaming the streets. He was all skin and bones, his fur was matted, and he was filthy and exhausted. The only thing shiny about him were his big eyes. They looked just like the eyes of a deer.

My family telephoned me to come look at him as soon as my sister brought him home. When I saw Jake I knew. My family didn't even have to ask, and I didn't need to say a word. "We knew you'd take him," said my sister.

The next day, I took Jake to the vet. After his examination, the vet said, "I'm afraid this dog has a serious heart condition. I don't expect him to make it to the end of the week." I'd only had him one night, but the news hit me hard. Jake looked at me and I at him and I said, "Let's go home, boy."

A month passed as Jake proved the doctor wrong. Jake blossomed; clearly he adored people and loved life. Grateful for his recovery, we simply took things one day at a time. Then, one morning, I noticed a newspaper article requesting dogs and volunteers for a pet-assisted therapy program. I thought this would suit Jake—and I must have gotten over twenty calls from friends and family who had seen the article and insisted that Jake would be perfect—

so I scheduled an interview. Jake was, as the interviewer said, "enthusiastic," and he went on to pass several more interviews, vet visits and discipline tests with flying colors. He was now an official hospital volunteer.

I was so proud, and Jake was too. For the next six years, we spent every Friday night at the hospital in the oncology/hematology unit; we saw hundreds of patients.

One particular visit stands out. We were working with another team, Sherry and her dog, MacDuff. It had been a long Friday night after a long Friday, and we were all tired. It was well past eleven o'clock, and as we passed the elevator, the doors opened and a man in his fifties and his grown son stepped out. They almost ran into Jake and Mac. "Oh, how beautiful," said the son. "Can we pet the dogs?"

"Sure, that's why we're here," Sherry replied.

The son knelt down and embraced the dogs, then jumped up and asked, "Can they visit a patient?" He glanced at his father, lifting his eyebrows to seek approval.

His father looked down at the floor and said slowly, with emotion, "My wife is very ill."

I placed my hand on his shoulder and said, "We've seen lots of very sick patients. Which room is she in?"

They led the way down the hall, and as we entered the silent room, we saw the patient lying on her side under the covers. She was asleep, twisted in a fetal position. She was very pale, and we knew instantly that this should be a short visit.

I pulled a chair over next to her head. I sat down and Jake hopped right up into my lap. I gently took the woman's clenched fist and let her knuckles stroke Jake's long soft ears.

I spoke directly to her, "This is Jake, and he's got very long ears. We think he's part cocker spaniel and part Irish setter." Her hand relaxed, slowly opened and lightly gripped onto Jake's ear. Jake glanced at me with his big deer eyes; we knew we'd made contact. I asked the woman, "Did you ever think you'd see a dog in the hospital?"

She opened her eyes just a bit and answered very slowly, but clearly, "No, I never thought I'd see a dog here." She started to gently pat Jake's head unaided, with a completely open hand. I smiled. She smiled. Jake smiled.

I said, "He's got a partner here. MacDuff would like to see you if it's okay with you." Sherry lifted MacDuff up. The patient's face filled with delight when she saw Mac, a beautiful sheltie.

She exclaimed, "My father used to raise shelties." She asked her son to help her up so she could hug Mac. Every eye in that stark hospital room was on them. Her husband and son beamed.

We didn't stay much longer after that hug, but the once-solemn room was now filled with warmth. For Sherry and I, this was an absolutely lovely visit with a devoted family. But as we enthusiastically told the nurse about the patient talking and hugging Mac, she interrupted, "You must have the wrong room." We confirmed the name and the room. The nurse stood very still.

"What is it?" Sherry asked.

She replied, "I have goose bumps."

The nurse went on to explain that this patient was very sick. Only 5 percent of her brain was functioning. On her arrival, they didn't think she'd make it through the first night. She'd been there a week, but had not awakened— she wasn't expected to awake. Family and friends had been keeping a vigil by her bedside the entire time. Now we all had goose bumps.

As the nurse scurried down the hall to check on her patient, we saw the father and son holding tightly to each other outside the room. They were jubilant. We turned and looked down at Mac and Jake sound asleep in the middle of the nurses' station. I guess miracles are exhausting.

For the next six years, I was blessed with Jake's company, and I'm grateful for every second. My dog, and others like him, had a power that left me in awe: He lay with people as they prepared for death. He listened as a young mother rehearsed her words to her children, telling them that she wouldn't be there to celebrate their joys or comfort them in their sadness. He had the ability to help patients overcome pain even morphine couldn't mask. He comforted family members as they said their last goodbyes to loved ones.

I felt so privileged to be a part of our therapy team, not only because I witnessed what Jake was able to do, but because I had the voice to tell of it, and to celebrate it, both during his lifetime and even now, long after he is gone. It's simple: My dog Jake worked miracles with his love.

Terry Perret Martin

Medicine Cat

I have felt cats rubbing their faces against mine and touching my cheek with claws carefully sheathed. These things, to me, are expressions of love.

James Herriot

The doctors sent my mother home to die. A fifteen-year survivor of breast cancer, she had suffered two heart attacks when advanced cancer was found in her lung.

Mom had struggled to raise three daughters while holding a full-time job, yet worked hard to maintain a cozy home for her family. Growing up, I knew only two things about my mother: She had an iron will, and she loved nature. During her days of illness, she told me a third: "I've had a miserable life."

My dad was a difficult man to live with, but my mom did not complain, probably because she could not put words to her own need. But when it became clear that because of her progressive deterioration, my dad regarded her as a burden, she and I decided that she would move to my home.

I had three weeks to make a myriad of arrangements. I

changed my work schedule, found transportation, an oncologist, cardiologist, hospice care, medical equipment, a caregiver and bather. My plan for Mom's final days was simple: She would live with love, and die with grace.

Upon her arrival, after an exhausting five-hour trip, Mom was examined by the home health-care nurse. The nurse took me aside and asked, "How long do you think your mother has?"

"Two, maybe three months," I said.

The nurse looked at me sadly. "Adjust your thinking," he said. "She has days, maybe a week. Her heart is weak and unstable."

My home, small and comfortable, was a haven to four cats and a golden retriever. The animals had the run of my house. During my parents' infrequent visits, they'd seen the cats prowl the kitchen counters, the dog snooze on the couch and knew the cats shared my bed. This made my father angry and my mother uncomfortable. I was worried my mother would be bothered by my pets.

We installed the electric hospital bed and oxygen machine, which frightened the cats from the bedroom. I'd moved their furniture, and they were peeved. The retriever, on the other hand, an immature dog with bad habits, was excited by all the changes in the house. She jumped up, barked and shed more profusely than usual.

One cat, however, seemed to adjust perfectly. Otto had been an ugly, smelly kitten adopted from the animal shelter, but he grew into a handsome cat. His short coat was white with black and tan tabby patches, accented by bold orange spots. The veterinarian decided he was a calico. "Unusual," she said, "because calicos tend to be female."

Otto was as smart as he was unusual. He had learned to retrieve paper balls, ran to the telephone when it rang and even gave useful hints about how to fix the toilet. Once when I was trying to repair the toilet, he kept reaching into the open tank, pushing on the float with his paw. Since I was not having any success with the repair, I decided he might be on to something. I went to the hardware store and bought a new float mechanism. It worked.

Otto was the one cat who was not afraid of the hospital bed, the oxygen machine or the medicinal smells. Nor was he afraid of the frail woman who had scolded him down from the kitchen counter. Otto jumped onto the foot of Mom's hospital bed, and stayed.

He was not startled by the nurses. He did not interfere when Mom was fed, nor when she was transferred from bed to commode and back. Whether the disturbance was from changing her bed or because of bathing, he simply waited to resume his post. With the exception of eating and using the litter box, Otto never left Mom's room.

Days passed, and Mom started to rally. "Not unusual," I was told, "a rally is often a sign of imminent death."

I grieved. But Otto would not give her up so easily. He used her improved condition to reposition himself from the foot of her bed to her side. Her thin fingers found his soft coat. He leaned into her body, as if clinging to the threads of her will to live. Though weak, she caressed the cat and would not allow me to take him.

Days turned into weeks and Mom continued to fight. Once, after the nurses had gone for the day, I heard the sound of Mom's voice coming from her room. I found her with the head of the bed raised. Otto was tucked into the crook of her elbow, listening adoringly as she read from the newspaper. I will forever cherish the memory of Mom's face with Otto's paw, claws retracted, caressing the side of her chin.

Being vigilant, I made sure juice, water and pain medications were always available. One evening I was surprised to find Mom unassisted in the bathroom, filling her empty medication dish with water. "Mom, what are you doing?" I asked.

Without looking up, she replied, "Getting a drink set up for Otto." I helped her back to bed. Mom sipped apple juice while Otto drank from the stainless steel dish. Getting that drink set up became her evening ritual.

Eventually, using a walker, Mom began to take walks through the house. She was trailed by oxygen tubing and Otto. Where she rested, Otto rested. Where she moved, Otto shadowed. It seems I had forgotten my mom was a mother. Somehow, Otto knew, and during those days he became her cat child, giving her life purpose. We had come a long way from the days when she used to chase him off the kitchen counter.

Exactly three years have passed since then. The hospital bed and oxygen machine are long gone. The medicines and nurses are gone, too. But Mom's still here. And so is Otto. And so is the bond that united them in days of sickness.

"You know, I swear that Otto knows my car when I drive up!" Mom says.

He does. Whenever Mom returns home from running an errand, he greets her car at the curb. She carries him up the driveway. They just pick up wherever they left off, with his front paws wrapped around her neck.

Happily, I prepare meals with Mom watching from a stool, and Otto next to her on the counter.

When we saw the oncologist a while ago, he patted himself on the back. "I can't believe it, Lula," he said. "I can't find your cancer and your heart is strong. When your daughter brought you to me, I thought you were a ship that had sailed."

We let the doctor think what he likes, but Mom gives the credit to Otto.

Thankfully, my mother has put off dying, and Otto continues to share his gift of love—a medicine more potent than any drug a doctor could prescribe.

Joan M. Walker

Sweet Pea's Mama

The Colorado Boys Ranch (CBR) is located in the southeastern part of the state, a sparsely populated area with flat plains reaching out to the horizon in all directions. For the boys who come here, mostly from the inner cities of this country, I think it must seem like another planet. Not only is the vastness of the terrain unsettling, but many of the boys are living around animals for the first time. Nothing in their previous experience has prepared them for "life on the Ranch."

I, on the other hand, spent my entire boyhood on a ranch here in Colorado, one of fourteen children. I spent most of my time with animals—horses, cows and dogs— and I know firsthand the magic in the interaction of boy and animal. Now, as the head of the horsemanship program at CBR, I witness again the power of animals to heal broken spirits.

The boys at CBR are what I call "last-chance kids." Sent by social welfare services, educational systems and private agencies, they are boys in trouble; some have spent time in jail or reform schools, many are escaping severely dysfunctional families, while others have no family at all. Yet all the boys share one basic trait—they don't trust or believe in adults. They've learned from hard experience that no one is *truly* there for them.

Martin was a typical new arrival. He had been in "lock-up" prior to coming to the ranch for a variety of offenses, including assault. The fifteen-year-old had difficulty keeping his temper, as well as a serious attitude problem.

He chose to join the horsemanship program, but obviously he had no experience at all with animals, especially horses. He seemed to consider a horse a strange form of motorcycle, useful only as a vehicle for speed and thrills. He pushed his way to the front of the line every day, knocking down smaller children in his frenzy to get up on the horse and start moving—fast. We tried to work with him, but he seemed oblivious to anything but his own need for excitement. I wasn't sure how much longer we could put up with his behavior.

I was wrestling with my dilemma about Martin one morning, when one of my staff flew into my office and told me that one of the mares was ill. I ran to the mare's stall, and although we summoned the vet immediately, nothing could be done and within the hour she was dead. This mare had recently foaled so even though we were all very upset, we had no time to grieve as we had to immediately turn our attention to her young baby whose first need was to eat.

We made up some formula and, putting it in a bottle, offered it to the foal. But the little horse was difficult and would not accept the bottle. We had to put our hands in the formula and let her suck the formula off of our fingers. It was a painfully slow and inefficient method of feeding, but we had no choice if we wanted the foal to survive.

At that moment, Martin, finished with his daily hot-rod-style riding session, walked into the barn. Muscling his way through the crowd of kids who were watching us feed the foal, he got to the front and started yelling, "Let me feed it! Let me feed it! I want to feed it!"

I showed Martin how to put his hand in the bucket and offer his fingers to the foal. He put his hand in the bucket and thrust his fingers towards the foal's mouth. When the baby closed her mouth around his finger, Martin yelped with surprise and drew back, shouting, "Hey, it bit me!"

But seeing the tiny little horse groping with her nose in the air for more food, he immediately re-wet his hand and put it near her nose, where she again latched on to his finger and sucked greedily. This time, Martin's face relaxed into a smile of pure pleasure. Again and again, he put his hand in the bucket and gave it to the foal. "She's so hungry," he said softly. Eventually, the foal had enough formula, and like all babies with a bellyful of nourishment she fell into a satisfied sleep.

I looked over at Martin and a jolt of surprise ran through me. He looked like a different person, his face radiant with tenderness. His eyes never leaving the baby horse, he asked me, "What's going to happen to her now?"

I told him she had lost her mama and she needed someone to take care of her. Then we talked about how it feels to lose a mother, how scary it is to be alone. I'm convinced that some of the best therapy at the ranch happens in situations like these.

We sat quietly together, watching the foal sleep and then Martin said to me, "She's my baby now. I'll be her mama."

And he was. Martin was the best surrogate mother a foal could have had. He came every day to feed the baby horse we named Sweet Pea and to clean her stall. He brushed her, sat with her, held her and played with her. They had a wild game where they took turns chasing each other, which was wonderful to see. Every time I turned around, Martin was there—I think that boy would have slept out there with Sweet Pea if we had let him.

When it was time to halter-break the little filly, Martin asked me if he could do it, and I said yes. When he had started taking care of Sweet Pea, he had begun reading everything he could about horses. In a short time, he had become one of the horsemanship program's star pupils. As I watched Martin—now a competent and gentle horse-man—work with Sweet Pea, it was hard to believe that only a few months ago I wouldn't have trusted him around *any* horse, much less a young filly.

Martin was different with the other boys as well. It was now common to see him helping a younger boy to saddle and mount a horse, and encouraging the boys as they learned to ride. And if anyone was as rough and wild as Martin had once been, he immediately told the boy in a firm tone to "Act right around the horses!"

Everyone at the ranch knows that the animals trans-form these boys. Time and time again, boys who are hav-ing a rough time run out of their classrooms and find their special animal, a horse or a dog or even a goat or sheep. The boys will throw their arms around that animal's neck and bury their faces in a soft coat, and talk and talk and talk, knowing that their animal friend will listen, patiently and silently, eyes full of love and acceptance, for as long as they are needed. The animals are simply "being there" for kids who could never count on that in their lives before.

I've always known that the animals can act like mamas for the boys, healing hearts that yearn for close contact and love. But now that I've met Martin, I see that for some boys, it takes *being* a mama to become whole.

Jim Kerr

Meant to Be

A few years ago, we had a Lab puppy named Blue whom we loved very much. But because everyone in the family spent so much time at work or at school, it soon became obvious Blue wasn't getting the attention and training she needed. It was a difficult decision, but we decided to see if we could find her a better home than we could provide at that time.

I asked around at our church and at work, looking for a special home for Blue. A coworker told me that she had a friend whose old dog had recently died. The family was looking for a puppy. I knew of the family: the husband was named Frank and his wife, Donna, was a Lamaze instructor who worked at a local hospital. Their children, my friend told me, were crazy about dogs and missed their old dog tremendously. It sounded like the perfect place.

I spoke to Donna on the phone, and she was thrilled about taking Blue. I arranged for my husband to deliver the puppy the following day, which was a Friday. Frank gave my husband their address, 412 Adams, and told him that he would be home all day, doing work on the house, so my husband should look for ladders in the front yard.

The next morning, my husband took Blue and set off in the car. Our sad good-byes were lightened by the knowledge that she was going to a wonderful home.

Donna and Frank lived an hour away, on the other side of the nearest big town. My husband found the house; the number 412 was clearly displayed and there was a ladder in the front yard. Taking the puppy in his arms, he went up to the house and knocked on the door. There was no answer. He waited a moment and knocked again.

A man in the next yard called over to him, "Who are you looking for?"

My husband said, "Frank."

"Oh, Frank went to the hospital," he said. "I don't know when he's coming back."

My husband was irked. Frank had said he'd be home all day. Maybe he'd had to give Donna a ride to work at the hospital. But my husband couldn't wait around. He had made appointments for the rest of the day and had to get going. Something of this must have shown on his face, for the man in the next yard said, "What's the problem, young fella?"

My husband explained his predicament and the neighbor offered to keep the puppy at his house until Frank returned. The neighbor had a fenced yard and said it'd be no trouble at all. He was a nice man with dogs of his own, and my husband decided it would be all right. He gave the puppy to the neighbor and left for his appointments.

The following Monday when I returned to work, my co-worker said to me, "Did you change your mind about giving away Blue?"

Surprised, I answered, "No. Why?"

"Well, Donna told me you never delivered her on Friday. They figured you'd had a change of heart when it came time to really say good-bye."

I told her we certainly *had* delivered Blue. I called Donna and told her about the neighbor taking care of Blue until Frank returned.

"But Frank was home all day!" she insisted. "And we haven't heard from any of our neighbors."

What on earth was going on? We finally figured out that my husband had made a wrong turn and had gone to 412 on the next street over. There had been a storm not long before and many people had ladders out to do roof and gutter repairs. Could it possibly be that the man in that house was also named Frank?

My husband and I got into the car and drove over to see what had become of Blue. We saw immediately that that he'd gone one street too far and we knocked on the door of the house where he'd left Blue.

A red-faced man in his sixties answered our knock. When we explained that we were looking for a puppy that had been delivered here last week, the man answered, "Oh, you mean the one that Frank ordered."

Realizing that the man at 412 on this street was also named Frank, we explained the mix-up. The man's face grew somber.

"What's wrong?" I asked. "Is the puppy all right?"

"Oh, the puppy is fine. In fact, I'm sure the puppy is great. But . . . well, I hope you don't want it back," he said seriously. Seeing the question in our eyes, he continued, "When you came with the puppy on Friday, my neighbor Frank was at the hospital. He'd been out in the yard working and had started having chest pains, so his wife took him to the hospital. Frank never did come home. He died of a massive coronary Friday afternoon. It was a terrible shock for his family, and I decided not to bother them until things had settled down a bit. Yesterday, I brought the puppy over and knocked on their door. Frank's eldest daughter came out. I told her that her father had ordered a puppy and since he hadn't been home, that I'd taken delivery on it for him. I said I didn't know what to do with the little dog now that 'things had changed' at their house.

"The daughter just couldn't believe it. She said, 'My father ordered a puppy? This is Dad's puppy?' Then she reached out and I gave her the pup. She hugged that little dog real tight, stuck her face in its fur and just began to cry.

"I wasn't sure what to say, so I just stood there. After a while, she looked up at me and thanked me. She said, 'You don't know what this means to me. I'm so glad to have my father's dog.' The puppy was wiggling around, trying to kiss the daughter any way it could and her face was just lit up with love."

Amazed at the story I turned to my husband, "We can't take Blue back now."

The man nodded in agreement. "Folks, some things are just meant to be. I'd say that puppy is in exactly the right place."

Cindy Midgette

Is Holly Working Today?

For Holly and me, it started with a stray kitten. Abandoned in the harsh winter weather, she huddled in a ball on the front steps of our building, an elementary school for emotionally disturbed children where I provided therapy three days a week.

That morning, I kept the kitten in my office while the principal figured out where to take it. Little did I know that this tiny bundle of fur curled next to my desk would inspire a project that would affect the entire well-being of the school.

It started as the children soberly traipsed into my office that day for their therapy. When they spotted the kitten, their faces suddenly brightened. Their reticence and tenseness seemed to melt away as they petted the stray, and our sessions were relaxed and open. The kitten's effect was astounding, and, by the end of the day, I was hatching a plan. My dog, Holly, was a gentle, gregarious, well-behaved seven-year-old of mixed parentage. Couldn't she have the same relaxing effect on the children I counseled? The more I thought about it, the more I was convinced that Holly was perfect for the job. She loved to ride in the car, could follow basic commands in English and Spanish, and could tolerate small, sticky hands running their fingers through her short, brown hair. Enthused, I began paperwork requesting permission to bring Holly to school with me, providing documentation of the benefits of companion animals.

The enthusiasm stopped short at my supervisor's desk. "What if it bit one of the children? What if it had an accident?" she asked me curtly. Obviously skeptical, she pushed my proposal through the proper channels. The project was approved, but my supervisor clearly let me know that Holly and I were on trial. The responsibility for any problems with the "dog experiment" would land squarely on my shoulders.

Optimistic nonetheless, I smiled at the signs pasted on my office door as I unlocked it on Holly's first morning with me at school. "Holly is happy to be here," the children had carefully stenciled. Already the children were responding positively to the idea of a dog counselor. Holly sniffed out my office, and we settled in for a day of work.

At a knock on my door, Holly jumped up and barked loudly. I hurried to calm her down, wincing at the noise; I was sure my supervisor would not consider the barking therapeutically productive for insecure children. We would have to work on that. A small boy entered, and he and Holly stared at each other warily.

"Does that dog bite?" he asked.

"No," I assured him. "Why don't you give her a treat?" I handed him a bag of multicolored doggie treats. "Pick any color you like," I said. The boy chose a red treat and tentatively held it out to Holly. She neatly and gently took the treat, swallowed it quickly and licked the boy's hand. The boy smiled. Holly's critical debut had been a success.

After the bell rang, a succession of little visitors came to our door, vying to see Holly. As they took turns handing treats to Holly, she wagged her tail and licked their hands, showing her approval. It was no wonder the children were drawn to her: For many of them, it was their first encounter with unconditional acceptance.

During the days that followed, Holly learned not to bark at the children's knocks on my office door. I set up a corner for her in my office on a piece of carpet remnant. The children eagerly came to me for their counseling visits, sitting on the floor by Holly and petting, brushing, playing with and confiding in her. As they relaxed with Holly, they let down their defenses. Our counseling sessions became smooth and productive.

Little by little, Holly's influence reached beyond her little corner of my office. Absences at school began to drop, and the children's disruptive behaviors softened. Even the teachers ducked in for some pet therapy throughout the day, giving Holly a short pat and restoring their spirits in her presence.

I didn't realize how loved Holly was, though, until I missed two days of work with strep throat. When I called in sick the first day, expecting a touch of sympathy, I was immediately asked if that meant Holly would have to stay home, too. The second day, I was seriously asked if I could at least send Holly to work in a cab. Apparently, the teachers were tired of answering the question: "Is Holly working today?"

One morning before school, nine-year-old LeMar, a third-grader who visited Holly regularly, was shot and killed in a domestic dispute. His classmates learned of the tragedy while they were still on the school bus, and by the time they arrived at school, they were terrified and in tears.

I hurried to LeMar's home classroom, Holly trailing behind me. LeMar's teacher stood there with tears streaming down her face. "My degree didn't prepare me to handle something like this," she sobbed. I mustered all my resources and expertise to come up with the right words to soothe them.

"Crying is okay for adults and children," I began, "especially when something like this happens." Still seeing the pain on their faces, I continued to tell them that it was okay to be scared, that fear is a natural response. For a while, we talked about how we would miss LeMar. It was at this point that I realized what Holly was doing.

She was working her way around the room, going from child to child—and the teacher—putting her front paws on their laps and stretching up to lick the tears from their faces. Unconsciously, the children hugged her back, running their fingers through her fur with such intensity that she would have gone bald if they'd done it all day. She called no significant attention to herself, but quietly expressed love and consolation. She diligently kept up her silent comfort throughout that long, difficult day.

As I slid into the front seat of my car that afternoon, I leaned back, exhausted from the emotional trauma. I just wanted to be home. Glancing briefly into the backseat, I was surprised to see that Holly had already fallen asleep. She was just as drained as I was, if not more so, and, not for the first time, I felt a pang of guilt. *Was it fair to ask my dog to take on the emotional responsibilities of troubled children? Shouldn't she be allowed to stay home and enjoy the carefree life of a house pet?*

Those doubts may be why, even now, I occasionally stop in my rush to leave for school in the morning and, instead of ordering Holly into the car, look at her, asking, "Do you want to go to school today?" When she leaps up eagerly, all wags and excitement, I figure she's answered that burning question for all of us. Yes, Holly is working today.

Barbara J. Wood

The Healing Touch

As a veterinarian making the journey from physical medicine to spiritual understanding, I found it was the animals who were my greatest teachers. I owe an especially large debt of thanks to an old gray tabby who was once brought into my practice for treatment.

The old tabby's pelvis was fractured so badly he couldn't stand. He had been sideswiped by a car, but luckily his fractures were such that they would heal naturally over time without an operation. Although he didn't appear to have any other injuries, it was critical that I keep him in the clinic for a few days just to be sure there was nothing else wrong.

"You don't understand," his owner said pleadingly. "This cat is seventeen, and I have another one just like him at home. They were littermates, and they've never been apart a day in their lives. You've *got* to let me bring him home."

There was no way I could release the cat, no matter how emotionally wrenching the separation might be. Until he was able to stand and had bladder and bowel control, I had no choice but to keep him under observation.

"I'm sorry," I said. "It's best for the cat if he stays."

By the next morning, I wasn't so sure. The tabby gazed into space with such a vacant look in his eye that it seemed he had already given up and died. His vital signs were normal, but there was no life in him. He didn't meow. He didn't purr. He just lay there without eating, staring into some distant place where all hope was extinguished.

As I pondered what to do next, the phone rang. It was the tabby's owner, and he was frantic. "My other cat's been screaming nonstop," he complained. "He never went to sleep—just prowled around searching and meowing. You have to *do* something."

"I don't know if it will make a difference," I said, "but why don't you bring the other cat here?"

The owner made it to the clinic in minutes. When he walked in with the other cat under his arm, I thought I was seeing double. The brother cat was the image of his littermate—a fluffy pearl-gray with stripes. But while his injured sibling lay in a cage torpid in depression, this one was taut with anxious energy.

The minute I opened the cage door, the healing began. The electricity between the two cats was palpable. At the sight of his brother, the ailing cat's eyes brightened, his ears perked up and he struggled in a futile effort to get up and draw near to him.

But it was actual contact with his brother that really made the injured cat come alive. The healthy cat bounded into the cage, rushed up to his brother and, meowing with joy, began licking and sniffing him all over. With the all-important physical link reestablished, the hurt cat mewed in response, and mustering all of his strength, recipro-cated by licking any part of his brother's body that brushed by him. A leg, a tail, an ear, a shoulder—all were touched by his tongue.

The two cats couldn't seem to get enough of each other. They kept licking and cleaning and smelling, oblivious to anything but each other. They made it clear that for the rest of the clinic stay, they would be in the cage together.

That night, I peeked into the cage and saw that the cats were still inseparable. They were huddled close together, purring in unison, as the brother cat encircled his hurt twin with the loving warmth of his body.

After about three days, the hurt cat began to display normal body functions, which suggested that he had no further significant internal injuries. By the fourth day, he was able to stand on his own, with the help of his brother. The brother nudged him with his nose a few times, and the injured cat got the message. Haltingly, he struggled to his feet, leaning briefly against his brother for support. A few seconds later, he stood proudly on his own and took a few wobbly steps.

The next day, they went home. I didn't see them again until two years later, when they came in for a checkup. By then, they were nineteen and still in good health. The injured cat had fully recovered and never showed any ill effects of the accident.

It was clear that the old gray tabby's recovery resulted not from some medical breakthrough or traditional veterinary science, but from the tender touch of a brother—a profound caring that had been transferred from one to the other through the touch of a tongue and the contact of warm fur. It was these physical acts of love that had brought the gift of life.

Allen M. Schoen, D.V.M.

The Language of the Heart

Soapy Smith is a twenty-four-pound calico rex rabbit. A rex rabbit's coat lacks the stiff guard hairs of other breeds, resulting in a fur texture that is as soft as a cloud. People look startled when they first touch him and remark how soft he is. I've noticed he seems to make everyone who meets him a little softer, too.

One day, Soapy Smith and I visited a shelter for battered women located in a bedraggled section of the city. The women in the shelter looked at me through downcast eyes. No one smiled a greeting, and they appeared uninterested in Soapy's carrier. Everyone seemed tense and ready to flee. One little girl in particular moved like a wisp in the background. Never raising her eyes, never reaching out, she drifted in and out of the gathered group. The staff informed me that she had been there for over a month and had not spoken the entire time. Nothing they tried had any effect. Her mother said she had talked at one time but not in recent memory. I didn't want to imagine what could have happened to rob this little girl of the natural curiosity and enthusiasm so natural to childhood.

Spreading a blanket on the floor, I sat down and opened Soapy's carrier. As the silent child circled past me,

I told the group that Soapy would come to talk to them if they sat on his blanket. Several children did this, including the silent girl. In a short time, Soapy emerged from his carrier and slowly hopped from one child to another. Unlike visits at schools where the first touches produced squeals of delight, this visit was unusually quiet. After touching Soapy, these children looked down and sighed softly or smiled into their hands. Soapy continued his rounds, and the children and their mothers gradually began to talk about Soapy and ask questions.

I chatted with the women and children as I kept one eye on the little girl. She sat rigidly at the edge of the blanket, legs held stiffly out straight in front of her. She was staring hard at Soapy. It appeared that he kept making eye contact with her. He would hop from child to child, each visit taking him a little closer to the girl. I began to wonder if he was pausing to give her time to watch him. During all other visits we had given together in schools, his usual behavior was to hop around the circle letting each person pet him. When he got back to me he would wash his face and then start the circle again.

That day, I watched as Soapy finally worked his way toward the girl. She didn't reach out to him or encourage him in any way. Rather she sat tensely, just staring.

Finally Soapy came to a stop about two inches from her thigh. He quietly reached out and laid his chin on her knee. I was astonished. While a common behavior for dogs, this is not a behavior exhibited by rabbits, especially not by this rabbit.

The child did not reach out to pet Soapy. Instead, she slowly leaned toward him. When her face was within inches of his, she carefully reached out and circled him with her arms. So softly that no one in the room could hear, she began to talk. Folded around the rabbit, she pillowed her head on his back and whispered to him. Soapy remained motionless.

I looked up and noticed that the shelter workers had stopped talking. Every adult in the room froze in place. Time seemed suspended. Then quietly the child unfolded and sat back up. Soapy sat up too, reached forward and briskly licked her knee. She did not smile. She did not reach out to him, but the rigidity of her back relaxed, and her shoulders rounded into a comfortable slope. The little girl stood up and walked over to her mother and began to suck her thumb.

The little girl reappeared when I was preparing to leave. She reached her hands out and looked me directly in the eye. I held Soapy out to her. She wrapped him in a big hug and pressed her face against him. Suspended from my hands as he was, I was concerned that he would begin to struggle. Instead he reached out his head again and laid it on the child's shoulder. His breathing slowed and he closed his eyes. As quickly as it happened, the little girl released her hug and stepped back. As she turned away, I thought I saw the beginnings of a faint smile.

The rabbit in his cloud of soft, warm fur had touched something deep in the child—something that had died from too much hard experience. Soapy's innocence and trust appeared to kindle those very same qualities in the little girl.

Numerous times, I've seen how the loving presence of an animal can heal where words have no effect. It seems the language of the heart is simple after all.

Maureen Fredrickson,
program director for the Delta Society

Body and Soul

I was fifteen years old when I began my long battle with anorexia nervosa and bulimia. As a teenager, I succumbed to the intense peer pressure to be thin. But when I started dieting I soon lost control, and I couldn't stop losing weight. When I dropped below ninety-five pounds, my frightened parents took me to the hospital. Back in 1969, few people had even heard of eating disorders, and neither my parents nor the doctors knew how to help me.

Finally, after four years and several prolonged hospital stays, I forced myself to get better. I managed to gain back every pound I'd lost and resolved to get on with my life. I even had a boyfriend.

Then one day my best friend told me she'd seen my guy out with another girl. "He hates me because I'm so fat," I sobbed.

And so it wasn't long before I'd all but stopped eating again. My family watched in helpless horror as I repeatedly collapsed from malnutrition. I felt so ashamed and couldn't bear the pain I was causing them.

Finally I left home, hoping to make a fresh start. I packed my car and drove until I ran out of money in Phoenix, Arizona. I liked the Phoenix climate. The warm sun felt good on my emaciated body.

Unfortunately, hot sunny weather also meant lots of short shorts and halter tops. I was painfully thin, but whenever I looked in the mirror I was horrified by what I saw. "I need to lose more weight," I panicked.

Whenever I went out with friends I ate and drank normally, but afterward I always raced to the restroom to purge. The more I purged, the more depressed I became. Depression led to binge eating, which led to even more purging. I knew I was slowly killing myself. I didn't want to die, but my illness was stronger than my will to live.

I went to psychologists and attended support groups, but they didn't help. Ultimately, I grew so weak I had to quit my job and go on disability. My health steadily deteriorated as I lost irreplaceable muscle tissue. My seventy-eight-pound body was so ravaged from malnutrition, my kidneys began to shut down and I was in constant pain.

"There's nothing more I can do," my doctor said bluntly. "Barring a miracle, you're going to die."

My brother Robert brought me home to Michigan, where I took an apartment, crawled into bed and waited for God to take me. I hated my life and could hardly wait for it to be over.

The first morning I opened my eyes in my new place, I discovered a pair of liquid brown eyes looking back at me. It was Cassie, the Australian shepherd a friend in Phoenix had given me just before I'd left town.

"I suppose you need to go out," I sighed, struggling to my feet and putting on a robe.

At the front door, Cassie just sat there gazing up at me. *Ruff!* "You come, too," she seemed to be saying, and grudgingly, I shuffled off to get dressed.

A few days later in a nearby field, Cassie started pouncing at my feet and barking, eager to romp. "Go on ahead," I said, but Cassie wouldn't leave my side. She barked and barked until I finally got the message and began walking with her. Daggers of pain shot through my nutrient-starved bones with every footfall. I cried out in agony, but every time I stopped moving Cassie waited at my side and wouldn't quit barking until we were again on our way. As painful as it was, I felt my blood—life—stirring in me for the first time in a very long while.

Somehow, Cassie knew there was something terribly wrong with me. She sensed my every mood and refused to leave my side. When I grew despondent, she curled up beside me. When I sobbed in pain, she licked away my tears.

Once, on one of my bad days, I asked my sister Pam to adopt Cassie. "I don't have enough strength to take care of her anymore," I explained.

Pam shook her head no. "I won't take her," she said firmly.

"Please reconsider," I begged. "Cassie needs a good home and someone who will love her."

"She already has both of those things," Pam insisted. As hot tears filled my eyes, she hugged me and said, "Don't you understand, Cynthia? Right now that dog is the only thing keeping you alive."

She was right. I needed a miracle to stay alive, and Cassie was that miracle. She was my constant companion, my best and truest friend.

For Cassie's sake, I forced myself to eat. A few raw vegetables. A dry turkey sandwich. *After all,* I thought, *if I died, who would take care of my Cassie? Who would brush her fur, romp with her in the fields or cuddle with her on the sofa at night?*

Cassie refused to let me surrender to despair. Her confidence in my ability to overcome my illness became infectious. Our daily walks made me physically stronger. Cassie's love and understanding gave me the will to fight on.

In time, I ventured out to church and made several friends. At a singles' dance, I met a man named Philip. When he asked me out I said yes. We fell in love, and a year later we were married. And even though the doctors said that because of my health it could never happen, miraculously I got pregnant—not just once, but twice.

Today, I still battle my anorexia, but now I have four more reasons to fight my disease: Philip, my teenaged stepdaughter, Corrie, and my two young sons, Trevor and Zachary.

Cassie is still my constant companion. Wherever I go, she's always right there by my side. But at ten years of age, Cassie's health has begun to go downhill.

Cassie once took care of me, but now the tables are turned; it's my turn to take care of her. Often, with an understanding look, with a gentle paw on my arm, she seems to tell me it will soon be time for her to go.

This wonderful dog once gave me the courage to live. Now she's giving me the courage to live on without her when she goes. I won't let her down.

Cynthia Knisely
As told to Bill Holton

For Better or For Worse®
by Lynn Johnston

Dolly

When my son was small, we purchased a lovely pearl cockatiel as a pet. We named her Dolly because she had large orange dots on each side of her face like a doll. (Also, she liked to puff out her chest, which reminded me of another Dolly.)

Dolly grew in our hearts with her endearing and loving ways. She loved to sing and whistle and always looked for someone to scratch her little head. Dolly and I were especially close, and each time she heard my voice she let out a long, shrill wolf-whistle. It was our own special greeting. Although we loved her very much and knew she was special, we did not yet realize quite how special she was.

One day, we were saddened when we found out that our friends' little daughter, Shayna, was stricken with leukemia. Shayna's parents were devastated; she was just four years old. Wanting to help my friend, I began to visit Shayna at the local children's hospital each time she underwent her chemotherapy. There was little I could do other than cheer her up and be by her mother's side. Each night, I prayed for Shayna's cure.

Several weeks later, my family lost our beloved Dolly when her cage was left open and she got outside. We searched the neighborhood diligently but to no avail. Our pet was gone, and we had to face the fact that such a delicate little bird could not possibly survive the wild for very long.

Five days passed with no sign of Dolly. We lost hope of ever finding her, and we missed her so very much.

That evening I received a phone call from Shayna's mother.

"I think we've found Dolly," she said.

"*You've* found Dolly?" I could hardly believe it. "Where? Are you sure it's her?"

"Orange dots either side of her face, right?"

"That's Dolly!"

"I'll tell you the story when I see you. Come over now."

Their house was five miles away, and I drove over immediately, hoping with all my heart that it really was Dolly.

When I arrived, if I couldn't believe my eyes, I certainly believed my ears because when the bird heard my voice she let out a long wolf-whistle. . . . It was my sweet little bird!

My friend explained what had happened.

"I've been out most of the day, but our baby-sitter told us that Shayna was in the backyard. She was just sitting quietly, since she doesn't have much energy these days, when she saw a small bird in a tree. She told me she had been feeling a little lonely and had said, 'Look at the pretty bird. Wouldn't it be nice if it came down to see me?' Of course, it was Dolly, although Shayna didn't know. And the bird flew directly to Shayna, landing on her shoulder and giving her a kiss on the cheek. Shayna was ecstatic."

My friend continued, "Our baby-sitter saw that the bird was domesticated and managed to tempt her into an old cage we had in the garage—she was going to find a home for her.

"I got home in time to tuck Shayna into bed, and she told me the whole story. I was stunned. I knew how upset you'd been about losing Dolly."

I was silent, trying to take it all in. I was grateful to see my lovely bird again, but there was more. I knew something that neither Shayna nor her mother knew. After watching that poor child suffer so much, and praying for her every day, I had finally asked God for a sign that Shayna would be healed. I considered it miraculous that we had really found Dolly again, but that he had sent our simple little bird to rest on Shayna's shoulder seemed truly wondrous. I took it as his promise, and I felt in that moment that Shayna would recover.

Today, Shayna is thirteen years old and cancer free. Dolly is getting on in years for a bird, but we see to it that she lives a life of luxury because it was through her that we were all given the greatest gift—the gift of hope.

Renée Sunday

The Cat Doctor

Dr. MacFarland, a veterinarian who goes by the name The Cat Doctor, has a practice in my hometown, where we bring our cat, Ragamuffin. At one point, we had to put Ragamuffin on a strict diet of prescription food, sold only at the vet's office. One time, when I went there to get a refill, I saw one of the saddest sights I have ever seen—a cat whose hind quarters were paralyzed and could get around only by dragging his back legs behind him.

I asked the receptionist about the cat. She told me his name was Slick, and that some people had found him by the side of the road a couple of years earlier and brought him in. The poor little guy had been shot and left for dead. The Cat Doctor treated him and when he recovered, they decided to keep Slick as the office mascot.

At first, it just broke my heart to see him pull himself around the office, using just his front legs. But Slick has such spirit, that each time I saw him, I seemed to notice his difficulties less and less.

Not too long ago, Ragamuffin became ill and I had to take him to the vet. The cat was scared to death to leave our house. Although he was in horrible pain from his illness, he put up a terrific fight. He fought his way out of the cat carrier three times before I could secure it.

I finally got Ragamuffin into the car and headed over to see The Cat Doctor. Ragamuffin howled and cried the whole way. Even as I carried the carrier into the office, my cat was putting up a fight. He was terrified of being in this strange place filled with new cat and people smells.

As I looked around, I noticed Slick sitting on a little cat bed across the room, oblivious to all the commotion I'd brought into his kingdom. He ignored us, continuing to groom himself.

Setting the carrier down on the floor, I tried not to listen to Ragamuffin's strident pleas for help as I filled out the proper paperwork.

Then suddenly it got quiet. Really quiet. No more screaming. No more howls. I cocked my head to listen as I continued to calculate Ragamuffin's weight in my head. Still, silence.

A sudden fear rushed over me as I realized that the front door to Dr. McFarland's office was still open. *Omigosh,* I thought, *Ragamuffin must have gotten out of the carrier and run outside!* I dropped my pen and turned to bolt out the door. I hadn't taken more than two steps when I stopped short—captivated by the scene before me.

Ragamuffin, still in his cage, had his pink nose pressed up against the bars. He was exchanging a calm little cat greeting with Slick, who had managed to crawl all the way across the room to comfort the agitated Rags. Slick, with his paralyzed hindquarters splayed behind him, pressed his nose to the bars as well. The two cats sat quietly, Slick continuing to soothe Ragamuffin's fears in a way only another cat would know how to do.

Smiling, I realized that there was more than one Cat Doctor around this place.

Norma and Vincent Hans

4

PET-POURRI

*Dogs come when they are called; cats take
a message and get back to you later.*

Mary Bly

Paw Prints in the White House

The White House became home to our family on
Inauguration Day—January 20, 1993. Our black-and-white
cat, Socks, is only the fourth cat to live here since Franklin
Roosevelt took office in 1933, so he became something of
an international celebrity. He has been immortalized in
poems, commemorated on postage stamps in a foreign
country, and has even become a well-known figure on the
Internet, where his cartoon persona takes children on
cybertours of the White House.

Socks had been with us for awhile before our move to
Washington. One day when I took Chelsea to her piano
lesson, we spotted two kittens rollicking in her teacher's
front yard. Although the teacher had been making calls
for several days to try to reunite the small strays with
their mom, she hadn't had any luck and didn't know who
else to phone. As we were walking to the car, Chelsea
reached out to the kittens and the black one with white
paws—Socks—jumped right up into her arms. That
clinched our decision to make him part of our family. We
also arranged a good home for Socks's sibling, Midnight,
with the help of a local animal shelter.

When he became "First Cat-elect," as the press dubbed

him after the 1992 election, he had to adjust quickly to becoming a public figure. And although the Secret Service protects the White House and its inhabitants, Socks and Buddy don't have their own cat and dog agents.

Socks loves to spend sunny days in the yard behind the Oval Office, under a beautiful, historic pin oak planted by President Dwight Eisenhower and his wife, Mamie. When the weather gets too cold or rainy, the cat usually saunters over to the Visitors' Office in the East Wing. He's discovered that the high back of a Queen Anne chair there makes the perfect window seat for him to keep tabs on what's going on outside. Sometimes, he jumps up on a staff assistant's desk to look over her paperwork or take a sip of water from a vase of flowers (which he once inadvertently sent crashing to the floor!). The Visitors' Office is home to a plush three-story "cathouse" complete with scratching post, a gift handcrafted by a devoted F.O.S.— Friend of Socks—in Florida.

A few weeks after Bill, Chelsea and I moved in, letters and postcards from across the country began arriving, first by the bundle, and then by the bin. A lot of the mail was for Socks—a spontaneous outpouring of affection for the first feline to live in the White House since Amy Carter's Siamese, Misty Malarky Ying Yang.

Over the years, Socks has heard from animal lovers of all ages, including admirers from England, Bangladesh and nearly fifty other countries, who have written asking for celebrity shots and "paw-tographs" (his paw print signature).

Children of previous generations wrote to F.D.R.'s dog Fala or the Kennedys' dog, Pushinka. Today's children who write to our pets often ask: "How does it feel to have all the food you want?" "Do you have a Secret Service agent?" "Do you ever annoy the President?" "Are there any good mice in the White House?" "What do you do for a living?" Children and their animal friends have extended many invitations to our cat and dog to fetch sticks, chase squirrels or simply to get away from the White House for what they perceive as some much-needed R & R. And Socks has even received his share of marriage proposals.

Soon after Buddy arrived, Socks was deluged with messages from children who wanted to console him about having to share the White House with another pet—a *dog,* no less. "Maybe you need to teach that dog some cat manners," a young letter writer suggested. Others offered support to Buddy. "I got used to my brother," wrote one child, "so I'm sure you will get used to Socks."

Before Buddy joined our family, we often talked about getting another dog. Finally, after Chelsea went off to college, we decided it was the right time. When we thought about what kind we'd like, a big dog seemed to make the most sense. We also had heard that Labs are particularly smart, loving and playful. Buddy arrived at the White House one afternoon for a tryout with the President. Within minutes, he convinced Bill that he was the perfect candidate for First Dog. They bonded so quickly that when they sat down on a bench in the backyard, it looked as if they were two friends catching up on old times.

Our first challenge was to pick the perfect name. We received hundreds of clever suggestions in the mail. A few of my favorites were "Barkansas," "Arkanpaws," and "Clin Tin Tin." One little girl came up to me and offered "Top Secret." We had to laugh when we imagined the President running around the South Lawn calling "Top Secret, Top Secret." Finally, we settled on Buddy, the nickname of my husband's favorite uncle who had passed away. We think Uncle Buddy would have loved his namesake as much as we do.

When Buddy and Socks met for the first time, both animals were caught off guard. Socks was hanging out in his usual spot behind the Oval Office when Buddy returned from an event with the President. Intent on protecting his turf the cat hissed and got ready to spring while Buddy, just as taken aback, barked and strained at his leash. Things got so heated between them that Bill and other peacekeepers had to step in. Concerned allies set up several summits in an effort to broker a truce between the pets. It wasn't until the day that Socks swatted Buddy on the nose and sent the puppy off yelping, though, that they began to get along fine.

Although there are thousands of visitors to the White House, our cat and dog lead as normal a life as possible. Neither animal keeps an official schedule. When they do make a special appearance, they seem always to rise to the occasion. Socks, especially, likes to pose for pictures. While he has an uncanny ability to sense when someone of any age needs a little extra attention, one of his most endearing traits is the extra bit of patience he musters for children.

Among the frequent visitors to the White House are children and their families sponsored by the Make-A-Wish Foundation and other organizations that help youngsters suffering from life-threatening illnesses fulfill their fondest dreams. They're often as thrilled at shaking the paws of Socks and Buddy as they are at meeting the President.

When we moved to Washington from Little Rock, we brought our family traditions, favorite pictures and personal mementos to make the White House feel more comfortable. But it wasn't until Socks arrived with his toy mouse and Buddy walked in with his rawhide bone that this house became a home.

Pets have a way of doing that.

Hillary Rodham Clinton

Church Dog

Sunday mornings are a leisurely time in many house-holds, but they certainly weren't in our Ogilvie, Minnesota home back in the late 1920s.

Church services began at nine-thirty in the morning. Mother was the organist, so she had to be there early. That meant all of us kids had to be washed and dressed with our hair neatly combed by the time mother left the house.

As you'd expect, there was a lot of hurrying around to make sure everyone was ready on time. That was trouble enough, but one day we had another problem on our hands—our dog, Brownie.

Every morning, Brownie was let out by the first person who got up. When we called him back in, he'd usually come running right away . . . but not on this particular Sunday.

We called and coaxed for as long as we could, but Brownie was simply nowhere to be found. Unable to locate our disappearing dog, we gave up in despair and headed off to church, leaving Brownie outdoors somewhere.

We arrived at church and got settled in, with Mother at the organ. After some hymns and prayers, the minister began his sermon. We kids tried to sit still, just as we had been told to do, and not fidget. But as the preacher began to warm to his subject, I thought I heard something unusual. No one else seemed to hear it though. But then it came again, louder. It sounded like something was scratching at the church door. We kids all exchanged silent glances and stifled our giggles. Then the scratching sound was followed by the plaintive sound of a lonely dog howling. All the grown-ups pretended not to hear anything, leaning forward in their pews so they could hear every word of the minister's oration. But we kids knew that howl. Only one dog in the neighborhood made that sound.

The wailing continued and the minister paused for a moment, furrowing his brow in frustration. He didn't want to have to compete with a howling hound, so he signaled to the usher to open the door and shoo the dog away. But the usher was not quick enough for Brownie. As soon as he opened the door, in bounded our dog with a smug look on his face! He strolled up the aisle, cool as you please, as congregation and minister looked on aghast. When Brownie got to where Mother sat at the organ, he just plopped down and sat quietly. A murmur went around the church and there were some smiles and nodding of heads. The minister, determined to ignore this unusual canine caper, resumed his sermon.

The following Sunday happened to be one of those rare Sundays when we didn't go to the morning service. However, no one had informed Brownie of the change in our schedule. After we attended the evening service, we heard the story: In the morning, Brownie had made a commotion at the church door until once again he was let in. Again, he sauntered down the aisle until he reached the organist, who was about to begin playing. Brownie stood stock-still for a moment, staring at the female organist. Then, when he had determined to his satisfaction that she was definitely not Mother, he returned to the church door and made it clear that he was not interested in attending this particular service.

There were many Sundays when Brownie repeated his demonstrations of religious piety and family loyalty. As you can imagine, this was quite embarrassing for Mother. There were some people who weren't all that happy to see a dog in church. And each time we got a new preacher, Mother had to explain our unusual dog to him. Since Brownie lived to be nineteen years old, quite a few preachers got used to having that little brown dog interrupt their Sunday services.

Shortly after Brownie passed away, our minister came to call. After consoling us over our loss, he said, "If there is a heaven for dogs, you can be assured Brownie will be scratching at the door—and when it is opened, he will be given a place right up front with the best of them."

Evelyn Olson

Bahati: The Lucky One

In early 1994, my wife Margaret and I were living in
Rwanda, in central Africa. We were working with an
American-based organization, Morris Animal Foundation,
to save the endangered population of mountain gorillas
that lived in that region. There were fewer than 650 of
these gorillas left in the world.

One morning, I'd received radio communication that
my services as a veterinarian were needed to help an
injured young gorilla in the neighboring country, the
Democratic Republic of the Congo, then known as Zaire.
Margaret and I prepared for the long and often difficult
trip that lay ahead.

Travel in central Africa is never simple, and since the
recent war in this particular part of Africa, we could never
be sure what to expect or if we would reach our destination
at all. Sometimes, official barriers were insurmountable.

That day as we finally approached the border of the
Congo, we hoped we would not be stopped, since the little
gorilla we were traveling to see needed our help sooner
rather than later. After a rather lengthy delay, the soldiers
let us pass, amused when they finally understood that we
were on our way to help a gorilla.

We turned off the main road onto a wet, grassy track and headed for the base of a large volcanic peak ahead of us, where the Virunga National Park headquarters is located. As we climbed the incline to the village, the roar of our laboring engine alerted the villagers that we were approaching. As we passed by, children ran to the edge of the track, smiling and waving and calling out, *"Jambo! Jambo!* Hello! Hello!" and jumping on to the back of our slow-moving truck for a free ride up the mountain.

We arrived at the headquarters and parked the truck. The next part of our adventure would be on foot. Along with a few guides and porters, who helped us carry our supplies, we started the steep climb into the rainforest where the gorillas lived.

When we entered the forest, we were struck by the sudden quiet—no more sounds of village life—and soon we discerned the buzzing of insects and the sound of small animal movement around us. We walked a long way on our path, noting signs that a group of gorillas had recently made "night nests" in the bushes and had only left them a short while before our arrival. They couldn't be far.

Soon we reached a clearing, where we could see a group of gorillas resting—dark black shapes sitting up in the trees, oblivious to our presence. We stood quietly, observing the group and trying to find the injured gorilla.

Then I spotted a young gorilla whose hand had a red, raw appearance. Taking up my field glasses, I saw the wire of a snare twisted around his hand. We had found our patient. We quietly discussed our plan of action, and then I prepared the tranquilizer gun and stood ready. I had to watch for the right moment when I could be sure to hit just the one gorilla and hit him squarely. There were rarely second chances in situations like these; a miss could cause the group to scatter in fright or prompt the silverback, the large male leader of the group, to charge.

Suddenly, the youngster showed himself, following his mother, and I fired. The dart hit him, causing him to yelp, but it fell out as he scrambled, already a little wobbly, onto his mother's back. Luckily, he had absorbed enough of the drug, for the next moment he slipped gently off of his mother and lay in a drowsy heap on the ground.

The adults of the group came over to investigate his strange behavior. They stood in a semicircle around him, looking at him in a perplexed way. Why was he so sleepy? One by one, they came forward to touch him. We watched from a distance as the little gorilla, still trying to move, rolled down the slope towards us.

I immediately ran out and threw a cloth over him to hide him from sight. I knew that gorillas lose interest in an object if they cannot see it. And indeed, the adult gorillas, who had been so interested just a few seconds before, began to withdraw from the scene.

Now, we had to act quickly, before the silverback became aware of what was going on. With several guides standing as sentries to warn us if any gorilla approached, we started working on our already-anesthetized patient. It took only minutes to remove the snare and clean and disinfect his severely wounded hand. I was distressed to see that three of his fingers were damaged beyond repair. Yet, in spite of the loss of his fingers, I thought the youngster would make a quick and complete recovery.

It started raining and we retreated to spots under trees to watch the little gorilla wake up. After a while—a cold, wet, miserable while—the young gorilla was able to get up and crawl toward the other gorillas, who were hunched under trees just as we were, trying to stay out of the rain.

I followed the youngster to make sure that he found his way back all right. When I saw him reach the other gorillas, I turned to rejoin Margaret and the others. I was almost to them, when I heard an enormous roar right beside me.

The silverback suddenly appeared, charging at me from out of the dense undergrowth. His immense bulk—he must have weighed close to five hundred pounds—and his fierce manner were terrifying. His charge was a warning; next he would attack. I had to convince this powerful creature that I meant no harm. I immediately pulled back into the vegetation around me and cast my glance downward in a gesture of submission. Holding my breath for a tense few moments, I crouched perfectly still, waiting.

Accepting my gesture as it was intended, the gorilla moved back a few feet. My shoulders sagged with relief. Thinking he had already turned to go back, I lifted my head from its downcast position, and for a moment, my blue eyes gazed into the deep-set and penetrating dark eyes of the enormous gorilla before me. As I glimpsed the great depth and comprehension evident in his eyes, I felt a rush of joy. But I quickly lowered my eyes again to avoid any suggestion of challenge.

The next moment, the gorilla turned and moved towards his group. I watched him go, admiring his broad silver-haired back, then rejoined my own group.

The danger past, we were all delighted that the young gorilla had gotten safely back to his mother, and that his group had accepted him without any problem. As we walked back through the rainforest, I realized I had another personal reason for elation. Sometimes lately, I'd wondered if our work here in Africa could really make a difference, but my moment of connection with the elder gorilla had deepened and renewed my sense of purpose and commitment. I felt in that instant that everything we had gone through, or would go through in the future, to save this remarkable species was worth it.

As we continued homeward, the guides told us that they had named the little gorilla, Bahati, the Swahili word for "lucky," because he'd had the good fortune to be treated by a veterinarian who'd come halfway around the world to find and heal him.

Bahati *was* lucky that we had found him. Our work that day had given him the opportunity to grow up to become a magnificent creature like that great silverback, and perhaps, I thought with pleasure, he would someday even lead a group of his own in this beautiful mountain setting that was his home.

John E. Cooper, D.T.V.M., F.R.C.V.S.

Hamster on the Lam

Friday. The weekend beckoned. But when I walked through the door, I heard the sniffling of a traumatized child. Amy, our eight-year-old, was sobbing. And for good reason. Hammie the hamster was inside our bathroom wall.

One major complicating factor: Hammie was not ours. He was the class hamster. He had come to our house as part of the great second-grade pet cultural exchange, having survived more than a dozen home visits with the kids in Mrs. Blackwell's class. A hamster with peer pressure attached.

Now, though he had been in our house only a few hours, Hammie was performing his own version of the Hamster Olympics inside the walls of our home. He was where no paw should tread—on and under pipes, stirring up drywall dust, munching on whatever looked tasty.

As great tragedies often do, this one started with a small act of kindness. Amy had uncaged Hammie in the bathroom for an early-evening romp as she guarded the door. With only one exit, the bathroom had seemed the perfect place for a romp. Unfortunately there was the teeniest hole where the sink cabinet meets the wall. We'd never known it was there, but to Hammie, it must have looked like the Florida Turnpike.

A quick sprint and he was gone: down the linoleum, over the baseboard and into the wall. And now the little squirt's telltale scratching seemed to move in rhythm to the sobs outside.

Midnight. The family was fast asleep while I maintained the hamster watch. Poking my finger into the hole, I felt a hamster paw. I bent over and, startled, gazed right into Hammie's eyes. He seemed to be smiling.

At first I thought that by baiting Hammie with some hamster fast food—carrots, apple, a huge piece of lettuce—the little guy would pitter-patter back into the bathroom.

He went for the lettuce. Unfortunately, he took it right back into the hole.

After a restless night, we swore one another to a tell-and-you-die oath. We had forty-eight hours to capture Hammie. Monday would be bad enough without kickstarting the second-grade rumor mill.

Saturday afternoon brought a new plan of attack: Lure Hammie into the Mice Cube, a small plastic rectangle. Bait it. The hungry rodent goes in the trapdoor, but he doesn't come out. This night brought less sleep—more scratch, scratch, scratch—no Hammie. I guessed he still had plenty of lettuce.

Sunday morning. The pressure was on. We prayed for Hammie. Amy said that under no circumstances would she ever go to school again if we didn't catch him.

A visit to Dad's secret weapon, the Pet Store Guy, now seemed crucial. When I told him of our crisis, he barely batted an eye. Clearly he knew a lot about hamster psychology. In his opinion, Hammie was either (a) on the lam and loving it, (b) playing a game of catch-me-if-you-can or (c) lost in the wall. But he would come out. Hunger would win.

The Pet Store Guy told me to take a two-gallon bucket and place an apple inside. Douse a towel in apple juice. Put the bucket a few hamster steps from the hole and drape the towel over the side—a kind of hamster ramp, if you will. Just enough towel should stick into the bucket to allow the hamster to fall in but not crawl out.

Bedtime Sunday. The trap was in place, but the bathroom wall was eerily quiet. Was Hammie alive in there? I sat in a chair, feeling defeated. I had been beaten by a pint-size rodent. How would I break this news to sixteen second-graders?

Then, in what seemed like one of those slow-motion *Chariots of Fire* moments, my hamster-loving, sweethearted girl was motioning to us from the door. Amy had heard the hamster drop in the bucket.

She looked first. Her anxiety as she peered over the edge of the bucket, followed by the sheer euphoria of her realization that he was there, was indescribable.

Hugs and kisses. Hero Dad. Hero Mom. Hamster high-fives.

There are moments in your children's lives when your heart bounces through your throat—the first step, the first bicycle ride, the first sentence read, the first hamster drop.

I never did win a stuffed animal at the carnival for my sweetheart. But now I know how it feels.

Amy and Jim Grove

The Dog Show

Recently it was my great honor to serve as a judge in the Key West Kritter Patrol Dog Show, which is considered one of the most prestigious dog shows held in the entire Key West area on that particular weekend.

This is not one of those dog shows in which serious, highly competitive dog snobs enter professional dogs that can trace their lineage back 153 generations and basically spend their entire lives sitting around being groomed and fed, like Zsa Zsa Gabor. The Key West show—it benefits the Kritter Patrol, a local group that finds people to adopt stray dogs and cats—reflects the relaxed attitude of Key West, where the term "business attire" means "wearing some kind of clothing." This is a show for regular civilian dogs, most of whom, if you had to identify them, technically, by breed, would fall under the category of: "probably some kind of dog."

When I arrived at the show, the last-minute preparations were proceeding with the smooth efficiency of a soccer riot. There were dozens of dogs on hand, ranging in size from what appeared to be cotton swabs with eyeballs, all the way up to Hound of the Baskervilles.

Naturally every single one of these dogs, in accordance

with the strict rules of dog etiquette, was dragging its owner around by the leash, trying to get a whiff of every other dog's personal region. This process was complicated by the fact that many of the dogs were wearing costumes, so they could compete in the Dog and Owner Look-Alike category. (There are a number of categories in this show, and most of the dogs compete in most of them.) Many owners were also wearing costumes, including one man with an extremely old, totally motionless, sleeping Chihuahua; the man had very elaborately dressed both the dog and himself as (Why not?) butterflies. The man wore a sequined pantsuit, antennae and a huge pair of wings.

"Look at that!" I said to the other judges, pointing to the butterfly man.

"Oh, that's Frank," several judges answered, as if this explained everything.

Perhaps you are concerned that I, Dave Barry, a humor columnist with no formal training or expertise in the field of dogs, was on the judging panel. You will be relieved to know that there were also two professional cartoonists, both of whom have drawn many expert cartoons involving dogs. Another judge, named Edith, actually did seem to know a few things about dogs, but I believe she was not totally 100 percent objective, inasmuch as her own dog, Peggy, was entered in most of the events. Edith consistently gave Peggy very high ratings despite the fact that Peggy is—and I say this with great affection and respect—the ugliest dog in world history. I think she might actually be some kind of highly experimental sheep. Nevertheless, thanks in part to Edith's high marks, Peggy did very well in several categories, and actually WON the Trick Dog category, even though her trick consisted of—I swear this was the whole trick—trying to kick off her underpants.

Actually, that was a pretty good trick, considering the competition. The majority of the dogs entered in the Trick

Dog event did not actually perform a trick per se. Generally, the owner would bring the dog up onto the stage and wave a dog biscuit at it, or play a harmonica, or gesture, or babble ("C'mon, Ralph! C'mon boy! Sing! C'mon! Woooee! C'mon! Woooooooeeee! C'mon!") in an increasingly frantic but generally futile effort to get the dog to do whatever trick it was supposed to do, while the dog either looked on with mild interest, or attempted to get off the stage and mate with the next contestant.

As you can imagine, it was not easy serving as a judge with so many strong contestants, both on the stage and hiding under the judges' table. Nevertheless, when it was all over, approximately forty-three hours after it started, we had to pick one dog as Best in Show. It was a big decision, and although there was a strong and objective push for Peggy, we decided, after agonizing for close to three-tenths of a second, to give the top prize to Sam, the old, totally motionless, sleeping Chihuahua dressed as a butterfly to match his owner, Frank. Frank got quite emotional when he accepted the trophy, and we judges were touched, although we did ask Frank to make Sam move his paw so we could see that he was, in fact, sleeping, and not actually deceased. Because you have to have standards.

Dave Barry

Moving Together

I was on a hillside whipped by wind, soaked in dew, beyond disgusted, all because of that wretched cat. I'd only opened the door for a moment. I'd been groggy with motel sleep, eight hundred miles from our last night's bed, so I wasn't thinking clearly.

I had been in the rented box of a room, and I needed something real to look at for a few moments. But when I opened the door there was nothing but sky and high-way—gray on gray with scrub bush in-between.

I closed the door just as Lisa was coming turbaned out of the bathroom.

This was the big trip, her return to Winnipeg from Montreal where she had what she repeatedly called "the best year of my life."

My mail and phone campaign had coaxed her to return. Now, packing hopes, memories and her smoky tortoise-shell cat into my station wagon, we were heading back west together. She had been reluctant to leave, dawdling for sips of café au lait, strolling down the boulevard of St. Denis to sigh *au revoir* and kiss her friends on both cheeks as they eyed me with deepest suspicion.

It was a little later that we discovered the cat was missing from the motel room. "I only opened the door for thirty seconds," I pleaded.

"That's all it takes," she snapped.

That's all it took to feel like a complete failure. Eternal vigilance, the price of loving a woman with a cat.

Moreover, it was no ordinary cat. Not when it had been raised by Lisa, the social worker. Its every response had been scrutinized. A nap in the pantry was a sulk, a scratch on the hand was a plea for attention, a walk out the window onto the second-story ledge was a suicide attempt and cause for Lisa to cancel our date.

"I should have seen it coming," she'd said. "Chloe's been alone too much."

And how would Lisa analyze this blunder during our very act of moving together? A cat's jealous rejection? A dark flaw in my character? This could affect our future together. I had to find that cat.

We called out in cat sounds along the bushes. I prodded the underbrush. It opened into a jungly ravine. Where would I go if I were a cat?

"She's gone!" Lisa cried into the wind. "I just know she's gone! I loved her so much!"

If only I had a reputation for being reliable—for locking doors and mailing letters, finding my car in a parking lot—but I didn't.

Ashamed, I stared into bush and vines thinking how Chloe was really just a vulnerable creature, frightened of the car, anxious in the cage. She just wanted some peace. I could empathize. A quiet rabbit hole, soft leaves. She could sleep for days. And so could I.

But we were late. We had to meet the movers. We had family waiting and friends taking time off work to help. We had jobs.

I crashed into the ravine. Never mind the branches and nettles. Scratches were good. Blood could draw sympathy.

Could that cat really want to linger in this wilderness? She was a consumer cat, supermarket-wise in the ways of Kat Chow and Miss Mew. What did she know about hunting mice and sparrows?

Then I stumbled through the tangles and discovered another world. It was a housing development—streets with names like Buttercup Bay and Peony Drive and children on skateboards staring at my muddied clothes.

"Hi, kids." They looked suspicious. "I lost my cat." They stayed frozen. "I'll give you fifty bucks to find her."

Sudden acceptance. "Wow! Was it black?"

"She's smoky tortoiseshell grey. She has a hot-pink collar with toy sunglasses attached."

"I saw her!" hollered one of them. "She was right here. I *knew* I should have grabbed her!" The boy was furious with himself. Never again would he let a cat get away. He'd pack his garage with them for years to come. The kids scrambled into full alert.

I found Lisa and told her Chloe was spotted up the hill from the motel. She suddenly came to life. "That tramp!" she said. "What's she doing way up there?" Where there is anger, there is hope. Where there is hope, there is action. We put up reward posters, knocked on doors, phoned the local vet and police. As the day wore on, we left a reward if she was found later, hired someone to drive her to the airport, arranged plane fare and a flight cage.

We finally ate. The fast-food franchise overlooked the development. We watched children on skateboards and bikes cruising the lanes below. Some were checking shrubs, trampling a flowerbed. It was comforting.

We were both pretty quiet. Lisa finally spoke, "She was a good cat."

"Lisa, it's not over."

"She can live here okay. As long as she finds someone to care about her."

"I wish we could find her," I said. "I'd give more than money."

Lisa lowered her eyes. "I've been bargaining in my head. 'Give me back Chloe and I'll be better to my mother. I'll do volunteer work.'" And then she added, looking straight at me, "And I'll stop blaming you."

My secret thought welled up. "I've been making all this into a test. Lose the cat, lose Lisa. Find the cat, keep Lisa. I'm almost ready to give up everything—the move, the house, whatever. I guess I can't handle tests."

Lisa cupped her hand as if she were speaking to me through a microphone. "This is not a test. I repeat. This is not a test." We smiled to each other. "I'm not coming back for you," she said. "I'm coming back for us."

Dusk was settling in. The hills were gray—smoky, tortoiseshell gray. Chloe was nowhere, but it felt as if she were everywhere.

We were already packed so it didn't take long to clear the motel room. I only had to call the radio stations and leave an announcement about Chloe. Lisa took out the last bag.

That was when Chloe appeared. She simply walked out from under the bed, blinking in the light. She had been asleep inside the box spring all that time. It seems there was an opening we couldn't see. Lisa shrieked. The cat fled back into the mattress but we pulled her out. Then we left in a run.

As we pulled out of the motel driveway, we saw a pack of kids heading up the hill towards us. They probably had cats with them. At least two or three. We didn't stop to check. We already had everything we needed.

Sheldon Oberman

Dogs Just Wanna Have Fun

My husband Daniel and I travel frequently. When we first got our dog, Buddha-tu (we call him Buddhi), we were concerned that he would be lonely or perhaps feel that we'd abandoned him when we left him at home during our trips away.

When we left, we always had someone stay in our house and look after Buddhi, so we knew he was well taken care of, but we still felt guilty. I even used to leave my husband's T-shirt for Buddhi to sleep with and made sure he got extra goodies each day we were gone. Still, I used to wonder what he made of the whole thing—did he miss his lovin's, "his rub-a-dubs and belly pats," sleeping by our bed, taking walks with us—and who was going to play ball with him while we were away? Was our absence too traumatic for him? I supposed I would never know.

But then one night when we called home, Buddhi made it quite clear what he missed the most when we were gone.

We reached our housesitter, Barbara, and had her put us on the speakerphone, so that we could talk to Buddhi. He immediately started barking and howling when he heard our voices. We were jabbering at Buddhi like a pair of fools, when we noticed we couldn't hear him anymore. Barbara told us that he had run out of the room.

What was he doing? I wondered uneasily. Maybe it hadn't been such a good idea to call home—perhaps Buddhi was confused and was searching the house for us. *When he couldn't find us, would he become upset and try to get outside to continue the search? What if he tried to jump through a window?* My imagination ran away with me, and I couldn't stop it. I thought, *Poor baby, he misses us so much, hearing our voices had just made it worse.* I urged Barbara to go and find him. My husband and I decided to try and coax him back into the room by continuing to talk to him.

Barbara ran after him to see what was going on and almost tripped over him as he raced back into the room, holding something in his mouth. He bounded to the phone, where we were still spouting endearments in a highly embarrassing manner.

We heard Barbara laughing in the background, and then she picked up the phone and told us that Buddhi had approached the phone, and had stood for a moment, head cocked. Then he carefully put his front paws up on the desk and set down the object in his mouth. It was his favorite ball. He put it directly on top of the speakerphone and stepped back—waiting for us to throw it.

Susan White

FRANK & ERNEST ® by Bob Thaves

IF YOU DON'T MIND THROWING TENNIS BALLS FOR ETERNITY, I DO HAVE AN OPENING IN DOGGIE HEAVEN.

FRANK & ERNEST *reprinted by permission of Newspaper Enterprise Association, Inc.*

The Cat Lady

I have lived in my neighborhood for twenty years. It seems to me that I've spent at least ten of those years looking for a lost pet, either mine or one I'd seen listed in the newspaper's lost-pet column.

Recently, I was at it again, going door-to-door looking for one of my own lost kitties, a little black cat named Nicholas who'd slipped out the door before I could stop him. I made my rounds, visiting with all the neighbors, describing Nicholas. Familiar with this routine, everyone promised to keep an eye out and call me if they spotted him.

Two blocks from my house, I noticed a gentleman raking leaves in the yard of a home that had recently been sold. I introduced myself and presented my new neighbor with the plight of the missing Nicholas, asking if he had seen him.

"No," he replied, "I've not seen a little black kitty around here." He thought for a moment, looked at me and said, "But I know who you should ask. Several of my neighbors have told me that there's a woman in the neighborhood who's crazy about cats. They say she knows every cat around here, probably has dozens herself. They call her 'The Cat Lady.' Be sure to check with her."

"Oh, thank you," I said eagerly. "Do you know where she lives?"

He pointed a finger down the street, "It's that one."

I followed his finger and started to laugh.

He was pointing at *my* house!

Patti Thompson

When Puss Comes to Shove

Cat owners like to describe their felines in superlatives. One person has the smartest cat in the whole world; another boasts of the biggest or the loudest cat in the whole world. I have Humphrey, the ugliest cat in the whole world.

Humphrey was a little crumpled when I got him. He was sitting in the middle of the road, suffering from a nasty case of failure to grant the right of way. His head was crooked, his jaw broken and one eye looked straight out into the twilight zone. The little fella had enough road rash to be an honorary Hell's Angel. He was the hurtin'est cat in the whole world.

I didn't think he would make it, but after four months and three hundred dollars he was doing quite well. He almost died three different times, but he never gave up. His head is still shaped like the last potato at the fruit stand, and the vet had to grind some teeth to let his mouth close, but Humphrey just wouldn't quit. He's got an eye on one side and a fur-lined depression on the other, and part of his nose is still out on Route 16, but that doesn't faze Humphrey. He's a cat, and he's tough.

Obviously I like cats, but a lot of men don't. Cats are not

macho. Cats are not rough and tough. Cats, I am told, are
sissies.

But let me tell you something, cats can rearrange your
face and hand you your lips. Ask my dog.

My dog weighs eighty pounds and has a smile like the
keyboard on Dracula's piano. He has too many teeth and
not enough jowl. He's not afraid of anything. Except cats.
So many ill-tempered Toms have tap-danced on his face,
his nose looks like a country fair after the tractor races.
Among the legions of slit-eyed mouse-molesters that
trouble Shep's dreams, Humphrey ranks pretty high.

Some years ago, Shep and I were living with the afore-
mentioned "puddy," a second cat named Bugsy Moran, and
Lynn, the nice lady who saw dutifully to their every desire.

The five of us were happily ensconced in a modern,
well-appointed duplex. Among the more admirable features of the place was a thick, springy carpet that covered
every inch of floor space except for a small area inside one
bedroom closet.

One still day in the dead of summer, it was oppres-
sively hot. Flowers were limp and lifeless. The ice cream
man wore a greedy smile. As for Shep, the combination of
lying on a thick rug and wearing one at the same time was
too much for him. He retreated to the uncarpeted closet
and stretched out on the cool cement, secure in the
assumption that, among the fur-bearing four-by-fours
present, his rank, guaranteed by his size, would ensure
that he was undisturbed.

Bugsy had pushed Lynn's knickknacks aside and was
resting peacefully on the third tier of a teak bookshelf. But
Humphrey was having a problem. Generally, on warmer
days, Humphrey sprinted down the hall, through the
bathroom door and leaped into the tub, where he played
with the faucet drips before passing out till dinner was
served. Unfortunately, on the previous day, without

Humphrey's knowledge, Lynn had filled the bathtub with water. The result was an abrupt feline behavior modification involving a very wet cat and a slightly torn shower curtain.

As the morning melted into afternoon, Humphrey got more and more annoyed. He paced the house glancing nervously into the bathroom and longingly into Shep's closet space. Faced with the choice of confronting twenty gallons of cold water or eighty pounds of hot canine, Humphrey opted for the latter.

Lynn and I were sorting laundry on the bed. She was marveling at how each of my socks was unique, when Humphrey stalked into the room and positioned himself in the open closet doorway at the edge of the carpet. One of Shep's eyes opened momentarily. He blinked uneasily in the face of Humphrey's baleful stare, then, seemingly reassured by his five-to-one size advantage, drifted back to sleep.

After several long minutes the cat stood up and stretched thoroughly like a Kung Fu priest preparing for combat. Carefully, Humphrey took one step toward the sleeping black hulk. Shep's ear twitched, and again both eyes popped open. An almost inaudible rumble came from deep in the dog's throat. Humphrey sat down and waited.

After several moments, Shep's eyes closed again. He groaned and shifted to a more comfortable position. I know what he was thinking. Cats are afraid of dogs. Right?

Shep is not tall or long. He's thick. Almost his entire body is protected by dense fur and heavy muscle. He has only one window of vulnerability—his feet. The ferocious and powerful Shep has delicate tootsies. Very slowly Humphrey stretched his mitt out as far as it could reach. It gently touched against Shep's front paw.

Shep's foot jerked immediately in toward his body. His head came up as he showered Humphrey with a long and ominous snarl. The cat held his ground.

After a minute, Shep's head sank slowly to the floor. His eyes began to droop, but each breath was exhaled as a low, moaning growl. Again the cat stretched his paw into enemy territory. This time Shep's rear leg was the victim. With a sharp and frightening roar, Shep jerked upright and tried to tuck all four feet under his body. His ears lay flat against his neck and a ghoulish row of gleaming white teeth were exposed and at the ready.

Humphrey pulled his head back and squinted. Behind the still-extended paw his face wrinkled. Shep continued growling and snapping his teeth. Humphrey moved in closer and reached one of Shep's exposed toes. Shep jumped to his feet and crowded against the closet wall, growling and glancing nervously about. Humphrey moved in quickly and began hitting at the backs of Shep's rear legs, like an elephant trainer at the circus.

Shep trampled some high-heeled shoes and bellowed uselessly as he beat a hasty if not honorable retreat. Humphrey sat down in the middle of his conquered territory and proceeded to wash his ears.

In some corner of the universe, I'm sure a scoreboard lit up: Cats—1, Dogs—0. Cats may not be macho, but just ask Shep if they're sissy.

Joe Kirkup

The Day We Almost Didn't Go

Any glimpse into the life of an animal quickens our own and makes it so much the larger and better in every way.

John Muir

Almost—almost—we didn't go. The afternoon was right for it: clear, not cold, a veil of sand blowing off the dunes into the restless sea along our strip of Georgia coast. All the three youngest children wanted was for me to take them across the river and through the winding tidal creeks to the deserted beaches where they could look for shells, gather sea oats or watch for wild goats.

Just a fifteen-minute run in our little outboard skiff. But the tide was out, and getting the boat into the water would be a struggle.

Besides, there was a televised football game that promised a degree of entertainment with much less effort. So I had said, "We'll see," in the vague tone that parents use. And the children knew from long experience that this means *no*.

But then I saw their forlorn faces, huddled in a sad triangle.

"All right," I said, feeling noble and self-sacrificing. "We'll go. But just for a little while."

Faces brightened. "Can we take Tony?" Tony is a Shetland sheepdog, unacquainted with sheep, who loves boats.

"I guess so," I said. And automatically, "Wear something warm."

We dragged the boat to the water, getting muddy feet. The engine coughed morosely for a while, then picked up with a splendid roar and drove us through the waves so fast that spray soaked everyone, including the sheltie, who stood in the bow, ears pinned back by the wind, tongue waving with delight.

For three minutes, the skiff pranced and bucked in the river. Then suddenly we were in the sheltered network of creeks, skimming around the silver corners, flying down amber aisles of marsh grass where black birds flared in silent explosions, finally into a broad estuary where the engine bellowed happily at full throttle.

The skiff eased into a quiet cove. I cut the engine, and at once the surf thundered in our ears. The dog sprang ashore and sank to his astonished chin in damp and porous sand. The children floundered after him, carrying the anchor. A fearsome crew, really. Kinzie, thirteen, was wearing blue jeans scissored off raggedly at the knee, and on her head a once-white sailor hat with down-turned brim pulled low. Dana, eleven, wore an old cashmere sweater of mine, full of holes, with sleeves so long that she seemed to have no hands at all. Mac, eight, wore a sweatshirt with a bulldog stenciled on it. As always, he needed a haircut.

They raced away through the sea oats, so many things to find or do: fiddler crabs to catch and carry home; marsh swallows' nests, skeletons of rowboats resting their weary bones against the dunes; starfish and sand dollars, conchs' eggs and horseshoe crabs, all flung carelessly by the lavish hand of the sea.

I watched them go and was tilting the engine to keep the propeller out of the sand when I heard the sheltie barking, hysterical high-pitched yelps. A moment later Mac came rushing back, eyes dark with excitement. "Daddy, come quick . . . a bird, a big one . . . he can't fly . . . he's hurt or something . . . hurry!"

Through the soft sand, into the dune grasses, up over the shallow rise, and there on the beach, the two girls and the sheltie surrounded a strange, penguin-like silhouette that lurched and flopped awkwardly, long neck and javelin bill lunging defiantly at the dog. I came close and saw it was a loon, feathers matted into a hopeless, tarry mass.

Looking at it, I felt something wince inside me: The worst that can happen to any creature is to be made incapable of doing the thing it was created to do.

"What's wrong with him?" cried Dana, not far from tears.

"He got too close to civilization," I said slowly. And I told them how sometimes a ship discharges fuel oil that makes a heavy slick on the ocean, and how a diving loon might come up under this deadly film and have its plumage so saturated that it could not fly.

"Will he be all right?" Mac asked fearfully. "What will happen to him?"

I knew that after sundown a roving raccoon would answer these questions, but I could not bring myself to say so.

"There's a towel in the boat," said Kinzie, the practical one. "Maybe we can wipe him off."

"He'll bite us!" cried Mac with delight and terror.

"Not very hard," I said. "Get the towel. We'll give it a try."

But the towel made little impression. "We need something to dissolve the oil," I said finally. "Mineral spirits, maybe."

"There's some at home," both girls said at once.

"Let's take him home!" shouted their brother deliriously. "We'll clean him up and put him in the bathtub and feed him some dog food and make him a pet!"

"He's a wild bird," I said, parental resistance rising up in me. "He doesn't want to live in a bathtub and be a pet. Besides, I'm not sure we can get this stuff off."

"But we *found* him," Kinzie said a little desperately. "We can't just leave him here to die."

We found him, that was true—or perhaps he found us. Either way, out of all of the millions of possible space-time curves, something had caused his and ours to intersect in this unlikely place. Chance? Of course. But still . . . "Who'll hold him?" I asked a bit grumpily. "I can't run a boat with one hand and hang onto a wild loon with the other."

"I'll hold him," all three of them said instantly. And they did, the bird wrapped firmly with a corner of the towel over its head (which seemed to quiet it). The sheltie crouched, disapproving and dejected, at my feet.

"We've got a loon!" Mac shrieked to his unsuspecting mother as we entered the house. "An oily one! We're going to wash him in the bathtub!" He hesitated, his masculine radar picking up dubious vibrations. "But then," he added more quietly, "we're going to let him go."

The next hour was chaotic. Preparations were immense: sponges, cotton pads, warm water, cool water, soaps and elixirs. Theories were advanced and demolished. Advice was endless. The loon, unappreciative, bit everyone at least twice. But finally, when the last rinse disappeared from the stained tub, the dark feathers were parallel and distinguishable.

We took him, wrapped in a clean towel, to the ocean's edge. When we put him in the water, he bobbed uncertainly for a moment. He turned his head and raked his back feathers swiftly with his bill as if to align them properly. Then he started swimming strongly out to sea, toward the distant sandbar where shorebirds were settling for the night.

"Why doesn't he fly?" Dana asked worriedly.

"I think his feathers are too wet," I said. "When the sun dries them tomorrow, he may be all right."

The sheltie, spirits revived, went bounding off, and the girls followed him. The boy and I turned back toward the house. "He would have died, wouldn't he, Daddy?"

"Yes, he would."

He shook his head slowly. "And we almost didn't go, remember?"

"Yes," I said. "Yes, I'll try to remember."

Arthur Gordon

5

CELEBRATING PETS AS FAMILY

To get the full value of joy, you must have someone to divide it with.

Mark Twain

"Bless my pork chop and my rice and Spot's broccoli."

Letters from Vietnam

One of the least pleasurable aspects of a military career are the extended family separations. The agony of saying good-bye to my wife, Mycki, and my son was compounded by the fact that I nearly always had a favorite dog that required (or at least I thought so) my sitting on the floor and explaining that Dad had to go away for awhile, but would surely return. Such was the case in 1970 when military orders directed me to Vietnam and I had to break the news to Roulette, our one-year-old miniature poodle.

Non-dog people raise their eyebrows when I tell them that dogs understand more of our speech than animal behaviorists give them credit for. Roulette understood. I watched her eyes and expression as I told her I was going away and she showed a sadness that I didn't see again until the final days of her life. When I promised to write often and return in a year, she acknowledged this with just one slow and deliberate wag of her tail. Then she sighed deeply and laid her head in my lap. That moment remains indelibly imprinted in my mind.

After my arrival in Vietnam, I wrote home two or three times a week. But Mycki soon began to complain that I wasn't writing very often. She told me that at first my letters arrived at intervals of a week to ten days, but now there were often no letters for two weeks at a time.

I was puzzled and began to imagine all sorts of things, including the idea that the Viet Cong were shooting down all mail planes carrying my letters.

My wife knew from previous experience that I was a pretty faithful correspondent. Even when sent to remote areas, I always managed to find a postal drop somewhere. So she was as puzzled as I was about what was happening to my letters.

Over time, Mycki began to notice something odd. It became clear that if she was actually at the front door of our house when the mail came through the slot, the probability of a letter from me was greater. Puzzled, she decided to experiment by monitoring the front door more closely around mail delivery times. Things began to fall into place when she noticed that a little four-legged critter seemed very irritated when "momma" got to the mail first.

Our postman usually arrived between eleven o'clock and noon, and the next time he came up the walk to the front door, Mycki hid behind a partition where she had a good view of the front door and the floor of the entryway.

As Mycki peeked around the edge of the wall, she saw Miss Roulette saunter up to the several pieces of mail that had fallen on the floor beneath the slot. Roulette sniffed at a couple of items and then gently, with one front paw, pulled an envelope out from the stack. She gave a quick glance around and then scooped up the letter in her mouth. With a mixture of mild outrage and stifled hilarity, Mycki followed Roulette into the living room. She was close behind the pom-pommed tail as the poodle rounded the end of the couch and slipped in behind it with the letter.

"The game is over, Missy—get out from behind the couch," Mycki ordered. But Roulette was not a dog that responded immediately to orders. Moving the couch away from the wall, Mycki sternly requested, "Come on Rou, out of there." Reluctantly, like a momma dog protecting her pups, Miss Roulette rose and cautiously left her clandestine lair, revealing a number of letters where she had been lying.

The mystery was solved, but for Roulette, the game wasn't over, not by a long shot. With each subsequent mail delivery, it became a race to the door between Mycki and Roulette to pick up the mail. If Roulette won, a chase ensued, unless of course, Mycki was busy or not at home when the postman arrived. Then it became a matter of search and seizure.

Roulette tossed in another twist that made the game even more interesting. Whenever Mycki received a letter, she would retire to her recliner in the living room to read it. But if she left the letter on the end table afterwards, the artful dodger would strike again. Even when Mycki left the letters on the kitchen table where she did much of her writing, Roulette managed to appropriate them as soon as Mycki's attention was elsewhere. No place Roulette could reach was safe for my letters. Mycki finally resorted to storing them in a shoebox and putting the box inside her armoire.

Roulette retaliated by attempting little hunger strikes. Mycki really became concerned until she found out that Roulette was actually conning her—our son was sneak-feeding the little letter-napper at night in his room.

When Mycki explained all this to me in one of her letters, I had to laugh. It was rather nice to have two ladies fighting over me.

But things reverted to normal pretty quickly when I returned home. Roulette suddenly lost interest in the mail. However, while packing and preparing to move to our next duty station, we did discover a few more postal hideaways containing unopened letters from Vietnam—a reminder that as far as a dog's nose is concerned, a small object sent by a beloved human that travels nine thousand miles, though handled by dozens of other people, still bears a treasured message. I had never realized during all those months when I thought I was writing just to Mycki that I was also sending a uniquely personal greeting to one smart and sharp-nosed little poodle.

Joe Fulda

Reprinted with special permission of King Features Syndicate.

I Love You, Pat Myers

He deserves paradise who makes his companions laugh.

The Koran

Pat Myers had been away in the hospital having some tests. "Hi Casey, I'm back," she called as she unlocked the door of her apartment. Casey, her African gray parrot, sprang to the side of his cage, chattering with excitement.

"Hey, you're really glad to see me, aren't you?" Pat teased as Casey bounced along his perch. "Tell me about it."

The parrot drew himself up like a small boy bursting to speak but at a loss for words. He peered at Pat with one sharp eye, then the other. Finally he hit upon a phrase that pleased him. "Shall we do the dishes?" he exploded happily.

"What a greeting," Pat laughed, opening the cage so Casey could hop on her hand and be carried to the living room. As she settled in her chair, Casey sidled up her arm and nestled down with his head on her chest. Pat stroked his velvet-gray feathers and scarlet tail. "I love you," she said. "Can you say that? Can you say, 'I love you, Pat Myers?'"

Casey cocked an eye at her. "I live on Mallard View."

"I know where you live, funny bird. Tell me you love me."
"Funny bird."

A widow with two married children, Pat had lived alone for some years and kept busy running a chain of successful dress shops. But when she developed serious health problems she had to give up her business and was scarcely able to leave the house.

Always an outgoing woman, Pat was reluctant to admit how lonely she was, but finally she confessed to her daughter, Annie. Annie suggested a pet.

"I've thought of that, but I haven't the strength to walk a dog, I'm allergic to cats and fish don't have a whole lot to say."

"Birds do," said Annie. "Why not a parrot?"

That struck Pat as a good idea, and she telephoned an expert who recommended an African gray, which he described as the most accomplished talker among parrots.

And so it turned out. Only days after Casey's arrival, he began picking up all kinds of words and phrases, like "Where's my glasses" and "Where's my purse?" Every time Pat scanned tabletops, opened drawers, and felt behind pillows, Casey set up a litany. "Where's my glasses? Where's my glasses?"

"You probably know where they are, Smarty Pants."

"Where's my purse?"

"I'm not looking for my purse. I'm looking for my glasses."

"Smarty Pants."

When Pat found her glasses and went to get her coat out of the closet, Casey switched to, "So long. See you later." And when Pat came home after being out in the Minnesota winter, Casey greeted her with "Holy smokes, it's cold out there!"

Pat began feeling better. It was so much fun having Casey; he could always be relied upon to give her four or five laughs a day.

Like the day a plumber came to repair a leak under the kitchen sink. In his cage in the den, Casey cracked seeds and eyed the plumber through the open door. Suddenly the parrot began reciting, "One potato, two potato, three potato, four."

"What?" demanded the plumber from under the sink.

Casey mimicked Pat's inflections perfectly. "Don't poo on the rug," he ordered.

The plumber pushed himself out from under the sink and marched to the living room. "If you're going to play games, lady, you can just get yourself another plumber." Pat looked at him blankly.

The plumber hesitated. "That was you saying those things, wasn't it?"

Pat began to smile. "What things?"

"One potato, two potato . . ."

"Ah, well, that's not too bad."

"And don't poo on the rug."

"Oh, dear, that's bad." Pat got up. "Let me introduce you to Casey."

Casey saw them coming. "Did you do that?" he said in Pat's voice. "What's going on around here?"

The plumber looked from the bird to Pat and back again. Then he shook his head slowly, speechlessly, and retired back under the sink.

Casey's favorite perch in the kitchen was the faucet in the sink; his favorite occupation, trying to remove the washer at the end of it. Once, to tease him, Pat held a handful of water over his head. Casey swiveled his head to look at her. "What's the matter with you?" he demanded sharply.

Often when Pat wanted him to learn something, however, Casey could be maddeningly mum. For her first Christmas back on her feet, Pat tried to teach Casey to sing "Jingle Bell Rock."

"It'll be your contribution to the festivities," she told him.

"Where's my glasses?"

"Never mind. Just listen to me and sing." But as often as Pat coached him, the bird simply looked at her and said, "Wow!"

A week before Christmas, she gave up. "All right, you stubborn creature, you probably can't carry a tune anyway."

Taking a beakful of seeds, Casey shook his head and flung them around his cage. Then he cocked his head and demanded in Pat's voice, "Did you do that? Shame on you, you bad bird!"

On Christmas day, he inquired, almost plaintively, "What's going on around here?" amid the noise of laughter and packages being ripped open, but all through dinner he was silent. When it was time for dessert, Pat touched a match to the plum pudding. The brandy blazed up. At that moment, with impeccable timing, Casey burst into: "Jingle bell, jingle bell, jingle bell rock!"

With her health so much improved, Pat decided on a three-week vacation. Casey was sent to stay with Annie. The day Pat was due back, Annie returned the parrot so he'd be there when Pat came in.

"Hi, Casey!" Pat called as she unlocked the door. There was no answer from the den. "Holy smokes, it's cold out there!" she shouted. Still silence. Pat dropped her coat and hurried into the den. Casey glared at her.

"Hey, aren't you glad to see me?" The bird moved to the far side of the cage. "Come on, don't be angry," she teased. "Shall we do the dishes?"

She opened the door of the cage and held out her hand. Casey dropped to the bottom of the cage and huddled there.

In the morning, Pat tried again. And the next day, and the next. Casey refused to speak. But finally, on the fifth day, he consented to climb on her wrist and be carried to the living room. When she sat down, he shifted uneasily. "Please, Casey," Pat pleaded. "I know I was away a long time, but you've got to forgive me."

Tentatively, Casey took a few steps up her arm. "Were you frightened I wasn't going to come back?" she said softly. "Darling Casey, I belong to you just as much as you belong to me." Casey cocked his head. "I'll never not come back."

Step by step, Casey moved up her arm. After a while, he nestled down with his head on her chest. Pat stroked his head, smoothing his feathers with her forefinger. Finally Casey spoke. "I love you, Pat Myers," he said.

Jo Coudert

Jake and the Kittens

It is a very inconvenient habit of kittens . . . that, whatever you say to them, they always purr.

Lewis Carroll

From the beginning, Jake made his feelings clear about the subject of cats: they were best served on a plate, with a side order of fries!

Jake was our resident dog, a large dominant male, part Border collie and part Labrador retriever, with a little German shepherd thrown in. Jake was about two years old when he adopted us from the local animal shelter. He came into our lives shortly after I lost my beloved dog Martha to an unexpected illness. One day we went to the shelter searching for a shaggy-haired female (like Martha) to bring into our home. Instead, we found Jake, a short-haired male, sitting tall, proud and silent in the middle of all that barking. We told the shelter worker that we wanted Jake to come home with us because we could sense he had a lot of magic inside of him. "That's great," she said. "Just don't bring him back when he shows you that magic!"

Jake immediately became a cherished member of our family. He loved watching the birds we attracted to our yard with numerous feeders and birdbaths. He played with the puppy next door and other dogs in the park, but made it extremely clear that cats would never be allowed on his property, chasing any feline that came too close.

One day I found a litter of wild kittens in our woodpile. Although I had been a "dog person" all my life and had never had the privilege of sharing my life with a cat, my heart went out to these little furballs. They were only about four weeks old, and had beautiful gray-striped bodies and large, frightened eyes. Their mother was nowhere in sight. I put them into a box and brought them inside. Jake heard the meowing and immediately began to salivate. And drool. And pant. Every attempt to introduce him to the kitties ended in near disaster. It was clear we couldn't keep the kittens in the house, even long enough to help find them homes. Our veterinarian told us, "Some dogs just won't accept cats under any condition."

A year after the kitty experience, I looked outside onto our deck and saw Jake with his ears up and his head cocked sideways, staring at the ground. There at his feet was a tiny kitten, sitting very still. Using soothing words to try and keep Jake calm, I moved in closer, hoping to prevent the ugly attack I felt sure was coming. The kitten had badly infected eyes, and it probably couldn't see where it was or what was looming over it. But Jake just looked at the little creature, then looked up at me, and then back at the kitten. I heard some meowing, and discovered another kitten under the deck. So I scooped them both up and brought them into the house, depositing them into a box that would be their temporary home. I put the box in the garage and started making calls to all the animal people I knew, telling each the same story—my dog would never allow these cats into our home, and

I needed to relocate them right away.

I bought baby bottles and kitten milk, and as I fed my two little bundles of fur, I told them how much I would have loved to welcome them into our family. But it could never be.

The next morning, we found three more kittens lying in a pile outside the door, huddled together for warmth and protection. So I took them in and added them to the box.

My heart was very heavy. Now we had five little kittens, all with infected eyes, who would be sent out into a world already crowded with unwanted little creatures. I spent the day making phone calls, only to be told over and over that no one had room for more critters. I knew I'd run out of options, so with tears in my eyes, I picked up the phone to make the call to the vet that would take the kittens out of my life forever. At that same moment, my eyes fell on Jake, calmly observing everything going on around him. There was no drooling, no panting. He didn't seem upset or anxious. He was definitely interested, but not in a calculating, just-wait-until-I-get-them-on-my-plate kind of way. I felt something was different. *Slow down,* I thought. *Don't react. Just sit for a minute. Be still.*

So I became still and I sat. And I heard a voice in my heart telling me what to do. I called our veterinarian and made an appointment to bring the kittens in and get their eyes checked. On the way home from the doctor, I went to a pet store and bought my first litter box. I came home and brought the box of kittens back into the house. Jake was waiting. The time had come, so I carefully put the babies on the floor of the kitchen and held my breath, ready to come to the rescue if necessary.

Jake walked over and sniffed each of the kittens. Then he sat down in the middle of them and looked up at me with a sweet, sappy grin on his face. The kittens swarmed over him, happy to find a big, warm body of fur to curl up next to. That's when Jake opened his heart to the five little kitties and adopted them as his own. I wondered if he remembered a time when he, too, had needed a home. I knelt down to thank him for his love and compassion and tell him how grateful I was he'd come into my life. But it would have to wait until later—Jake and his kittens were fast asleep.

Christine Davis

"This is a song about love, betrayal and the day they brought home a kitten."

Reprinted by permission of Randy Glasbergen.

We Are Family

When I broke up with yet another boyfriend, this time after a three-year relationship, I decided it was time for me to face the facts—I was just not lucky in love. Yet even though I had given up on men, I wasn't ready to go without love in my life, so I decided to get a dog.

I found the perfect puppy after a careful search, and one hot June day, I brought home the little golden retriever puppy I'd named Cognac.

Like all puppies, Cognac was adorable; immediately, I felt love and sweetness flowing in my life again. Why hadn't I thought of this sooner?

A few days later, I received a call from a man who'd gotten my name through a computer-dating club. I had joined the club before the start of my last relationship and had never cancelled my membership. I hadn't been very impressed with the people I'd met through the club's services, but this guy, Brad, seemed nice enough on the phone, so when he asked me to meet him at the lake in a nearby park the next evening, I thought, *I've got to walk Cognac anyway . . . sure, why not?*

Brad had said he was no longer in the service, but that he had been an air force tech sergeant. That wasn't the kind of guy I usually dated, but I had liked his voice on the phone and decided to keep an open mind. When I got to the park for our date, I looked around for a blond man with a buzz cut and a military bearing. There was no one like that at the park—the only blond man was a gorgeous guy with hair almost to his shoulders. I thought, *Now why can't a guy like that ask me out?*

Then the gorgeous guy walked over to me and said, "Are you Jan?"

I immediately decided to give men another chance.

Cognac's enthusiastic greeting made our introductions easy. He jumped up on Brad's legs and ran in circles, wagging his whole body madly while trying to lick every part of Brad he could. We started to walk around the lake, and everybody we met fussed over the puppy. By the time we were halfway around the lake, Brad was holding Cognac's leash, and he and I were chatting away like old friends.

At the end of our walk, we weren't ready to say goodbye, so we found a café and picked an outdoor table so the puppy could be with us. From the very start, our relationship included Cognac.

Things went from good to better. One evening, three months later, Brad and I went to a restaurant that we liked for dinner. It was one of those places that have paper over the tablecloths and when they bring you the menu, they also bring crayons so that you can draw or write poetry while you're waiting for your meal. Brad and I always played Hangman while we waited and that night, we were playing our usual game. As I guessed the letters and the words started to form themselves, a sentence emerged: *Will you marry me?*

I gasped and turned towards Brad, "Are you kidding?"

Brad looked nervous, but his eyes were shining and he smiled at me. "No, I'm not kidding—what's your answer?"

I took a crayon and wrote a huge YES across the paper.

We sat grinning at each other for a few minutes and then began to plan our wedding.

From the start, we were sure about two things: We wanted an outdoor wedding and we wanted Cognac to be a part of the ceremony.

The day of the wedding dawned perfect and clear. Our families and friends gathered near the natural spring that we'd chosen as the spot where we would say our vows. My bridesmaids were dressed in rich purple gowns. I had on my wedding dress, and my heart felt as if it were over-flowing with love and joy. Yet I was slightly apprehensive, wondering if we had lost our minds expecting Cognac, now ten months old and goofy in the way that only young dogs can be, to handle his responsibilities as ring-bearer without creating chaos.

Cognac wore a white collar and a purple satin bow tie. My bridesmaids, who *knew* we had lost our minds having a dog at the ceremony, ran around with lint rollers, trying to keep their dark gowns free of golden hair—an almost impossible task.

Cognac's job was to carry a heart-shaped basket con-taining our rings to Brad. The basket held a heart-shaped pillow to which Brad had secured our rings with pieces of wire. This would prevent a disaster, in case Cognac decided to go for a swim in the spring, basket and all, instead of delivering it to Brad as we'd planned. As I began to walk to the aisle, in preparation for following the bridesmaids, I panicked. I realized I needed another hand! I held my bouquet in one hand, Cognac on his leash in the other, but I needed to hold the basket as well. If I gave the basket to Cognac to carry, he would take it as the signal to run to Brad, just as he'd been trained and I'd be dragged after him—spoiling the effect I'd had in my mind for my appearance on the scene.

Somehow I managed to get to the aisle, unhook

Cognac's leash and put the basket in his mouth. He was off like a shot, racing toward Brad with his beautiful golden ears streaming behind him, as if he was hot on the trail of a speeding rabbit. There was a swell of laughter as our guests appreciated the dedication of our furry ring-bearer.

When Cognac reached Brad, he dropped the basket at his feet and, panting, looked up at Brad for approval. As Brad reached down to pick up the rings, a suddenly quiet Cognac solemnly raised his paw to meet my almost-husband's hand—a canine "Way to go, Brad."

Our guests, dog-lovers and non-dog-lovers alike, were completely undone and to this day, when anyone talks about our wedding they may not remember what year it was or what I was wearing, but they *always* mention the dog's pawshake.

For me, it was the perfect start to our new life together. Just the way I always dreamed it would be—Brad and me . . . and Cognac.

Jan Paddock

Me and My Mewse

According to my dictionary, a "muse" is any of the nine Greek goddesses who preside over the arts. This means that, as a writer, I not only get to work in my pajamas, I can also claim my own goddess who will answer my prayers in times of literary distress.

Luckily, there's no need, since I have Necco, a peach-colored tortoiseshell cat to serve as my own personal "mewse."

The cat discovered us at the local animal shelter. We were looking for a quiet, neat pet to complement our boisterous dog, Emma. We found Necco instead.

As soon as we entered the shelter, she called to us in a noisy chirp that made it clear she required immediate attention. The yellow tag on her cage—the symbol showing that this was her last day—backed up her urgent request. When the cage door swung open, she stepped into my arms and settled back with a look that clearly said, "What took you so long?"

Six months old and barely three pounds, Necco wasted no time establishing herself as the one in charge of our lives. The leather chair was her scratching post. The Christmas tree was her playground. And the mantel, neatly decorated with a collection of brass candlesticks of all shapes and sizes, was where she discovered the Feline Law of Gravity: Cats go up; candlesticks come down. The first dainty swipe of a paw resulted in a satisfying crash. So did the second, third and fourth. By the fifth crash, Necco's face bore the cat equivalent of a grin. She had discovered her purpose in life.

It happened that Necco's skills reached their peak just as my life reached a low point. My twenty-year marriage had shuddered to a stop, leaving me with a ten-year-old daughter, Katie, and a large home to support on an advertising copywriter's salary. Although I worked full-time, the pay was modest and I often found myself with more bills than paycheck. I soon realized I would have to work as a freelance writer just to meet expenses.

That meant getting up at 4:00 A.M., writing for two hours, and then getting ready for work. Eight hours later, I would return home, fix dinner, help Katie with homework, clean the house and get ready for another day's work. I fell into bed exhausted at 11:00 P.M. only to crawl out of bed when the alarm sounded at 4:00 A.M. the next day.

The routine lasted exactly two weeks. Despite gallons of coffee, I couldn't seem to produce anything. I was cranky, frustrated, lonely and ready to admit defeat. Writing was hard. Paying bills was even harder. The only answer was to sell the house and get an inexpensive apartment. Unfortunately, that would mean more losses for Katie and me. Especially since no apartment in town allowed pets.

I hated the thought of finding another home for us all, and I especially hated the thought of telling Katie about the changes in store. Depressed, I slept right through the 4:00 A.M. alarm the next day. And the next and the next. Finally, I quit setting it.

That's when Necco did a curious thing. Knowing that a sudden crash would make a human jump, she decided that the perfect time to make that crash was at 4:00 A.M. Her bedroom bombing raid was timed with military precision. First she set off a small round of artillery in the form of two pencils and my eyeglasses. I rolled over and covered my head with the blanket. Then she moved on to an arsenal of notebooks and the alarm clock. Each crash forced me deeper under the covers. Finally, she brought out the big guns. A half-filled glass of water splashed to the ground. A hardbound book crashed beside me. How could I sleep with the world literally crashing down around my ears? My mewse said it was time to get to work.

Wearily, I made my way to the computer. Necco hopped up on the desk, seeming to feel her job wasn't done yet. Sitting on a pile of unfinished story ideas, she watched with apparent satisfaction as I began to type. Whenever the words seemed slow in coming, she helped me along. Gliding across my keyboard with the grace of a goddess, she produced sentences like: "awesdtrfgyhub-jikpl[;' dtrfgbhujni guhnj!" My translation? "I woke you up for a reason. Now, write!" I wrote. And wrote some more.

From then on, every day Necco got me up at 4:00 A.M. sharp, when the ideas were freshest and the world slept around us. With her watching over me as I wrote, I didn't feel so alone. My goals didn't seem so impossible. Slowly, over months of early mornings, stories were born, and polished, and sold.

Today the old house still surrounds us. Katie and I are both doing fine. And although both pets are treated like the cherished family members they are, whenever another story is sold, I give thanks to my muse—a little cat with a mischievous grin, who kept me company in my "darkest hours."

Cindy Podurgal Chambers

Step-Babies

It had been scheduled. Muffie, our seven-month-old Lhasa apso, was to be fixed. But as luck would have it, we didn't schedule it soon enough. Five months pregnant myself, I sat at the kitchen table staring at my beautiful pet and reprimanding myself for not doing something sooner.

My ten-year-old daughter walked into the room and saw me staring at Muffie. "What's wrong?" she asked.

I thought Nina, an animal lover, would be thrilled to have puppies in the house. And lately I'd noticed her mood had seemed a little down. But when I told her, she simply looked from Muffie to my protruding stomach and stated, "I don't know how I feel about babies right now."

My heart squeezed. "What do you mean? I thought you wanted a brother or sister."

The expression on her young face turned anguished, and deep down I sensed her fears. Steve and I had married when Nina was six years old and because her biological father had long since severed the ties, Steve had become the daddy she had always wanted.

"What if Daddy loves the baby best?" she asked and tears filled her brown eyes. "It will be his, you know. Not just some stepchild he got stuck with."

My own eyes grew moist, and I reassured her that Steve had enough love to share and he would love them the same. But I still saw the doubt in her watery eyes, and it broke my heart. It seemed nothing we said or did could convince her.

Two months later, Muffie had two beautiful puppies and although Nina was fascinated, and I'd occasionally find her visiting with the puppies, she still remained somewhat aloof about the whole "baby" situation.

Then one day I came in and found Nina crying as she stood over the puppies.

"What's wrong?" I asked.

Through her tears she told me about a friend who had found a stray pregnant dog. After a few days, the animal had gone into labor and after several hours they took the dog to the vet. The puppies were premature: Two were born dead, and the other two were sickly. It seemed the mother dog was too weak to feed the puppies. "The vet is giving the mother until this afternoon, and if her milk doesn't come in, he's going to . . . put the puppies down. That means he going to kill them, doesn't it?" she asked.

Heartbroken, I took Nina in my arms, "Oh baby, I'm so sorry."

"They can't do that, Mama. They just can't," she cried.

She allowed me to hold her a second then she pulled away. "So I've been thinking. Maybe Muffie will take them as her stepchildren."

I was shocked at her idea. I'd heard that sometimes whelping animals would take other young, but I also knew it wasn't a sure thing.

"But honey," I told her. "Muffie's puppies are almost four weeks. And you said the puppies were premature."

"So, you told me I was premature, too. They didn't kill me."

"But honey," I said, "What if . . ." What if she doesn't accept them, I almost said, but right then my mind played back what Nina had said, "Maybe Muffie would take the children as her stepchildren. . . . I was premature." Somehow Nina related to this situation at a deeper level than I first guessed.

I stood there in a quandary. I wanted to say we'd try, but what if Muffie rejected the puppies? Would that send a message to my daughter? Yet would our not trying send a message? I thought of the puppies, the consequences, and then I met my daughter's pleading gaze. "I'll talk to the vet."

The vet was not reassuring. My Muffie could very likely reject the puppies.

Steve and I talked, and in the end we felt that not to try would be more damaging than to have tried and failed. We also discussed the possibility of attempting to save the puppies ourselves. But with our baby on the way and Steve's job situation, the around-the-clock care seemed too daunting. In spite of our doubts, the next morning Steve went to the vet and got the puppies.

Nina stayed home from school, and although we had explained to her that Muffie could very well reject the new additions, Steve and I both worried.

Removing a towel from Muffie's box, I placed the two new puppies on the towel in another box. Then I put the box in the middle of the kitchen, a room away from where Muffie was nursing her own litter.

When Muffie heard the new puppies' soft cries, she came bustling into the kitchen to investigate. She stared down in the box, and I can honestly say I've never seen a dog with a more befuddled expression. She ran back to her puppies and stared down in the box as if to count. Then she scurried back to the two other puppies and looked at us in total bewilderment. After a moment, she smelled them, nudged them with her nose, and then left the room as if to say, "These aren't mine."

I looked at my daughter. Her big brown eyes had begun to fill with tears. "She doesn't want them, does she?"

"Let's give her some time," I told her. We waited for fifteen minutes. The new puppies began to cry again, and I felt like joining in. The vet had said not to force Muffie to take them. It had to be her choice. Eventually, I took Nina's hand and Steve wrapped his arm around her shoulder.

"We tried," he told her. Then he looked at her, and I saw the beginning of tears in his eyes. "But hey," he said. "We can still try. We'll get those droppers. We can do this."

Nina looked up at him with love in her eyes, somehow sensing this was a sacrifice on his part. "Thank you," she said.

Sighing, he reached down to pick up one of the yelping puppies and when he did Muffie came running into the room. She barked at him. He quickly put the tiny newcomer down, and we stood back. Muffie jumped into the box and licked the puppies. We all started laughing and hugging. Then, with our arms around each other we watched as she carried her adopted family, one at a time, to her box.

Steve took Nina by the hand and led her to the puppies. "You gave Muffie something very special today. You gave her two more puppies to love. Just like your mother gave me you to love." In gentle words, he assured Nina one more time that she had a place in his heart, a place that couldn't be erased no matter how many brothers and sisters she had.

Nina looked up at Steve, and then down at Muffie, who was lying contentedly with all four of the puppies, and her face brightened, breaking into a radiant smile. As she returned his bear hug, I could see that her fears had finally melted away. In that happy moment, I knew our combined family was going to be just fine.

Christie Craig

"Nobody's the cutest, you're all cute."

Jet

"Will you save them, Mommy?"

As I looked down into the inquisitive, trusting faces of my two sons, ages four and seven, I was touched by their undeniable, little-boy faith in me. They had not asked, "Can you save them?" They just assumed that I could. I decided to try.

The mallard nest that we had stumbled upon that spring day along the wooded shore of my father's backyard pond was abandoned and strewn apart. Only five of twelve eggs were left unbroken.

We gently gathered the smooth, creamy-white, elliptical orbs into our hands. They felt cool against my skin, which warned me that the nippy spring air had probably finished what their unknown assailant had begun during the night.

Back in our kitchen, we constructed a primitive incubator from an empty fish aquarium, clamping a reflector light to its upper rim. After placing the eggs on a towel at the bottom of the aquarium and turning on the light, we began our patient vigil. A little research told us that duck eggs take about twenty-seven days to hatch, but since we had no clue as to when the "birth" of the eggs had taken place, we didn't know how long we would have to wait.

Day after day, several times a day, their enthusiasm never diminishing, the boys checked and gently turned the eggs. As we passed day twenty-seven, the disappointment on their young faces was only too visible. Not willing to abandon hope, we continued to watch and wait.

A day or two later, our patience was rewarded. I was summoned to the kitchen by shouts of excitement. One of the eggs looked different. Its once smooth surface was now covered with dark jagged lines. When we listened carefully, we heard tiny noises confirming the life within. Slowly but surely one little mallard was struggling to make its way into the world.

After several hours of scratching and pecking, the duckling finally freed itself of the eggshell. Wet and exhausted, it collapsed and slept in the warmth of the light. By the time it awoke, it was dry, soft and fluffy. Immediately, it began to try out its spindly legs and very large feet. Before the day had ended, it was walking around, eagerly flapping its tiny wings. After eating its fill of chicken feed, it slept once again, as we looked on with wonder and pride.

In the days that followed, it became obvious that in the duckling's eyes, I was its mother. When I moved, it moved with me; when I stopped, it sat on top of my foot. When it lost sight of me, its tiny panicked peeps would fill the air.

Even though we enjoyed the enthusiastic greeting we received each morning upon entering the kitchen, it soon became obvious that we needed to make new living arrangements for our little friend. In exchange for a quiet kitchen, my husband, who through the years has patiently endured an array of orphaned critters, constructed a chicken wire pen in a remote corner of our yard, complete with a "duck house" and a tub of water.

We expected that our duckling would be thrilled to

have so much space and so many amenities. Apparently, though, the adjustment from house duck to mere yard duck was not an easy one, and the duckling wasted no time letting us know how it felt about its new accommodations. In order to maintain some peace and quiet, during the day we gave the duckling free range of the yard under the watchful eyes of the boys and myself. At night, or when we were away from home, it was returned, protesting loudly, to its pen.

As the duckling grew, the soft fuzzy down that covered its body was slowly replaced by the coarser feathers of adulthood. Two things soon became obvious. The first was that our duck was a female, and second, that something about her wings was very unusual. Instead of folding neatly at her sides, her wing tips turned upside down and stuck straight out. We dubbed her Jet, because to us she resembled an airplane.

Jet assumed many roles as a member of our family. As resident comedian she was a constant source of amusement and giggles. She waddled behind whoever was walking in the yard, going as fast as she had to in order to keep up. She supplied our lawn with an abundance of fresh fertilizer. She also provided us with numerous fresh eggs, placed indiscriminately throughout the yard, though somehow we never found the courage to eat them. Jet was also an efficient bug-zapper and a terrific "watchdog." Head cocked, watching with first one eye and then the other, she was always on the alert and never failed to announce the arrival of visitors.

Jet quickly outgrew her small water tub, so we purchased a kiddy pool and propped a board on the edge to serve as a ramp. She relished her new pool and spent hours swimming, diving and flapping those misshapen, yet rapidly developing wings. As Jet reached her full physical maturity, her pool seemed suddenly small, and we knew the time had come to give her the freedom of the lake and the company of her own kind.

Wondering how long she would continue to recognize us, two quiet adults and two sad little boys loaded her into the car. As I carried her through the woods to the lake's edge, she quickly spotted her real family for the first time. I felt her heart beating wildly beneath my hands. As I placed her on the ground at our feet, the other ducks loudly beckoned to her to join them. Jet sat there, unmoving, glued to her spot in confusion. She seemed to have no clue as to what those noisy creatures were nor what she was to do. Jet had never seen a duck before!

I watched from the lake's edge as my husband and boys climbed into a small rowboat and began to paddle her out to where the other ducks had congregated. They carefully lowered Jet into the water and suddenly, with a splash, we learned another thing about her: with the right motivation, those bent wings were quite capable of flight. And fly she did. Before the boys could get their paddles back into the water, Jet was once again on the shore, tucked safely between the feet of the only mom she had ever known.

We tried many times that day to introduce her to life on the lake, but Jet had made her choice. So we left the lake in single-file and made our way through the woods and up the hill to the car, five "ducks" in a row . . . all happy and relieved to be going home together.

Lynn Pulliam

Obedience

For seven years my father, who was not yet old enough to retire, had been battling colon cancer. Now he was dying. He could no longer eat or even drink water, and an infection had forced him into the hospital. I sensed that he hated being in the hospital, but he hardly complained. That wasn't his way.

One night when he had no luck summoning a nurse, and tried to reach the bathroom on his own, he fell and gashed his head on the nightstand. When I saw his wounded head the next day, I felt my frustration and helpless anger rise. *Why isn't there anything I can do?* I thought, as I waited for the elevator. As if in answer to my prayers, when the elevator opened, two dogs greeted me.

Dogs? In a hospital? Personally, I couldn't think of a better place for dogs, but I was shocked that the city laws and hospital codes allowed it.

"How did you get to bring dogs here?" I asked the owner, as I stepped in.

"They're therapy dogs. I take them up to the sixth floor once a week, to meet with the patients in rehab."

An idea grew stronger and stronger as I walked out of the hospital and to my car. My dad had bought a springer spaniel named Boots for my mom for a Christmas present a few years before. My mother had insisted that she wanted a dog, and it had to be a spaniel. My dad had explained this to me when he asked me to go for a ride with him to pick out a puppy.

When he picked up a wriggly kissy puppy, I saw the tension ease from my father's face. I realized the genius of my mother's plan immediately. The dog was not for her; it was for him. Brilliantly, she asked for a spaniel so he could have the breed of dog he'd always wanted, and never had, when he was a boy.

By then, all of us kids had moved away from home. So Boots also became the perfect child my father never had. She was an eager, loving and obedient pal for him.

Personally, I thought she was a little *too* obedient. Boots was not allowed on the bed or any other furniture, and she never broke this rule. Sometimes I wanted to tell my dad when he was at home lying on his sickbed, "Call Boots up here! She'll give you love and kisses and touch you like I'm too restrained to do . . . and you need it."

But I didn't. And he didn't. And Boots didn't.

Instead, she sat near his bed, watching him protectively, as the months rolled by. She was always there, a loving presence as his strength ebbed away, till he could no longer walk or even sit up without help. Once in a while, he got very sick, and went to the hospital, and she awaited his return anxiously, jumping up expectantly every time a car pulled up to the house.

I decided that if I could give my dad nothing else, I was going to give him a few minutes with his beloved dog. So I went back to the hospital and asked a nurse about it. She told me that if I were to bring his dog in, she would not "see anything." I took that as a yes.

Later that day, I came back for another visit, bringing Boots. I told my dad I had a surprise for him in my car. I went to get her, and the strangest thing happened.

Boots, the perfect dog, who was as impeccably leash-trained as she was obedient, practically flew out of the car, yanked me across that snowy parking lot to the front door and dragged me through the hospital lobby. She somehow knew to stop directly in front of the appropriate elevator (I could never find the right one myself). And even though she had never been anywhere near that hospital before, when the elevator doors opened at the fourth floor, she nearly pulled my arm out of its socket as she ran down the hall, around two corners, down another hall and into his room. Then, without a moment of hesitation, she jumped straight up onto his bed! Ever so gently, she crawled into my father's open arms, not touching his pain-filled sides or stomach, and laid her face next to his.

For the first time, Boots was on my dad's bed, just where she belonged. And for the first time in a long time, I saw my father's broad smile. I knew we were both grateful Boots had broken the rules and finally obeyed her own heart.

Lori Jo Oswald, Ph.D.

A Cat Named Turtle

You will be lucky if you know how to make friends with strange cats.

Colonial American Proverb

I didn't grow up with cats. Or with dogs. We once harbored the dalmatian of a vacationing aunt and uncle. If all had gone well, we'd have gotten our own dog.

But all did not go well. My brother refused to clean up after the dog, and soon we were permanently critter-free. Not that my mother minded. Having been scratched by a cat when she was little, she feared anything that moved too quickly on too many legs. My father, a city boy, had no experience with animals and less interest in them.

But I married a cat-lover. In his meager walk-up flat in New York City, Roy had enjoyed the company of several marvelous felines, one of them a waif from the subway. I listened to his fond recollections in the same way I heard his tales of some other experiences: They were interesting, even compelling, but nothing I thought I'd ever experience myself.

And then we moved to Vermont and found the cats on

our land. Or they found us—and it was really *their* land. They were feral, having lived in the wild for who-knows-how-long. We extended a hand literally and figuratively to newly named Mama Cat, Honey Puss, Herbert and Sylvester, giving them food on the deck, shelter in the carport and veterinary care for the occasional ailment. Now we realized we should have neutered them, too.

We first saw Turtle trotting along behind her mother, in a parade that included several chubby kittens making their way from the blackberry thicket, across the driveway and into the pine trees. She reappeared briefly a year later, unmistakably the same tortoiseshell. The year afterward, she visited often. I named her when I didn't quite like her; she was nervous, pushy, eating Honey Puss's food. Turtle seemed a good name for a tortoiseshell, especially one who didn't yet have my affection.

I was already reading about feral cats. The universal opinion was that unless a feral cat becomes used to people very early in life, taming the cat is virtually impossible. But nobody told Turtle, who grew ever more comfortable with us. She'd fall onto her back with a thud, inviting us to pet her lovely white belly. She'd linger on the deck with our guests, on summer evenings, sampling one lap after another. Then, as soon as everyone had gone, she'd trot off into the darkness.

Could we bring her inside? Roy's on-again-off-again allergy to cats suddenly returned. But she wouldn't want to come inside anyway, I proclaimed.

Or would she? My office, on the second floor, looks out upon our hillside. Many times I'd put down my work to gaze out the window, and I'd see Turtle staring at me, her wide golden eyes and her dear, crooked little face—haphazardly splotched in black and tan—not twenty inches from my own face. Often I heard her talking to me before I saw her.

We were having a new wing constructed, and she found another route to my office one day, staring at me through the side window. Her muddy paw prints on the roofing paper led from my window to the builder's ladder at roof's edge. I was impressed.

She built a nest for herself in the developing new wing, settling into an open carton where the carpenter had tossed his sweaty T-shirt. She was so comfortable here that she barely lifted her head to greet us when we came looking for her. Roy started getting allergy shots.

With the new wing enclosed, Turtle was again outside. But the next time she looked in at my desk, Roy opened the window screen, waited for her to climb in and carried her downstairs. She was purring loudly. She walked through the living room, poking into all the little places: a cupboard, the bottom of a small bookshelf. She seemed oblivious to us, and indeed we were as dumb as chairs. After a few moments, Roy took her outside.

Later that day, she was sitting near him on the deck, when he got up and moved toward the kitchen. She reached the door ahead of him and scrambled inside. She didn't mind being taken out again. I didn't mind either. She might want to be inside (I now conceded the possibility), but did I want her? Wouldn't a feral cat, even a friendly one, shred everything to tatters? Wouldn't she scratch us at the slightest provocation? Wouldn't she yowl all night?

The deciding moment arrived after I'd been away for a few days. Turtle had stayed at the bend in the driveway for most of my absence. But barely fifteen minutes after my return, she was at the kitchen door! When Roy opened the door to bring her some food, she pushed past him into the kitchen and headed straight for me. No curiosity about the house this time. No interest in the food. She jumped into my lap, readjusted her weight and purred—

the kind of purring you could hear from twenty feet away. She *missed* me! She missed *me!* That was it. I was ready to share my house with her.

Very soon it was also Turtle's house as she figured out the best spot on our bed (between us, lengthwise) and the sunniest corner of our living room. She had a lot to learn. How to sprawl across my in-basket. How to awaken us for her breakfast. How to keep the house free of the tiny mice that sneak inside every autumn, when the cold air ruffles their rodential dispositions. How to launch a steady stream of complaints at the snow. How to stand guard at the bathtub until I could be meowed safely from the water. How to settle her weight on precisely the document I might be reading from, or typing from, or writing on. The litter box? A snap. She managed that in half a day.

I had a lot to learn, too. And to unlearn, from my mother's prejudices. But with Turtle's help, this cat was soon my dear companion, gentle and wise, considerate and affectionate. Roy was delighted to see how I loved her and how she loved us back. She became the subject of several chapters in the book I wrote on feral cats, and I wish she could have understood the gifts and letters she got from adoring readers. Roy however was convinced she understood everything we said, or even thought; he was sure she could read our minds. Once, he was only thinking of her, and was startled to hear her sudden purring from a nearby chair.

She knew plenty, our Turtle. In parts of the British Isles it is considered a good omen when a tortoiseshell cat comes into the house. The tortoiseshell is considered special. But Turtle was special beyond all other specialness. The sweetest pussycat we've ever known. And the smartest. Never a pest. Never seeking attention when we were heavily preoccupied with work or chores. But there in a flash whenever a lap became available, whenever a head hit a pillow. She was very special. I knew it, Roy knew it, and Turtle knew that we knew it.

She lived with us for ten sweet years, until kidney disease claimed her, and she is buried just up from the bend in the driveway, under a stone that has her coloring. We see the stone from our kitchen.

I bless the day that she decided to chance it with us. She knew so much more than I did, about the important things. She knew enough to make that running leap that day into my house, my lap, my heart.

Ellen Perry Berkeley

Woman's Best Friend

Qui me amat, amat et canem meum. *(Love me, love my dog.)*

St. Bernard De Clairvaux,
"Sermo Primus," 1150

At age thirty-two, I had just about given up on ever getting married. Over the years, I'd had numerous relationships. Some were wonderful—and some were real disasters. About the only thing they had in common was that they all ended.

The entire relationship and dating scene was wearing me down. I was tired of relationships with no potential. I was weary of putting my heart out there and getting it smashed. Getting married was starting to look like it wasn't in the stars for me.

Giving up on marriage was one thing. But I wouldn't, and couldn't, give up on my heart. I wanted to love and be loved. I needed to nourish my heart in a way that even my best-intentioned friends and family members hadn't done for me.

I needed a dog.

Soon, on an afternoon in early May, I found myself peering into a pen on a friend's farm, studying a litter of eight black and white puppies who were playing on and around their mother, a champion Border collie. The puppies were six weeks old and as cute as only puppies can be. I slid through the door and sat down. The puppies, wiggling with excitement and apprehension, quickly jitterbugged over to the safety of their mother's side. All except one.

The littlest one, an almost all-black ball of downy fur with two white front paws and a white breast, came sidling over to me and crawled into my lap. I lifted her up and looked into her puppy-hazy brown eyes. It was instant love.

"Just remember, Puppy, you chose me, okay?" I whispered. That was the beginning of the longest successful relationship I've ever had.

I named my puppy Miso. The next weeks of a glorious early spring were spent basking in the glow of literal puppy love while housebreaking, training and establishing new routines. When I look back, that whole spring and summer was spent incorporating her into my life and me into hers.

Miso's Border collie heritage dictated lots of time outdoors, preferably running. I'd been eager to have company while I ran my almost-daily three to five miles in predawn darkness, and now I had a running buddy. Miso and I were out in all kinds of weather, rarely missing a day.

Weekends and evenings were spent in quiet, loving solitude with Miso. At my writing desk or art table, Miso would lie relaxed at my side and sigh with contentment. Anywhere I went, Miso came too: camping, swimming at a local lake on weekends, long car rides to my parents' home in the summer. If an activity precluded taking a dog along, I wasn't much interested in it anyway. We were a happy couple . . . inseparable and self-sufficient. My heart was nourished, and I felt content and full. We spent two years this way.

Looking back, it's remarkable that I met my husband-to-be at all. I certainly wasn't looking for Mr. Right anymore, not when I was so happy being a "single mom" to Miso. Bob just kind of popped into my life, or rather, our lives, because Miso was definitely impacted by Bob's appearance on the scene.

At first, Bob accepted Miso as part of the "package." Our dating consisted of lots of outdoor activities where Miso accompanied us easily. But as fall and winter approached, and Miso needed to be indoors more due to cold and wet weather, trouble brewed. Bob wasn't enthusiastic about dog hair or mud on the furniture and insisted that Miso stay outside when we spent time at his house.

Since the amount of time spent there was increasing, it bothered both Miso and me that she was required to stay outdoors. This was an uncomfortable blip on the radar screen of an otherwise growing and loving relationship with Bob.

A crisis point was reached one particularly cold January night. Bob insisted that Miso bunk out on the enclosed porch for the night, a location Miso and I felt was unacceptable considering the temperature. I argued that anything less than Miso's admittance to the basement was cruel and inhumane treatment. He argued that I was being unreasonable, and he felt I should respect his "house rules."

We went back and forth like two lawyers arguing a Supreme Court case. Things got heated. Tempers flared. We reached an impasse and stood, staring steely-eyed at each other.

The next thing I knew I heard my own voice, thick with emotion, declare, "Don't make me choose between you and Miso, because you may be in for an unpleasant surprise!"

Bob looked shocked, and in the face of my determination, wisely backed off.

Miso was admitted to the warm basement for the night. The entire indoor/outdoor Miso arrangement was renegotiated over the next couple days and we reached a satisfactory compromise for all three of us.

That crisis was a turning point. I realized I had issued my ultimatum in all seriousness. Bob realized that I did not solely depend on him for love and affection—I had loyalties beyond him. And Miso found her new place in my life, no longer my one-and-only, but as a beloved member of a family.

For that's what we became. Bob and I married, and soon our threesome became a foursome with the birth of our daughter.

Eleven years later, Miso is over fourteen years old. Partially blind and deaf, she suffers the infirmities of old age now, enduring diabetes and arthritis with dignity and grace. The relationship between Bob and Miso has undergone an amazing transformation.

Now I watch Bob tenderly guide Miso to find me when she has "misplaced me" in our house, and lovingly help her up the front steps on a rainy night. I believe Bob has grown to respect the debt he owes Miso. For Miso held a place ready in my life for Bob. She gave love a foothold.

There was never any need to choose between Bob and Miso—both had already laid claim to my heart.

Sometimes now I look into Miso's eyes, which see only shadows, and speak in her ear, though I know she no longer hears, and tell her once again: "Remember, you chose me."

Holly Manon Moore

Bedroom Secrets of Pets Revealed

A long, long time ago, people slept in the house; dogs slept in a doghouse in the backyard; and cats, well, they "catted around" and slept in the barn or alley. That was before our pets migrated from the backyard to the bedroom to sleep, and from the kennel to the kitchen to eat. Now, the average doghouse has three bedrooms, two baths, a spa, an entertainment center and a two-car garage. Yes, the doghouse is our house.

Consider this: Before the arrival of our four-legged bed-partners, human bed-partners decided which side of the bed they would sleep on; we carved out property lines on the mattress. But then we decided to welcome pets into our homes, hearts and bedrooms.

That was the last day any of us got a decent night's sleep.

I was reminded of this recently when, after a hectic trip, I headed home from New York to Almost Heaven Ranch in northern Idaho. Between airplane breakdowns and storms, it was a nightmare trip that took two sleepless days of travel instead of the usual one.

Fighting extreme fatigue, I finally made it home, stumbled into our log house, and headed directly to my bed, ready to slip between the flannel sheets and nestle under the goosedown comforter next to my beloved wife, Teresa. Now at long last I would be able to sleep. It sounded great in theory, but I was dreaming!

Three formidable barriers to my sleep were sprawled across the king-size bed. Scooter, our wired wirehaired fox terrier, was lying perpendicular across the bed, while Turbo and Tango, our two Himalayan-cross cats, were asleep on each pillow. I shoehorned myself next to Teresa and collapsed into deep sleep. I was sawing the timber and dreaming sweet dreams when suddenly, I was shot in the ribs with a deer rifle! At least that's what it felt like.

It was actually Teresa's elbow that had poked into my side as a last resort to stop my snoring. Sleepily, I looked across at her. She was crowded onto the tiniest sliver of mattress at the edge of the bed. The cats were wrapped around her neck and face, and our twenty-pound, flabby, fur-covered, thorn-in-the-side, Scooter, was dreamily snoring away, her feet pushing against Teresa's head. But would Teresa shove an elbow into Scooter, or disturb Tango or Turbo? Are you kidding?

Now, if *I* snore, Teresa's sure to find a way of letting me know it, and if I cross over to her side of the bed, she waits only a nanosecond before shoving me back onto my side or onto the floor. But there she lay, unwilling to move a muscle or twitch an eye, because she didn't want to interrupt the fur-queen's sleep!

I turned over, pulling instinctively on the down comforter to make sure that Teresa let me have my fair share of it. Yet through this sleepy tug-of-war, I was careful not to disturb my "Scooter Girl," who slept lying across me, looking warm, toasty and content.

And who needs an alarm clock when you have pets? I had managed to doze off again, but Scooter woke me up before the crack of dawn to be let outside. Again, I looked across at Teresa. Turbo and Tango were kneading her hair and licking her face to show they were ready for break-fast—now!

It was clear that Scooter, Turbo and Tango had had another great night's sleep, while Teresa and I were battling for shuteye scraps. I knew the pets would fly out of bed fully charged, while my wife and I, chronically sleep-deprived, would crawl out from under the blankets to start another day on the hamster wheel of activity we call life.

And yet . . . that's not quite the whole story. I knew full well that our four-legged bed partners had as usual gotten the best end of the sleeping arrangements, but I regarded it as just a small payback for the great gift of uncondi-tional love that they give us, twenty-four hours a day, seven days a week.

So as I got out of bed, I paused to kiss Teresa's cheek, pat Scooter's furry head and stroke the cats' tails. Our bed was in purr-fect order and I had had a grrr-eat night's sleep after all.

Marty Becker, D.V.M.

Mighty Hercules

One April Sunday, my children and I picnicked in the park. I was pouring lemonade when I heard a shout. Andy, my towheaded eleven-year-old, ran toward us, holding what looked like a long, crooked stick. When the stick wriggled, the lemonade splashed across the picnic table.

"Mom!" Andy cried. "It's a garter snake. May I keep him? Please?"

My instinct was "No!" But the look in Andy's eyes made me hesitate. Andy was the youngest of my three children, and I worried about him. At four, he'd required surgery on his ears and subsequent speech therapy. A year later, his father died; the same year, doctors diagnosed attention deficit disorder. He had needed special schools in early grades and still required a tutor. And, like many ADD kids, he had grown up feeling "different" and "dumb," despite his very real intelligence.

From an early age, Andy possessed an affinity for animals. Growling dogs wagged their tails at his approach. Hissing cats purred. But dogs and cats were not allowed in our apartment complex. I looked from Andy's pleading eyes to the unblinking eyes of the snake. Its tongue flicked at me, and I shuddered.

"Where would you keep it?"

"In my aquarium. I'll put a lid on and never ever let it bother you, Mom." He held the striped, black snake up to his face. "Please, Mom. Please?"

I'm still not sure why I said yes. But Hercules, as Andy triumphantly named him, came home with us.

Andy set to work at once, cleaning the twenty-gallon aquarium, lining it with rocks and dirt, setting a branch upright in one corner for Hercules to climb on, installing a light bulb for warmth.

I admired Andy's industry, and once Hercules was safely behind glass I could even admire the long, striped snake. In the sunlight, his scales danced and glittered, the way sunlight catches on a dragonfly's wing.

"He's not trying to sting you," said Andy, when I jerked back from Hercules' flicking tongue. "Snakes use their tongues to sense things around them."

To a boy with dyslexia, reading can be an excruciating task. Andy had never read for fun, even though his tutor told us he had overcome his early handicaps. But after Hercules' arrival, Andy checked out every book on snakes in the library. We were amazed at all he learned.

Even more amazing were the changes in Andy, especially after his sixth-grade teacher invited Hercules to school. Andy was smaller than most of his classmates, but I saw his shoulders straighten as he proudly carried the snake to school.

Hercules spent all spring in the classroom, under Andy's charge, and adapted well. Before long, Andy had only to stick his hand in the aquarium for Hercules to slither to his outstretched fingers and glide smoothly up his arm. On the playground, he looped gracefully around Andy's neck, basking in the warm Kansas sunshine, his tongue flicking Andy's cheek.

Hercules returned home when school ended, to be

joined, for Andy's birthday, by a pair of boa constrictors he named Mabel and Sam.

The boas were young, about eighteen inches long, and beautifully mottled in rich shades of brown and tan.

"How do you know they're male and female?" I asked.

"I just know," said Andy confidently. "I'm going to put myself through college by selling baby boas."

College! I marveled again at the changes the snakes had wrought. Here was Andy, who had thought he was "dumb," suddenly talking about college.

As summer veered toward autumn, Herc became Andy's near constant companion. Often, when Andy went out on his bicycle, Herc rode with him, sometimes wrapped around the handlebars, other times tucked into Andy's drawstring snake bag.

Seventh grade is a tough year for kids, and for shy, insecure Andy, starting junior high could have been a nightmare. But now there was a difference.

The lonely boy of a year ago smiled now. He held his head high and stepped confidently into the crowded school hall, knowing that the other kids whispered of him, "He's the guy with the snakes."

I remembered what Andy's teacher had told us on the last day of grade school: "Hercules has given Andy value in his own eyes. For the first time he has something no one else has—something others admire. That's a new feeling for Andy. A good feeling."

The snakes were a regular part of all of our lives now. When Hercules disappeared from the bathroom one day, after Andy had let him out to exercise, the whole family pitched in for the snake hunt. We found him in the closet, wrapped cozily around one of Andy's sneakers.

And we all watched, fascinated, when Hercules shed his skin, slithering out with a smooth, fluid motion to leave behind the old skin perfectly intact, while his new scales glowed with youth and promise. Carefully, Andy collected the old skin and placed it in the shoebox where he kept his valuables.

We never learned what sent Hercules into convulsions that spring. As far as we could tell, nothing had changed in his environment. But one Friday afternoon, Andy ran to me screaming, "Hurry! Something's wrong with Herc!"

Mabel and Sam lay quietly curled in their corner of the aquarium. But Hercules writhed and jumped. His tongue flailed the air wildly.

I grabbed my car keys while Andy wrestled Hercules into the snake bag.

Our veterinarian injected some cortisone, and it seemed to work. Gradually Hercules grew calmer.

Andy gently stroked his snake, and slowly Hercules reached up and flicked Andy's cheek with his tongue. He flowed again into a graceful loop around Andy's neck.

For several weeks thereafter, Hercules seemed fine. But then the convulsions returned, and we raced to the vet for another shot of cortisone. Once again, Hercules recovered.

But the third time was too much. Although the cortisone quieted the massive convulsion, it was apparent as we drove home that Hercules was dying. His long, lean body lay limp in Andy's lap. His scales, instead of catching the light, were clouded and gray.

He tried to lift his head as Andy stroked his back, but the effort was more than he could manage. His tongue flickered once, weakly, like a candle flame about to go out. And then he was still.

Tears rolled silently down Andy's cheeks. And mine.

It would be another year before Andy blossomed, seemingly overnight, into the six feet of linebacker's build that would carry him through high school. He went on to college, made good grades and, later, earned an M.B.A.

Andy never did raise baby boas, but Mabel and Sam stayed with us all through high school, bequeathed, at the end, to Andy's biology class. They never took the place of Hercules, though.

In Andy's top drawer, there is still a dried snakeskin. Before he left for college I suggested it might be time to throw it out.

Andy looked at me in horror. "Don't you dare!"

He touched the skin gently. "Ol' Herc . . . he was sure one splendid snake, wasn't he?"

Yes, he was. He gave a shy, lonely boy the first intimation of all he was—and all he could be.

Barbara Bartocci

Angie's Dog Always

The mountain folk didn't know what to make of Dr. Gaine Cannon at first. All they had heard was that the stranger had left a good practice in another state because he wanted to come up to an isolated community here in the North Carolina mountains and build a hospital. They were used to traveling twenty-five miles over one-lane dirt roads to the nearest clinic at Brevard. But only if it was urgent, because even if they could get there in time, the cost was out of the question for families living on three or four thousand dollars a year, like most did way back in the coves and hollows.

Cannon knew all that when he moved up to Balsam Grove, but he was of mountain stock himself and he cared about these people. Today, bouncing along in his black Jeep over the gravel road on his way home from his last call, he flicked on his windshield wipers as snow started to fall from a darkening sky. He was glad he had no calls to make that day.

Walls were already raised for the Albert Schweitzer Memorial Hospital. Dr. Cannon had become fast friends with the great doctor during the summer he spent working with him at his hospital in Africa. The inspiration of

Dr. Schweitzer kindled Cannon's desire for a similar ministry to the people of Appalachia. He didn't worry about his patients not having money to pay. He asked them to bring river stones for the walls of the hospital, or whatever they had—a home-cured ham from their smokehouse, or some fresh vegetables.

Now, the snow was falling faster. An old man walking beside the road raised one gnarled, arthritic hand to hail him, and Cannon slowed the Jeep.

"Evenin,' Doc. Did you know Annie Neal's little Angie is bad sick?"

"No, I didn't, Rufus."

"Yep. I jest heard it at the store."

"Well, why in heaven didn't her daddy come for me, then?"

"He's up takin' care of his Ma in Boswell this week. Think you could get over to see Angie, Doc?"

"I'll give it a try. But if this snow gets much heavier, I can't promise I'll even see the turnoff to get up to their cabin."

Doc Cannon turned the Jeep around and headed back into the mountains. He wished the Neals had a phone so he could call and ask them to put some kind of flag out where the road branched off to their cabin, but he thought he would recognize it anyway. He wasn't too worried about getting stuck. The new snow tires on the Jeep should make it.

When he reached Jackson County it was snowing harder, and he couldn't see any distance. The Jeep lurched through potholes and along deep rock-laden ruts on the dirt road. It was one lane and narrow, with a drop of several hundred feet to the left. He found himself leaning in toward the mountain, hugging the side of it with his Jeep.

He thought about Angie, hoping he wasn't too late and that he had everything in his bag that she might need. He felt his isolation in this white world of snowy, swirling flakes. Where was the grove of wind-twisted trees on the left just before the Hughes turnoff? Had he missed it? He wondered if he would get there tonight or freeze to death instead.

A faint sound came from behind the Jeep. He heard it again and slowed to a stop. Through his open window came the barking of a dog, sharp, insistent. Then he saw him. He would have known that dog anywhere. He looked like a cross between a golden retriever and a large coon dog, a long reddish fringe of fur hanging from the underside of his snowy tail. It was Angie's dog, standing beside the road. He backed up a little more. The animal kept barking, coming toward him a few paces, then striking out on a trail among the trees. Gaine cut the wheel recklessly toward the slope of the mountain and followed. He hoped to God this was the road.

Gratefully he felt the tires of the Jeep settle into shallow ruts, and he drove on, the dog always keeping about twenty feet ahead. Then, in a clearing, he saw the dark shape of the little house. What luck! The dog had led him right to it.

He knocked, and after a minute Angie's mother opened the door.

"Doc! I near didn't hear you out there. Come in."

The air in the room was filled with the smoky scent of the wood fire, Dr. Cannon knelt down beside a golden-haired child who lay on a pallet of quilts. He placed his stethoscope against her chest. Eyes bright and face flushed, her little body almost burned his hand—pneumonia. Had he reached her in time? He gave her a shot. She stirred and then was up on one elbow trying to rise.

"Did you see him, Doc?" she asked excitedly.

He tried to ease her back down on the pillow. "See who, honey?"

"My Prince."

Doc Cannon glanced questioningly at her mother.

"She meant her dog, Prince. It's just the fever talking, Doc," and she clasped Angie's hand tenderly in hers. "Hush. You were dreaming. Now go to sleep."

"But Momma," Angie exclaimed. "I saw him waving his tail as he trotted along the road up to the house here, and then he came in the room and over to my bed. He licked my face. He did, Momma."

Dr. Cannon smiled. "He's a fine dog."

Her mother put a finger up to her lips and gave Dr. Cannon a look of warning that puzzled him.

At the door of the cabin, Gaine Cannon handed Angie's mother a paper packet of pills for the sick little girl.

"Is she going to be all right, Doctor?"

"Yes, I think she's going to be okay, but you send for me, now, if she takes a turn for the worse. By the way, as far as I'm concerned, Annie, that dog ought to be given a medal. I had already missed the road that leads up here when I heard him barking. He led me all the way up to your cabin. I would have missed it for sure without him."

The woman stared. "Doc, Prince was killed by a car almost a month ago."

"Killed!"

"Yes, down on the highway. The child took on so, Angie's Pa carved a wooden plank in the shape of a grave rock for Prince, and carved some words she wrote herself. Angie plumb loved that dog." Annie looked out the door and up at the sky. "Snow's stopped. Maybe you can see the marker. The grave is at the edge of the woods where you turn in to our place." She paused. "Doc, you don't think it really could have been Prince?" she asked quietly. "But he was the only dog I ever saw all the way up here, and there's not another house for five miles."

"I don't know."

"Well, however you got here," she said, "I want to thank you, Doc." She thrust a jug of apple cider into his arms.

"Take this for now, and I aim to see you get some river stones for your hospital."

Though he was eager to get off the mountain before dark, he saw the marker and could not help braking. The makeshift memorial to the dog stood beneath a big tree. Leaving the motor running, the doctor got out and plodded through the snow. He untied the bandanna scarf from his neck to flick the white flakes from the face of the board. The words he read were crudely carved:

PRINCE
Angie's dog always.

Nancy Roberts

6

PETS AS TEACHERS

By loving and understanding animals, perhaps we humans shall come to understand each other.

Dr. Louis J. Camuti

"It's always 'Sit,' 'Stay,' 'Heel'—
never 'Think,' Innovate,' 'Be yourself.'"

Lesson in Love

It was difficult to feel vexed by a creature that burst into a chorus of purring as soon as I spoke to him.

Philip Brown

Some people call me a cat shrink. I call myself a feline behavior consultant. Over the years, I've helped thousands of people and cats to have happier lives together. Mr. Vinsley was one of my most memorable clients. Originally from England, he lived in a beautiful mansion in Kentucky.

A widower for twenty-five years, Mr. Vinsley had no surviving relatives, so he was used to a life of solitude. He spent his days reading, listening to music and walking around the grounds surrounding his house. He was comfortable being alone and was not interested in making friends or engaging in silly chatter with neighbors.

One cold winter morning, Mr. Vinsley found a large gray cat sitting on his car. Having no fondness for cats, he chased the cat away and assumed that was that! But every morning for the next week, the same gray cat sat on the roof of his Mercedes.

The weather continued getting colder. Even though Mr. Vinsley didn't like cats, he hated the thought that the poor creature might freeze outside. Surely he must belong to someone—perhaps he has a collar, Mr. Vinsley thought. The next day he went outside, expecting to find the cat lounging on his car as usual. But there was no cat. Mr. Vinsley found himself checking outside every few minutes, waiting for the cat. All he wanted to do was to find the owner of this pesky feline or take it to the local shelter if it had no identification.

When the housekeeper arrived later that morning, she found Mr. Vinsley in the kitchen, spooning a can of tuna into a dish. Mr. Vinsley hurried outside and placed the tuna on the roof of his car, then went back to his warm house to wait. By late evening, he removed the tuna, now quite frozen, from the car.

"Have it your way, stupid cat," Mr. Vinsley said as he went back inside the house and dumped the tuna in the garbage before going to bed.

At about 2:00 A.M., Mr. Vinsley woke up. He swears it was a terrible thirst that drove him out of bed and down the stairs to the kitchen. Along the way, he stopped for a quick peek out the front door—still no cat. But just as he was closing the door he caught sight of something limping toward him. Hobbling up the driveway was the gray cat. His fur was matted and his right front paw dangled helplessly in the air. Mr. Vinsley stepped out onto the porch and the cat stopped.

"I'm not going to hurt you," Mr. Vinsley said. "Come here and I'll help you."

The cat just looked at him, not moving.

Leaving the front door open, Mr. Vinsley went into the kitchen, where he dumped some leftover chicken onto a plate. He placed the food on the porch and leaned against the doorway. The old man and the cat just looked at each other. The cat was a tough-looking male who had obviously seen more than his share of fights. He was tall and large. Both ears were torn at the tips and his nose bore several scars.

Mr. Vinsley really hadn't cared about anybody in a long time, and he didn't know why he was so concerned about this cat now. There was just something about him. And here they were, two tough old guys so used to being alone that they didn't even know how to ask for help.

A few minutes passed. Mr. Vinsley was shivering. The cat was watching him intently. Then warily, the old cat limped up to the porch, sniffed at the plate of food, then weakly hobbled past it and through the open doorway.

Amazed that the cat had come inside, Mr. Vinsley followed him in. After some hesitation, the cat allowed him to examine his injured paw. It would need medical attention in the morning. In the meantime, the scruffy old thing would spend the night in the kitchen. But as Mr. Vinsley bent down to scoop him up, the cat darted off on his three good legs. Before he could be stopped, he was clumsily hobbling up the stairs toward the bedrooms.

Cold and tired, Mr. Vinsley climbed the stairs too. He figured the cat would be hiding under a bed. But when he reached his bedroom, he found that the cat had decided that curling up at the foot of the bed would be much more comfortable.

"You could've at least chosen one of the guest rooms," Mr. Vinsley commented.

But he was too tired to argue, so he crawled under the covers, stretching his feet out next to the cat. "Don't get too used to this. You're leaving in the morning."

The following morning, on the way to his doctor's appointment, Mr. Vinsley dropped the cat off at the vet's.

It was at this visit to the doctor that Mr. Vinsley learned he had cancer. Depressed, he drove home, almost forgetting to stop at the vet's. In fact, when he realized he was near the animal hospital, he considered just leaving the cat there for the vet to deal with. But he stopped anyway.

The cat had a broken leg, which was in a large splint. Mr. Vinsley paid the bill and left with the cat. He didn't understand why, but he felt a tug at his heart as he held the cat. Despite his rough exterior, the cat was gentle. Wrapped in his new owner's arms, his loud purr sounded like an old car engine.

Three weeks later, Mr. Vinsley's health took a turn for the worse, and he was confined to bed. The cat, by now named Dancer—because he moved so gracefully despite his heavy splint—only left his side to use his litter box and eat.

The friendship grew deeper. When Mr. Vinsley was well enough, the pair strolled around the grounds or sat in the sun. Dancer loved to sleep in Mr. Vinsley's lap as he listened to classical music or read a book.

And another thing happened. Mr. Vinsley started chatting with his neighbors about pets. They'd share stories and advice. After all these years, Mr. Vinsley was caring about others again. Soon his neighbors became friends who would stop by for a cup of coffee or to play cards.

It was at this point that Mr. Vinsley called me. His doctor had told him he had less than nine months to live. He was not afraid to die, he assured me. After all, he had lived a good seventy-seven years and would face the end with dignity. All of his business was in order.

"There's just one important thing left to do," Mr. Vinsley told me sadly. "I need to take care of Dancer. Since I found him, we've been best friends. I need you to find him a home while I'm still alive. I want to know that he'll be getting the love and care he deserves. I'll provide for his medical and food expenses." He was quiet for a moment and then said, "I know anyone else would think I'm a foolish old man, worrying about some cat, but he's been by my side through the tough times. He's a wonderful friend, and I want to make sure he lives a good life without me."

There was something so sincere and compelling about this man's love for his cat that I couldn't refuse. After a lengthy search, I found a potential home for Dancer with Ruth, a sweet but lonely widow.

When Ruth met Mr. Vinsley and Dancer, all three of them hit it off. Mr. Vinsley took great pleasure in telling Ruth all about Dancer's likes and dislikes.

Eight months after I first met Mr. Vinsley, he was taken to the hospital. At Mr. Vinsley's request, I drove to his house and collected Dancer's things. As if he knew what was about to happen, Dancer was waiting for me in Mr. Vinsley's room. He sat quietly on the bed. The housekeeper walked me to my car. She touched my arm and thanked me for helping Mr. Vinsley. There were tears in her eyes. She'd worked for him for fifteen years.

Later that day I visited Mr. Vinsley to tell him that Dancer was in his new home. He smiled. We talked a little more and then he drifted off to sleep. I stood by the bed for a few moments. "I'll keep watch over Dancer for you," I whispered. Two days later Mr. Vinsley died.

I've since visited Dancer several times, and he's very happy. He follows Ruth the same way he did Mr. Vinsley. And I've noticed that Ruth looks more content than when I first met her. She proudly told me that Dancer sleeps next to her in bed.

Dancer, the tough, stray cat, had once taught Mr. Vinsley how to love again. Now, the furry gray teacher with torn ears and a purr like an old car engine was helping Ruth to learn that same lesson.

Pam Johnson-Bennett

More Than Medicine

Hear our humble prayer, O God. . . . Make us,
ourselves to be true friends to the animals and
so the share the blessings of the merciful.

Albert Schweitzer

Tuesday was my day to make the housecalls in our multidoctor veterinary practice—not my favorite thing to do. I felt isolated working outside the safety of the clinic, yet having to make crucial medical decisions on my own. The cats always hid, and the dogs were always meaner at home. And the people? Well, you never knew what sort you'd run into. I was uncomfortable dealing with the people on their own home turf. As a new graduate depending on textbooks and medical notes to get me through, Tuesdays were definitely a pain in my calendar.

This wasn't what I had envisioned when I'd decided to become a veterinarian. I'd had noble dreams of healing animals, which I felt at least semiqualified to do. But I was at a loss having to deal with people. Somehow my professors had failed to mention two very important facts: Every pet comes with an owner, and every case costs money. My boss, who always had one eye on the bottom line, constantly reminded me of the second.

Cheryl, our technician, had our schedule for the day and plotted our route. Handing me the clipboard, I could see she had saved the best for last, a sick dog in the not-so-affluent end of town.

Cheryl packed our supplies for the day, I packed my insecurities and a medical text, and we both piled into the house-call van for another day's rounds. The first several calls went relatively smoothly with the exception of one junkyard dog with a torn toenail. I was surprised we left with all our fingers intact.

As we parked in front of our last stop for the day, I sighed.

The house was old and rundown, and the lawn hadn't been mowed for a very long time. "Hope this dog isn't too sick." I said, " It doesn't look like these people can pay for veterinary services."

We knocked on the door that was presently answered by Mrs. Johnson, an elderly lady in a flowered-print house-dress. "Oh, doctor!" she exclaimed. "I am so glad you're finally here. Blackie just ain't doin' right. He can hardly pick his head up. He's back in the kitchen. Come right this way."

Mrs. Johnson led us through a remarkably neat and tidy home to the kitchen. It was a pleasant room with flowerpots in the window and fresh-baked bread on the counter. Blackie, a black furry Heinz 57, lay on a pile of blankets in the corner.

Cheryl got the necessary information from Mrs. Johnson as I took a look at Blackie. His gums were pale, his pulses were thready and his heart was rapidly beating. This was one sick little dog.

I explained to Mrs. Johnson that Blackie was very sick and would need to be hospitalized. "The hospital stay and the tests could be very expensive," I told her. "And I can't be sure that we'll be able to save Blackie."

"Doctor, I want you to try," she replied. "I just know you will be able to help him. You see, I'm gonna be praying for Blackie—and for you too, doctor."

Cheryl took a twenty-dollar deposit from Mrs. Johnson. It was all the old lady could spare, but she promised to come up with more in a few days and to pay the rest over time.

We carried Blackie out to the van with Mrs. Johnson calling "God love ya!" after us.

I shook my head wearily as I pulled away from the curb. Here I was with a hopeless case and an owner that couldn't possibly pay the bill. *I guess the clinic will just have to eat this one,* I thought. I wasn't looking forward to telling my boss. And Mrs. Johnson was a Bible-thumper to boot. I didn't place much stock in faith healing. Either we could cure the dog or we couldn't.

Back to the clinic we went and began treatment, running the necessary tests. The results were discouraging at best. I called Mrs. Johnson and told her that Blackie had a condition called autoimmune hemolytic anemia—his body was destroying its own blood cells.

At the time, dogs rarely survived this disease; I asked her as gently as I could if she wanted to put Blackie to sleep.

"No, doctor," she said. "You keep him going overnight. Tomorrow I have prayer group and we're gonna pray for you and Blackie. Just trust God on this one."

The next day Blackie began showing signs of improvement.

His blood cell count was up a bit, and he now sat upright in his cage. I felt my skepticism slip a notch as I phoned Mrs. Johnson with the surprising news.

"Oh, I'd no doubt he'd be better today. You just keep on doing what you're doing, doctor. Me and the girls will keep on a-praying."

With each day that passed, Blackie showed more and more improvement. Humbled, I had no explanation for it.

And Mrs. Johnson and the girls just kept on praying. After a week of hospitalization Blackie was back to his normal happy self, eating and wagging his tail.

I was shaken. Maybe there was something to this praying Mrs. Johnson and the girls had been doing. Many other dogs I'd seen had received the same treatment as Blackie and had died. Did God really care about this little black mutt?

We brought Blackie home to a jubilant Mrs. Johnson. "God bless you, doctor," she said. "God bless you."

I *felt* blessed. My experience with Mrs. Johnson and Blackie gave me the pieces I'd been missing—healing wasn't just about textbooks and medications. If it were, Blackie would never have made it. Now I knew healing was a team effort that involved God, me, the animals and the people who loved them. It was about compassion and faith and serving others.

The next Tuesday I found myself humming as I helped Cheryl load the van for our house-call rounds. What would the day bring? I didn't know, but I was ready to start on this week's adventure. I knew I wouldn't be alone.

Liz Gunkelman, D.V.M.

Wheely Willy

The dog in the cardboard box was incredibly tiny. Someone had brought him, box and all, into the vet's office. They had found him on Melrose, they said. Just one more unwanted animal in Los Angeles. But this one, a full-grown Chihuahua, was unusual in two respects.

Someone had gone to the trouble and expense of ensuring this dog would be a quiet pet by having his vocal chords surgically severed. Plus, the poor little guy had recently been in an accident of some sort, because he was paralyzed from behind his front legs all the way to his tail. But the dog had a good disposition and wasn't in pain, so the vet decided to see if he could find a home for him.

For a year, the Chihuahua waited. No one was willing to take on the burden of a special-needs pet. But right about then, Deborah Turner heard about the unfortunate dog. Haunted by the story, she came to look.

The first moment she laid eyes on him, something in his face moved her deeply. And it seemed the feeling was mutual.

She picked up the two-pound dog and held him to her heart. He was underdeveloped from lack of exercise and strangely mute, but his eyes said it all: I will love you with everything I have and more.

When Deborah's boyfriend saw her new dog, he was doubtful, "What are you going to do, carry that dog every-where?" he asked her.

"If I have to," Deborah answered. She had named the Chihuahua Willy, and he had seemed thrilled with every-thing she'd offered him. He squirmed with delight when she fed him, he sighed luxuriously when set in his new soft dog basket. He played enthusiastically with the toys she gave him. When she walked into the room, Willy pranced, lifting his front feet one at a time in an eager dance of greeting. He especially loved Deborah's cat, Stevie, and rolled over trying to get as close to the large silver Persian as he could. Sometimes he tried to walk, dragging his back legs behind him, but the weight of his hindquarters was too much for his tiny front legs.

Deborah's boyfriend had an idea. He bought three large helium balloons and tied them to Willy's hip area, hoping it would lighten the load. But Willy was so small, the bal-loons lifted his front legs off the ground as well. He hung for a moment, suspended with his back end higher than his front end, before they could take the balloons off of him. He didn't seem disturbed, just curious. Deborah could see that her dog was an exceptionally patient and trusting creature.

They tied the balloons to three of his toys and Willy bat-ted at them with his front paws. Now this was a great game!

Not long after the balloon experiment, Deborah read about a wheelchair for disabled pets called the K-9 cart. She ordered one and when it arrived, she was excited to try it on Willy. It was delivered to the pet store where Deborah worked. She always brought Willy to work with her and so she immediately strapped him into the con-traption and laid his back legs in rests built over the wheels. The instructions had warned her that sometimes an animal could be initially scared of the cart and refuse to take a step, but Willy took off like an airplane. For a full half an hour, the little dog raced around and around the store. Finally free of the limitations he'd so patiently endured, Willy's spirit soared and now his body could keep pace with his joy.

From that moment, there was no stopping Willy. Deborah began taking him to the local hospital, to the Starlight Room, where children who were ill as a result of accidents or disease—some in wheelchairs, some sitting in red wagons with their life-support machines beside them—received visitors. When Willy first arrived, the children were wide-eyed with wonder. A dog! In a wheelchair! Just like us! It was hard to say who was more excited, the children or Willy. Soon Willy was visiting schools, convalescent homes, and senior centers on a regular basis.

L.A. reporters wrote stories, took pictures and filmed interviews about "Wheely Willy." Deborah's dog was a local celebrity. One day Deborah was doing errands, Willy rolling along right by her side without a leash, when a woman stopped them.

"Is that Wheely Willy?" she cried. "I saw you on TV. Your dog saved my life."

Deborah was used to people making a fuss over Willy, but this was a first. "Saved your life?"

The woman explained, "Not long ago, I lost my job of many years. I felt helpless, betrayed and hopeless. I was sure I would never be able to find another job. I stopped bathing, I stopped going out—except to buy junk food—I guess I just stopped caring. Day after day, all I did was sit in front of the TV.

"Then I saw you on a talk show. You were talking about Willy, about this little dog in a wheelchair. You said, 'Dogs don't feel sorry for themselves. They do what they have to do to get what they want. Before Willy got his wheelchair, if he was across the room from me, he didn't collapse in a heap and whine, "Oh, I want to go over there, but I can't." He gladly did whatever he could to make his way to me. No question—he'd just do it with everything he had!'"

The woman continued. "It was like waking up. I looked at myself and said, 'What are you doing?' Then I took a shower, wrote a resume and went out to look for a job. I got the first job I interviewed for, and I love it. All because of Willy."

She bent over and petted her unlikely hero. Willy, as usual, jigged back and forth on his front legs, signaling his delight at meeting another friend.

That same year at the L.A. Marathon, this plucky Chihuahua led a group of people with spinal cord injuries. Moving along in front of the humans in wheelchairs, the small dog towed his own two-wheeled vehicle, which bore a heart-shaped sign that read: Wheely Willy. Their official mascot, red straps bright across his muscular chest, was stepping high as he pulled his cart over the finish line to the sound of thundering applause.

Deborah Turner
As told to Carol Kline
A story from Animal Planet's **Wild Rescues**

"He only watches the Animal Planet Channel."

The Education of Jeeves

*Thousands of years ago, cats were worshipped
as gods. Cats have never forgotten this.*

Anonymous

It's inevitable whenever cat lovers get together that the
topic of litter boxes comes up—the merits and drawbacks
of various brands of kitty litter, the best locations for the
boxes, the problems certain cats have using the litter box
and of course the debate over whether those new elec-
tronic self-cleaning models are really worth the price. It is
an awkward moment for me, for I have nothing to say to
my fellow feline fanciers on this subject, except to mention
as humbly as I can, that my cat, Jeeves, is toilet-trained.

This announcement always causes a stir. Some people
laugh, while others scoff. After insisting that it's true, I
explain that Jeeves uses—and flushes—the toilet like any
other civilized apartment dweller. I ignore the head-
shaking and envious mutterings, for it is a privilege and a
joy to live with this refined gentleman of a cat.

I must admit, though, there were times while Jeeves
was being taught this marvelous feat, when my husband

Tim and I realized that training a cat is not as simple as it seems.

One of those moments came in the final stages of Jeeves's mastery of the toilet. It had been a long, involved process. We'd started by setting the litterbox on top of the toilet, and then in various stages, we'd graduated to putting a spare toilet seat over the litterbox. It was a simple matter to eventually remove the litterbox completely—the cat recognized the toilet seat and *voila!*

Now we were attempting to introduce the ultimate nicety: learning to flush. We tied a string with a small empty film canister on the end of it to the toilet handle. The small canister was punctured all over and inside it we placed kitty treats. When the cat pulled on it, thereby flushing the toilet, he received a treat. This was straightforward enough, and Jeeves was really getting the hang of it.

It was a Sunday morning. Tim and I were sleeping late, a luxury for us on our constantly busy schedule, when we were awakened by a noise. As we slowly surfaced from sleep and our brains began to register what we were hearing, we realized it was the sound of the toilet flushing—and flushing—and flushing. Over and over again, the toilet gurgled and whooshed. Tim staggered sleepily from bed and made his way to the bathroom to investigate what we assumed was faulty plumbing.

Instead, when he opened the door, he saw an imperious Jeeves, paws wrapped around the film canister, pulling the string again, looking for all the world like a monarch using the royal bell pull to summon a servant to his bedside.

"Ah, there you are, my good man," he seemed to say. "Now, where's that treat of mine?"

My husband dutifully fetched a treat and the porcelain Niagara Falls was finally silenced.

Back in the bedroom, Tim recounted to me what had just happened. Up till this point, we had been feeling pleased with how successfully we were training our cat. It was then we sensed the hollowness of our victory.

The cat was doing what we wanted him to do, yet it was clear that somewhere along the way, we'd lost the upper hand. I began to wonder if we'd ever really had it.

To this day, it remains a mystery just who has been conditioned to do what, but one thing is certain: Cat training can be a very tricky business.

Debbie Freeberg-Renwick

Silky's Test

True mercy is nobility's true badge. He who does not restrict harmless conduct to man, but extends it to other animals, most closely approaches divinity.

Porphry

The dog was dying. Almost unconscious, she lay on the ground outside the door of our clinic in Jaipur, India. She was a purebred black Labrador retriever—a rarity in India and especially at our shelter. My assistant, Ramsaroop, told me that she had been left by her owners for our shelter doctor to euthanize. Ours was the only shelter in the region where people could bring their dying pets, in the knowledge that their animals would be able to die peacefully and without pain. As many people in India believed it was wrong to take the life of an animal, even if it was terminally ill, it fell to our veterinarians and staff to take on the role of mercifully releasing these creatures from their suffering.

Like so many of the dogs we dealt with, she was so thin she could not stand. I recognized the terrible symptoms of distemper, and knew that she didn't have long to live. Her breathing was labored, and she was so weak she did not want to move. If by some miracle the dog recovered from the distemper, it was almost certain that she would have neurological damage, which could result in either seizures or permanent spasms. Reluctantly, I decided I would have to follow the owners' instructions and euthanize the dog. I asked Ramsaroop to bring the needle.

Ramsaroop returned with the syringe, and I bent down to perform this final act of mercy. As I did so, the dog, with great and deliberate effort, slowly lifted her head so that she could look into my eyes. As she stared at me, I felt that she was asking me for one last chance. She was not ready to die; she wanted to try to live. As our eyes met, I felt a great love and affinity for her. At that moment, I vowed to do all in my power to help her recover.

I turned to a surprised Ramsaroop and asked him to put away the needle. Then I went and fetched a small bowl of milk and placed it under the dog's nose. She showed no interest in it and continued to lie without moving. It was critical that she take some nourishment, so I prepared an IV drip for her. I was about to begin the procedure when I suddenly had an impulse.

I walked out of our front gate and up the road to the small temple next door to our shelter. Inside the plain, square cement temple, under a huge and ancient peepal tree, was a very old image of the Hindu monkey god, Hanuman, so old that it was no more than a blob of stone, all its features eroded, and its form painted with orange and silver.

There was something in the air of this special spot, perhaps because so many people had worshipped here, and I found myself filled with the peacefulness that emanated from this symbol of the love between human and animal. I stood for a long while, offering my own prayers to God for the black dog's recovery.

I walked back to the shelter and saw the dog still lying there, not moving. Again I fetched the bowl of milk and held it under her nose, which rested on the dust. This time however, she lifted her head, and slowly drank the full contents of the bowl. I was amazed and delighted with this sudden change, but still I did not really believe that it was possible for her to live.

I wasn't ready to give up though. Every few hours, I fed her small measures of food—baby cereal, raw egg, some bread soaked in milk. Each time I fed her, I marveled that she was still breathing. Over the next twenty-four hours, the dog's strength slowly returned. As the days passed and it seemed that she might live, I began to worry that she would be left with a legacy of convulsing limbs, or a permanently nodding head. I watched her carefully for signs of these problems.

But after a couple of weeks, when no neurological damage had manifested, I knew my patient was out of danger. She was able to wag her tail vigorously, to walk stiffly and to smile, looking at me with love-filled eyes that said, "You saved my life."

I named her Silky and decided to adopt her as my own. Her original owners had indicated that they did not want her, even if she recovered and I did not want to send this dog away with strangers. So I took her home to our small cottage built on the grounds of the shelter.

As soon as she walked into our bedroom, I was surprised to see her climb onto the bed. "No, Silky," I said, and went to pull her off. As I pulled on her collar, she growled furiously and tried to attack me, almost biting my hand. Shocked and dismayed, I stood back, and contemplated the situation. It had not occurred to me that she might have an aggressive side to her personality; she had been so meek and docile in the clinic.

Clearly someone had mistreated her. Silky must have

thought that I, too, was going to brutalize her.

"Silky?" I asked in a soothing tone. She snarled and bared her teeth in response. It was painfully clear she knew how to be very frightening. I felt hurt that the dog, which I had so tenderly nursed, was now behaving in this way towards me. We were at a crossroads.

I have to show her who's boss, I thought, my mood hardening. *She must obey me—we can't keep her if she's a dangerous dog.* It was crucial that she pass this test.

Silky stared at me dolefully, no longer displaying any malice. Suddenly, as we looked at each other across a few feet of space, I realized that *I* was the one who had to pass the test. Others had mistreated her. Now she wanted to know whether I, too, would be a bully and a brute, or whether I would treat her with kindness and understanding.

My arrogance and desire to dominate melted away as I stood humbly before her. I had to win her loyalty now, in this moment. I had to show her, just once, that I was worthy of her love.

I wanted to communicate with her in the way I believe animals communicate, via thoughts and emotions. So I stood there, a few feet away from the bed, speaking to her gently. I explained that she would never be hurt again, and that she never need fear again. I consciously held to loving thoughts and images in my mind.

She watched me with her large, brown eyes, perhaps assessing whether she could truly believe me. At one point, I felt completely connected to her—as if we were one entity—both permeated by the same energy that suffuses all life. I was filled once again with the peace I had experienced in the temple.

The moment had come to discover whether I had passed her test. I leaned forward and took her collar. I saw her thinking, watching. She lay with front paws extended forward, her head slightly to one side. I held the collar, and tugged gently.

"Silky, come," I said. Without hesitation, as though she had never been anything but the most loving and obedient dog, she jumped down from the bed.

"Good Silky," I said, patting and fondling her ears. Slowly her tail began to wag.

That was many years ago, and Silky has now grown quite old. To this day, she has never again jumped on the bed. At night she sleeps at my feet on her own small mattress—my devoted companion and guard. And each time she pads softly beside me on a walk, or lays her dark head on my lap, I'm glad that, years ago, I had the wisdom to pass Silky's test.

Christine Townend
Managing Trustee,
Help In Suffering Animal Shelter, Jaipur, India

Cat's Paw

Ellen and Alex Petricone were house-hunting, and were driving past a long, empty field on their way to look at their fourth or fifth house. Ellen was just staring out the window when she saw what seemed to be a baby rat or squirrel—or even a chipmunk—climbing out of a ditch between the field and the road ahead of them. She was afraid it might dart in front of the car as they drove by, so she told Alex to slow down, so they wouldn't hit the little squirrel, if that's what it was. Alex squinted hard, and said, "That's no squirrel—that's a kitten."

So they pulled the car over and got out to investigate, walking on tiptoe and trying not to alarm the little animal. When they reached the kitten, it let out a pitiful cry. Ellen had never seen a kitten open its mouth so wide. She scooped him up, and he just about buried himself in her hair. He was shaking so hard. It was early November, and far too cold for a little kitten to be out wandering alone.

After having it examined by a veterinarian, the Petricones took it home and began calling area shelters and animal agencies to learn if anyone had reported a missing kitten. They took out an ad in the local newspaper, and posted flyers around their small New

Hampshire town. Receiving no response, they decided to adopt the white and black tom themselves. They called him Jack.

Jack, Ellen and Alex lived happily in their new home for several years. Then tragedy struck. One rainy March evening, Alex was killed in a traffic accident while driving home from work. He was twenty-nine years old.

As she grieved for her husband, Ellen was also plunged into a financial crisis. She had recently been laid off from her job, and she and Alex had been struggling to make mortgage payments, car payments, furniture payments. Now she had to cope with it all by herself. She began to get depressed and had trouble sleeping.

There was one small consolation. In the weeks and months following Alex's death, Jack rarely left Ellen's side. He followed her around the house, waited on the windowsill when she went out, and slept on the pillow next to her at night. Never intrusive, but plainly visible, Jack was always available when Ellen needed consolation of the furry, whiskered variety.

Ellen was amazed at his behavior. He had always been an affectionate little guy, but he liked his independence, too. But now he started showing the type of devotion she had associated with dogs. Ellen would get up, Jack would get up; she'd sit down, he'd sit down. He would even follow her into the bathroom at night, and hop up on the counter beside her while she washed up and brushed her teeth.

In spite of these consolations, however, the deep hurt of losing her husband still remained with Ellen. After one particularly grueling week, she found herself in extremely low spirits as she prepared for bed. She was standing at the bathroom sink with a bottle of sleeping pills in one hand, and her other hand, palm upward, in midair. She stood there for a long time, motionless. She felt defeated, without the strength to go on. Jack jumped up on the counter next to her, but she neither heard nor noticed. All she was thinking was that she could just take the whole bottle of sleeping pills and be done with everything.

At that moment, Jack lifted his paw and swatted at her open palm. Ellen was startled. She turned and saw Jack looking at her with his head cocked to one side. The look in his eyes was a strange mix of curiosity and concern. It was as though he were saying, 'What are you doing?' And all of a sudden, Ellen thought, *What* am *I doing?*

With a quick movement of her hand, she tossed the sleeping pills into the trash. Then she marched into the kitchen and made some good, old-fashioned warm milk— for her *and* for Jack. When she went to bed, she gave Jack a big hug and promised that she'd never even think about leaving him again.

A small gesture—the insistent tap of a cat's paw—had pulled her back from the edge of a huge abyss. And that night Ellen slept better than she had done in months.

Eric Swanson

Charity

When I first saw Phaedra, she was standing in a field of daisies, her fluffy white coat dusted with dried flowers and bits of grass. She looked like a tiny fairy, big-eyed, delicate and graceful as a deer on her tapered white legs. She was much smaller than any of the other llamas in the field, and I mistook her for a baby until her owner, a local farmer, told me that something had gone awry in her growth centers and she was dwarfed. To me, her babyish look only added to her unique appeal. Something about her seemed almost magical. Phaedra had a serene and delicate gentleness about her I'd never seen in a llama before or since, and my heart was instantly and hopelessly lost to her.

At the time, my husband, Lee, and I were still attempting to make our Brightstar Farm a going business concern. Llamas, however, were not in our business plan. So when Phaedra walked up to me, nuzzled my cheek with a nose as soft as feathers, I bit my lip and turned away. Although I left Phaedra standing in the field that day, my heart was with her constantly. A few times, I made excuses to go back to the farm where she lived, just to see her again.

Then time got away from me, and I didn't see Phaedra again for nearly a year. Late in the following fall, I managed to visit her. As she walked across the pasture to greet me, an alarming sense of urgency boiled up in my throat. I could hardly believe that this was the same animal I'd seen the year before. Her coat was caked with mud and burrs and had matted to a dull, lifeless gray. When I rested my hands on her back, rib and bone moved beneath my fingers. She was a skeleton.

Size and deformity had betrayed her. As the other llamas in the pasture had grown tall and powerful, Phaedra was no match for them at the hay and grain bins. Too small to compete for food, she waited and she starved.

The man who owned her had moved Phaedra away from the herd to her own small pasture, but she had continued to fail.

I attempted to ignore the voices that screamed inside of me to take her. I knew how important it was to stay within the limits Lee and I had set for our farm. Our animal family was enormous. Our financial resources were terribly limited. There was no money left for new animals. In tears, I told myself to be an adult while my heart cracked inside of me. "Susan, you can't save them all," I told myself. "You can't."

In the end, my heart won. Phaedra was a filthy, bony bundle of health problems and vet bills, yet I heard myself say, "Please, let me take her home." The next thing I knew, she was in the back of my van, kneeling quietly on a cushion of straw as we drove home to Brightstar. I imagined Lee would have a fit when I got there. Of course, he didn't.

Phaedra stumbled out of the van and into our pastures, a frail, unsteady creature with an uncertain future. She took a few hesitant steps toward our barn, and stopped a moment to sniff the branch of an apple tree. Her lips pursed into a Betty-Boop pucker, and she uttered a questioning sort of murmur and looked back at me. The heart performs miracles: Before my eyes I saw a dainty, glittering fairy blessing our pastures with beauty and tranquillity where anyone else would have seen a dirt ball on stick legs.

Phaedra became my summer project. I sang songs to her while I washed the dirt off her ears and eyes and worked the burrs out of her fur. Each day, I treated her sore, swollen eyes with drops and wiped bug repellent on her face and ears. One day, I got industrious and cut off her matted hair with a pair of blunt-nosed scissors. My hands blistered and my wrists ached for days, but the results were worth it. Beneath the old dead coat was a fine white blanket of soft fur.

Weeks passed and I asked myself—as Lee often asked—*what in the world was I doing?* There were countless other projects, other tasks that needed my time and attention. Yet I let them fall by the wayside, focusing my energy on Phaedra, my precious, gentle fairy. For reasons I could never hope to explain to anyone, myself included, Phaedra simply enchanted me. I found myself spending hours of time just watching her walk around the pasture or sprawl luxuriously in the sun. One day, in the soft breeze of a late-summer afternoon, I saw her leap around the pasture like a gazelle, all four legs straight beneath her, springing high up into the air as she tossed her head left and right in rapturous abandon.

Yet, despite all my loving care, Phaedra failed to thrive. She lived in a standstill state of frail health, not gaining much ground, occasionally losing some. Her vet and food bills were hitting the catastrophic mark when I told Lee, out of shame for my lack of more mature and logical behavior, that I wouldn't spend any more money on her. If she got worse, I would put her to sleep before I ran up any more big bills. Lee saw the pain in my eyes and, trying to spare me and our shrinking wallet, said, "No more charity cases, okay?" I turned away and muttered, "Yes, okay."

One evening later that week, I sat in the barn with Phaedra and watched as she ate, one small pellet or two at a time. I asked her, out loud, the questions I had only asked myself. I asked her what she was doing at our farm, why she had called so strongly to me and what she needed to teach me. Sitting on a bucket beside her, I closed my eyes and reached out my arms to her, waiting for whatever thoughts might come to me.

No more charity cases. Visions of a lifetime of hurt and lost animals drifted up before me. I had taken them all home— dogs, kittens, birds, injured toads—and spent my last dime on them. I loved them, found them new homes, sometimes healed them, too often buried them. Yet when I was stricken with cancer in my late thirties, it was my lifetime of experience with animals that offered me a vision of healing. In a very real sense, animals had given me my life.

I heard Phaedra finish the last of her pellets. In the out-stretched circle of my arms, she settled down on her knees and began working her cud. I stayed very still, continuing my reverie. Phaedra, for all the effort of her care, had brought me back to a sense of childlike mystery. With Phaedra in the pasture, I could believe in fairies again. I could stop and take time to sit and daydream. Her gentle nature seeped into the cracks of my own daily tension and she calmed me and brought me many moments of quiet and thanksgiving. She shared with me her joy and steadfast companionship. For what I had given her, she had given me back tenfold.

Tenfold. It struck me then—this is how I tithe. Not with money, but with time and love willingly given to a decades-long chain of animals who have found their way to me, who have chosen me, healed me and empowered me: the charity cases. God grant me a never-ending stream of charity cases.

My eyes flew open and met the quiet brown sea of Phaedra's kindly gaze. Her face was soft, her eyes clear and bottomless. The banana ears she swiveled toward me were white and clean. She leaned into me and gently sniffed my face. When I rubbed her neck, I realized that her bones were beginning to recede behind a new layer of muscle. There had been improvements, albeit small ones. She would be fine. We would be fine.

When I left the barn that night and returned to the house, it was to tell Lee that I would be cutting off my very arms and legs if there were no place at our farm for charity cases. And of course he understood. It was I who had needed to understand, and it was Phaedra who had chosen to teach me.

Susan Chernak McElroy

Killer Angels

I cannot avoid compassion for everything that is called life. That is the beginning and foundation of morality.

Albert Schweitzer

I had just graduated from veterinary school, and I was volunteering at the local shelter in Twin Falls, Idaho. As I looked down at the dog napping in her run, I knew I was going to have to wake her up to put her "to sleep." What a cruel euphemism.

She was a Heinz-57 mixed-breed with no name, no home, no hope. She was horrifically malnourished, and her coat was a mass of mats and burrs.

In a way, she was lucky to be here. Found on the side of the road—like living garbage—she'd been left to die in a remote area of our county.

The kind rancher who found her brought her to the local shelter where she joined dozens of other cuties and uglies pressing against the front of the cages hoping to catch the eye of someone who had a heart and home big enough to give them another chance.

Problem was there were too many homeless pets and not enough homes. Day after day for a week the dog waited and waited, her still-wagging tail marking the time.

But on this day, her time was up. No one had adopted her; like many in the shelter, the animals were too big, too small, too hairy, too young, too old. Without enough cages to hold all that came through our doors, we were prepared to end her life quickly and without suffering. "Better than starving to death in the country," I said, finding little solace in the words.

I was inspired to enter this profession because of a deep love of animals. I had been highly trained and entrusted to save lives and prevent pain and suffering. Yet here I was about to end the life of this innocent creature. I hated this part of the job, but I had to do it. Choking back my emotions, I readied myself to perform the procedure for which I'd been trained.

I set her on the table, and she wiggled her gaunt frame with delight as I spoke some soothing words and patted her head. The tempo of her tail quickened as she looked up at my face. Looking into her eyes, I saw total trust, unconditional love and absolute loyalty. I felt the cruel irony of what was taking place. God's precious creatures, embodying the kindest virtues on the planet, being killed for the crime of not being wanted. She held out her leg for me to inject and licked my hand. She was ready. I wasn't.

I collapsed onto the dog and held her tight as I bathed her with tears. Never, ever would I do a convenience euthanasia again. I'd euthanize a pet if it was suffering terribly, or had an incurable disease, but never again because of an uncaring owner's mere request.

I took the dog back to my veterinary practice and named her G. H.—short for Good Home. I'd observed over the years that people who raised litters of puppies or kittens always said, "I just want to find them a 'good home.'"

I soon entrusted G. H. to a loving client who had a heart and home big enough to welcome yet another four-legged family member.

Saving G. H. set me on a new path as a veterinarian. Although my hands still held the power of death, my heart didn't. Now, whenever I look into the dancing liquid eyes of a pet, brimming with love, I realize that looks can save. They did me.

Marty Becker, D.V.M.

7

AMAZING ANIMALS

Nothing is impossible for a willing heart.

John Heywood

"So far they've taught me how to sit, beg and roll over.
What I'd really like to learn is Swing Dancing."

Reprinted by permission of Randy Glasbergen.

Pampered Persian

For fifteen-year-old Kirsten Hicks of Adelaide, Australia, the most difficult part of a long overseas family trip was leaving behind her Persian cat, Howie. In fact, the only people she trusted to look after Howie were her grandparents—and they lived one thousand miles away.

Kirsten was relieved when Grandma and Grandpa readily agreed to take care of Howie for the entire period of her family's absence from Australia. Her grandparents had always liked the magnificent Persian, and they seemed happy at the prospect of having Howie as a houseguest.

When the Hicks family returned to reclaim Kirsten's furry friend, the grandparents greeted them with the terrible news that Howie had disappeared. They begged their granddaughter's forgiveness and hoped she would understand that they had made every effort to find him.

At first, Kirsten tried to nurture a feeble hope that Howie might still be alive, but she knew her pampered gorgeous Persian probably wouldn't have lasted five minutes in the streets by himself. He must certainly have been killed by a car or a dog. Kirsten did not blame her grandparents, but she was heartbroken over the loss of her pet.

Back in Adelaide, Kirsten continued grieving for months over her lost Howie. Even though her parents offered, she didn't want another pet.

A year passed. Then one afternoon Kirsten's mother made an unusual discovery. Lying miserably on the front porch of their house was a stray cat. The longhaired cat was obviously in a bad way. He was skinny, bleeding from a wound in his paw, filthy and very bedraggled. He was also ravenously hungry, as Mrs. Hicks found out when she put some canned tuna down for him. The thought struck her that if they could clean the cat up and fix his paw, he might make a good pet for Kirsten. Maybe Kirsten would accept the cat if she knew that he had just turned up at their house in dire need of help. Kirsten's mother was thinking about how best to clean him up when Kirsten came out of the house.

Kirsten took one look at the grubby, footsore cat before her and shrieked: "Howie! Howie!" And she went down on her knees and embraced the cat, dirt and all.

Her mother was startled. Howie? Was it possible?

Kirsten was in no doubt. Underneath all the grime and the matted fur was her beautiful Persian. He had found his way home! Gently, she picked him up in her arms and burst into unrestrained tears when she heard his happy purring.

In the twelve months it had taken Howie to make the one-thousand-mile trek home, the pampered Persian had somehow forded wild rivers, crossed hostile deserts and fought his way through the vast wilderness of the Australian outback. He knew where his home was and neither distance nor danger could deter him. He wanted to lie lazily once more on the soft couches he re-membered, and perhaps most of all he wanted to purr again in the arms of the young girl who loved him so. Such is the miracle of love.

Brad Steiger

Three-Dog Night

Everyone in Bricqueville-sur-Mer loved Pére Marie. Though his real name was Alphonse Marie, the villagers affectionately called him "Pére," a cross between papa and uncle. Ever since he moved to that village in northwest France in 1947 to start a modest sawmill, hardly a day went by without him cheering up or otherwise helping someone.

Pére Marie's kindliness was also reflected in his relationships with animals. To the amazement of local farmers, he talked to dogs as if they were children. When a customer once gave him a rabbit to cook, Pére Marie tamed it instead.

"Animals can do surprising things if we trust them," he often said.

After his wife's death in 1964, Pére Marie lived with his son, Louis, in a four-room bungalow off a country road. In 1972, when a large, automated sawmill opened in a neighboring village, the Maries were forced to close their small operation. Louis found work as a night watchman in a school in nearby Granville, and Pére Marie reluctantly retired. Although his doctor had warned him about his high blood pressure, at sixty-nine he still felt fit.

Father and son shared their home with three four-legged "children"—Rageur and Royal, nine-year-old littermates, part spaniel and part hound, and Rex, only three, who had the face of a lovable mutt and the large body of a black Labrador. The dogs had the run of much of the house. All were highly intelligent and, under Pére Marie's tutelage, could "almost talk." A thorn in a paw would cause one of them to stare at Pére Marie or Louis—with an occasional lick at the sore spot—until one of the men removed the irritation. Young Rex, especially, had an uncanny ability to understand and to communicate. Louis marveled at how rapidly the dog learned to fetch the morning newspaper at a one-word command. But, as the latest arrival in the family, Rex was lowest in the dogs' hierarchy. Cheerfully accepting his role, he let his elders have their way at play and at their masters' feet.

One March evening in 1977, Louis drove off to his watchman's job as usual and Pére Marie watched television. At 10:30 he picked up his flashlight, put on a woolen scarf and cap, and called the dogs for their evening romp. With the temperature dropping to below freezing, Pére Marie's companions frisked about in the tall icy grass as he made his way down the path to the meadow behind the house. Suddenly, a veil clouded his vision. Feeling very ill, he staggered a few feet and collapsed. He forced himself to his feet but fell again after a few steps. The pain, unlike any he had ever felt, seemed to come from inside his head, wringing a shriek from every cell in his body.

Having dropped the flashlight in one of his falls, he was lost in the darkness. He knew the cold would kill him if he didn't get back to the house. But when he tried to get up once again, he found his left side was paralyzed. Pushing blindly on his right elbow and right knee, he managed to drag himself some thirty yards—only to discover, when the moonlight peeked through the clouds, that he'd been moving in the wrong direction. Utterly exhausted, he could go no farther; only rest.

He had no idea how long he lay there before he sensed that he was not alone. His dogs were breathing above him. They circled him and barked. *They're here,* he thought. *They will not abandon me.*

At 6 A.M. Louis Marie finished his shift and drove toward home. When the Marie bungalow came into view, he stiffened. Why were the lights on inside? Something was wrong. He turned onto the dirt track to the bungalow and heard—even above his motor noise—a fearful howling from Rageur and Royal on the porch. As he came to a stop the two dogs rushed to the car and tried to pull Louis from it. He ran up the stairs, into the house and on to his father's bedroom at the back. There, stretched out on the bed, was Pére Marie, looking more a corpse than a living man.

He was half-naked, his undershirt and a seaman's sweater sodden with saliva and nearly bitten through at one shoulder. His body was covered with mud, bruises and blood. Rex was pressed tightly against his master, licking the old man's face and neck with long, steady strokes. Louis leaned over his father and heard him faintly mutter, "You're here, need hospital." His face was half paralyzed, his color ashen. Louis ran to get help. At the hospital, his fears were confirmed. His father had suffered a serious stroke, and his chances of survival were slim.

Pére Marie lay between life and death for several days. Then, slowly, his condition improved. With his speech more coherent, he was able to tell Louis what he remembered about that terrible night.

After lying for some time on the cold ground, he said, he felt Rex take his shoulder in his mouth and begin tugging. Gradually, he realized that the dogs would lead him to the house if he could muster enough strength to crawl.

He could only drag his useless left side, inches at a time, with his right. As he struggled along, he lost his shoes, his socks, his scarf. His loose trousers ripped off as he scraped along the ground. Blood streamed from a gash on his knee, and he passed out repeatedly. But whenever he came to, Rex still had him by the shoulder and the other dogs circled around as if keeping watch.

At least an hour of seemingly hopeless, half-conscious struggle must have passed. And still the dogs and the old man persevered. Suddenly, Pére Marie's hand brushed a wooden post in the darkness. He had reached the stairs! *Home,* he thought. But fear followed: how could he possibly drag himself up the nine steps to the porch? Pére Marie had no memory of what followed next, but long, deep gashes on every step told the story. The dog's toenails had torn the old wood, as they struggled to keep their foothold while straining against their master's weight. Pére Marie remembered crossing the threshold— with Rex still tugging at his shoulder. Then he passed out. Coming to later, he realized he was in bed and that Rex was beside him. *Thank goodness for the dogs,* he thought. Then he drifted off.

When Pére Marie was taken off the danger list at the hospital, his doctor told Louis that he would not have survived the cold night had he not made it back to the house. Louis then told him about the dogs. A week after the patient had passed his crisis, the hospital allowed all three to visit their master. Wriggling with joy, they jumped all over Pére Marie.

Gradually, Pére Marie recovered and his life returned to its familiar pattern. But something in the dogs had changed. Rex was now the unchallenged leader. He alone occupied the privileged spot at Pére Marie's feet in the evening. And he alone lay at the foot of the bed and guarded his master as he slept.

One afternoon, not long after Pére Marie returned home, a friend dropped by to visit. As they sat together in the living room, the old man cradled Rex's head on his knee, stroking the dog's ear.

"Thanks to him I'm here today," he told his guest matter-of-factly. Then he added, almost inaudibly, "Animals can do surprising things if we trust them."

George Feifer

King of Courage

Love is shown by deeds, not by words.

Philippine Proverb

"Go away, King," Pearl Carlson said sleepily as her German shepherd dog pulled at her bedding, attempting to rouse her. "Not now, I'm trying to get some rest."

Pearl vaguely wondered what King was doing in her bedroom at three o'clock in the morning, since he usually slept on the enclosed porch at night. It was Christmas night and the sixteen-year-old girl had been looking forward to a good night's sleep after an exciting day.

Pearl sat up in bed to give the barking dog a good push and realized that smoke was filling her room—the house was on fire. Bolting out of bed, she ran in panic to her parents' bedroom and awoke them both.

Her mother, Fern, got up at once and told Pearl to escape through her own bedroom window while she helped her husband, Howard, out of their window. Howard Carlson had a lung condition and could not move quickly. They realized that Pearl had somehow wound up in the living room where the fire was at its worst.

"I'm going after her," Howard said, but his wife, knowing his health made this impossible, told him to escape through the window while she went for Pearl. Fern led her dazed daughter to safety but saw that neither Howard nor King had gotten out of the house. Fern ran back into their bedroom and found Howard collapsed on the floor with King by his side. Fern and King struggled to lift Howard and finally the two of them managed to get the nearly unconscious man to safety. Fern later said she could not have moved Howard without King's help.

King and the Carlsons were saved. King had badly burned paws and a gash on his back, but seemed otherwise healthy. Yet the day after the fire, King would not eat his dog food.

The neighbors had come by with sandwiches and refreshments and were helping to rebuild what they could of the house. Then King did something he had never done before: He stole one of the soft sandwiches. Something was wrong.

They looked in King's mouth and saw that his gums were pierced with painful, sharp wooden splinters. Now the family knew how King had gotten into the house. That terrible night, King had, with sheer desperate force, chewed and clawed his way through the closed plywood door that separated him from the Carlsons. The splinters were removed and eventually King recovered fully.

What was most striking about the dog's heroic act was that night he had easy access to the porch door, left open to the outdoors. King could easily have just saved himself. Instead, he chose to gnaw and smash through the door to the house, and face blinding fire and choking smoke, all to rescue his family.

Stephanie Laland

Ginny, the Dog Who Rescues Cats

My dog Ginny is in the lifesaving business, and the first life she ever saved was mine. Ginny is a bright-eyed, tail-wagging, medium-sized mixed breed—mostly schnauzer and Siberian husky by the look of her—who came to me out of a Long Island animal shelter during the darkest days of my life.

I was a well-paid construction worker, content with my comfortable life, when an industrial accident cost me the use of my right arm. After my surgery, all I could do was feel sorry for myself until my good friend and neighbor, Sheilah, convinced me to adopt a dog from our local shelter. She knew I needed some responsibility to snap me out of my depression. I agreed to adopt a large, male dog of a pure breed, but once I was in the animal shelter some instant mysterious connection took place between me and a smallish dog of no pedigree at all. The next thing I knew, I was head over heels in love with a pup I named Ginny.

When I took Ginny home six years ago, I had no idea of how radically my life would change. It turned out that Ginny Gonzalez was put on earth to save the lives of abandoned and homeless cats, especially disabled cats and kittens. With her it is a sacred mission. Using a kind of sixth sense, she seeks them out in the hardest-to-reach places, where I am certain that nothing could possibly survive. Ginny has proved me wrong again and again, until I've learned to trust her instincts completely. Time after time, she has turned up some ill, injured, disabled, abused, helpless cat or kitten and demanded quick assistance for them. The more a cat needs her help, the faster Ginny is to respond.

Little by little, and at first with great reluctance on my part, Ginny increased my household from two—Ginny and me—to many more, all of the new ones being cats she rescued. When she started out, I was pretty much indifferent to cats, but it wasn't long before Ginny convinced me to love them as much as she does. We have a deaf cat, a cat with one eye, a cat with no hind feet, and a cat so brain-damaged it can't stand up or walk, but rolls across the floor instead. The more a cat is disabled or abused the more determined Ginny is to bring that animal straight home to our house, where she can look after it properly.

Now, in addition to my indoor cats, Ginny, Sheilah and I feed about eighty or more outdoor cats, homeless strays, twice a day every day no matter the weather.

One of Ginny's most dramatic rescues took place when we were out on one of our daily feeding runs. Across the street from one of our feeding stations is a glassworks where windows are manufactured, the Airtite Window Factory. Because there's a lot of broken glass around, I keep Ginny in the car when we feed there. I just tell her "stay." Usually she stays put, because Ginny is always very responsive to what I say to her, but this time she dashed out of the car and ran to my side.

First, she froze and stood at attention, staring at the loading dock. Her nose twitched and her ears stood up as stiffly as palace guards. I could tell she was even more excited than usual. Suddenly, Ginny was heading across the street at a dead run, straight for the loading platform. Before we knew what was happening, Ginny began digging furiously in a carton overflowing with broken glass.

"Ginny! No!" I yelled, and Sheilah let out a scream. We both ran toward the loading dock. I could tell my dog was cutting her pads on the sharp glass, maybe deeply; but Ginny paid us no attention. She kept on pawing through the knifelike shards. By the time we reached the platform, she had found something, picked it up in her mouth, and was already limping toward us with the something dangling from her jaws. Although it was dark out, there was a light on the loading dock, and I could see that Ginny was leaving bloody footprints. My heart sank. How badly was she hurt?

In her mouth was a curled-up ball of fur, barely moving. Ginny didn't seem to notice that her paws were bleeding as she laid the little bundle down at our feet.

It uttered a tiny little sound, an unmistakable mew. It was a kitten, very tiny, and it was covered with splinters of glass. Some of the glass had penetrated its skin, and its fur was bloody. Could this kitten possibly live?

We wanted to get Ginny and the kitten home right away so we could examine their wounds and treat them. Even though Ginny is no lightweight, Sheilah scooped her up and carried her to the car in her arms. I followed with the kitten.

As soon as we were safe in my apartment, Sheilah and I brought Ginny into the bathroom and turned on the light for a good look. My dog sat quietly letting us examine her without pulling her paws out of our hands, even though they must have been hurting.

There were pieces of glass stuck in the pads of Ginny's feet. We lifted them out very carefully, making sure to get even the tiniest piece out, washed her wounds, and applied a styptic pencil. We then turned our attention to the kitten, which couldn't have been more than a week and a half old. Gently, we brushed the glass off it, pulling out the pieces sticking in its flesh and examined its scratches and cuts. They didn't appear to be too serious, so we went the soap-and-water and styptic pencil route with the little cat, too.

We got out the little bottle we use for nursing kittens and gave the baby a decent meal. The kitten drank until it was full, and then curled up and went to sleep between Ginny's aching paws. It was already making itself at home.

Neither Sheilah nor I expected that baby kitten to live. Its wounds weren't serious, but it just seemed too young to have much of a chance at growing up. There was feistiness in that little fellow, though, and he surprised us by thriving.

A few days later he was as lively as a kitten ought to be, and eating enough for six. I made up my mind there and then not to put him up for adoption, but to keep him.

I named him the Chairman. The Chairman and Ginny have a very special relationship. She seems to think he belongs to her, the way she fusses over him all the time. And he thinks he belongs to her, too. It's almost as though the Chairman recognizes that he is Ginny's living reward for her brave dive into that box of broken glass to save him.

Philip Gonzalez with Leonore Fleischer

Jim the Wonder Dog

In 1925, Sam VanArsdale, proprietor of the Ruff Hotel in Marshall, Missouri, purchased an English setter puppy born of pureblood champion field stock in Louisiana. The puppy was considered the least promising of the litter and was sold at a throwaway price. The dog was nothing special to look at as he had unusually big paws and an ungainly appearance. Sam decided to call him Jim.

Jim grew to be a fine companion for Sam. The dog was smart and good-natured, and Sam was pleased with his "bargain."

One day, when Jim was three years old, he and Sam were walking through the woods. The weather was hot, and Sam said to Jim, "C'mon boy, let's go and rest a little under a hickory tree."

There were many types of trees in the woods, but Jim ran straight over to a hickory tree. Sam was a bit surprised. No doubt it was just a coincidence. On a whim, Sam said to Jim, "Show me a black oak tree." When Jim ran to the nearest black oak and put his right paw on the tree, Sam was amazed. This couldn't *possibly* be true.

"Show me a walnut tree," he said, and Jim ran unerringly to the nearest walnut and put his paw on it. Sam continued with everything he could think of—a stump, hazel bushes, a cedar tree, even a tin can. Jim correctly identified them all. Sam could hardly believe the evidence of his own eyes. How could a dog do such things?

Sam went home and told his wife what had happened. She said flatly, "Sam VanArsdale, you can tell me, but don't go telling anyone else."

Sam persuaded his wife to accompany them back to the woods, where Jim put on a flawless repeat performance. She shook her head in amazement—Sam's crazy story was true!

Over the next few days, Sam couldn't help telling his friends around town what his smart dog could do. They smiled at him indulgently and moved off pretty fast.

One man did listen, although of course he was skeptical. Sam, noticing that the man had parked his car on the street a few yards away, told Jim to show the man which car was his. Jim went straight to the car and put his front paw on it.

Then another man gave Sam the license plate number of his car. Sam wrote it down on a piece of paper and put the paper on the sidewalk. He told Jim to identify the car. Without hesitation, Jim walked to the car in question.

After incidents like these, Jim's reputation spread like wildfire around the small town. Soon he was demonstrating his powers in the Ruff Hotel for amazed crowds of up to a hundred people at a time. There seemed to be no limit to what Jim could do. When people were in the lobby, he could determine what room numbers they occupied in the hotel. He could identify people according to the clothes they wore, the color of their hair—in spite of the fact that dogs are thought to be color-blind—their profession, and, in the case of the military, their rank.

In addition, he could identify objects not just by name but by function. For example, at a command such as, "If

we wanted to hear Amos and Andy, where would we go?"
Jim would go to the radio.

Perhaps, the skeptics said, Sam was secretly signaling
to Jim. Although none of Sam's friends and associates
questioned his integrity, knowing him to be a plain-
speaking man who wouldn't dream of deceiving others,
one woman decided to test this theory. She had the clever
idea to write an instruction for Jim in shorthand, which
Sam did not understand. When Sam showed Jim the
paper on which the instruction was written, and told him
to do whatever it said, Jim went over to a certain man. The
woman shouted, "He's doing it!" Then she explained that
the instruction was, "Show us the man with rolled socks."

One year, at the State Fair in Sedalia, the editor of the
Joplin Globe asked for a demonstration. Since they were
near the bandstand where the musicians were putting
away their instruments, Sam said, "Jim, show us who
plays the tuba." Jim went to the tuba player and put his
paw on him. The citizens of the "Show-Me State" had to
admit Jim had abilities far beyond the normal.

By this time Jim's reputation had spread far beyond the
small town of Marshall. Newspapers and magazines from
all over the country sent reporters to cover the story.
They went away, like everyone else, amazed. Jim became
known as the Wonder Dog.

Jim's feats aroused scientific and medical curiosity. He
was examined by veterinarians at Missouri State
University, who said that there was nothing unusual
about Jim—physically, he was just like any other dog.
They could offer no explanation for his uncanny talent.

Later that same day, Jim gave an outdoor demonstration at the university, attended by students and professors. Various professors gave him instructions in different
languages.

In Italian, "Show me an elm tree."

In French, "Point out this license number."
In German, "Show a girl dressed in blue."
In Spanish, "Find a man wearing a mustache."
Not once did Jim err.

Sam watched the demonstration with quiet satisfaction. His bargain pup had become his dearest treasure, an extraordinary dog whom he loved and was proud of. But he had no explanation of how Jim could do all these things. When a friend at the demonstration asked him about it, he said, "All I know is that he has the power of doing whatever I ask him to do, and there seems to be no limit to his knowledge or ability."

One man who was deeply impressed by Jim's ability was Jack L. Jolly, a Missouri state representative, who invited Sam and Jim to Jefferson City for a joint session with the legislature. The politicians tried to trip Jim up. They gave him an instruction in Morse code. But Jim had no problem indicating the person they were calling for. Anyone who harbored any lingering doubts that Jim was simply reading his master's mind, or responding to secret signals, had to put them aside, because Sam knew Morse code no better than he knew shorthand. Sam was as astonished as everyone else by Jim's supernormal gift.

One day, some friends persuaded Sam to test Jim further. Could he possibly predict the future? Sam took an interest in the Kentucky Derby, so that year he wrote down the names of the horses on pieces of paper that he then laid on the floor. He asked Jim to select the horse that would win. Jim put his paw on one of the slips of paper, which was then put in a locked safe until after the race. It turned out that Jim had picked the winner. He repeated his success the following year, and so on for seven successive years.

Sam was not a gambling man and never attempted to profit from Jim's abilities to foretell the future. He received many letters and telegrams requesting Jim's predictions of winning horses. Some people offered to split the profits with Sam. But Sam never wavered. Nor was he interested in a lucrative offer from Paramount for Jim to work in movies for a year. Like the modest midwesterner he was, Sam said he didn't really need the money and didn't want to commercialize Jim.

As time passed, the bond between Sam and Jim grew. Sam's love for Jim was that of a man for his greatest friend. And the dog's ability to do anything Sam asked was just one facet of Jim's deep devotion towards Sam. So when Jim died at the age of twelve in 1937, Sam was devastated. And indeed, the whole town of Marshall was stunned by the loss. Jim was buried in the Ridge Park Cemetery, where his small white headstone reads: Jim the Wonder Dog.

Many people visit Jim's gravesite every year, leaving flowers and coins in remembrance of the Wonder Dog whose mysterious powers won him lasting fame and honor and love.

Bryan Aubrey

[EDITORS' NOTE: *The events in this story have been confirmed by eye-witnesses and documented in numerous newspapers, magazines and other publications. The editors have checked the author's sources and are confident that they are reliable.*]

"I told him to get down."

Ding, Dong, Bell

The painted cowbell Martha Agrelius found at a local craft fair made an attractive addition to her front porch—especially when suspended over the old metal milk can she'd bought a few months earlier.

Salem, Martha's cat, seemed to think so, too. He relished the sound the bell made when he leapt up onto the milk can and began swatting it with his paw.

Like Pavlov before him, Salem discovered that certain individuals could be conditioned to respond in a predictable manner to certain stimuli. After a while, he realized he didn't even need to ring the bell to bring sixty-five-year-old Martha scurrying out to the front porch. All he had to do was stand on the milk can and reach up. On quite a few occasions, neighbors could also be induced to respond to his summons. All in all, the experiment in behavioral conditioning seemed to be enormously satisfying to Salem.

Shortly before Halloween, Martha asked her son-in-law to raise the bell by about twelve inches, firmly out of reach of Salem's paws and the sticky hands of costumed children.

The following February, an ice storm coated streets, cars, trees and sidewalks with a slick, transparent glaze.

On the day after the storm, Martha bundled up and ventured out of doors. But just as she was walking alongside
the garage, she slipped on the ice and fell. Try as she
might, she couldn't raise herself up. She was sure she
must have broken something. And she was bleeding, too.
Traces of blood painted red webs in the cracked ice
around her head.

It got colder and colder. No one came. Martha realized
with a sinking feeling that because of the trees in her yard,
no one would be able to see her from the street. She closed
her eyes and began to drift into semi-consciousness.
Everything was a blur, and she had no idea of how long
she lay there.

Suddenly she was roused by a cold, moist touch on her
cheek. She opened her eyes and moaned softly, before
turning her head to gaze on Salem, who was standing up
close to her face, eyeing her intently.

"Meoow," the cat cried out. Martha was so cold she was
unable to respond.

"Meoow" came again. Then Salem rubbed his face up
against Martha's. Still she could manage no response.
Salem turned his attention to Martha's hand, nudging it
with his cold nose, trying to get her to pet him. Martha felt
like crying, but she still could not move.

Looking out of half-closed eyes she watched as Salem
gave up trying to get her to respond and stepped gingerly
across the ice. He made his way to the front porch and
leapt onto the swing suspended from the porch roof by a
set of rusty chains. For a few moments the swing swayed
beneath his weight. As the movement gradually ceased,
Salem stepped from the swing onto the ice-covered top of
the milk can, and positioned himself directly underneath
the bell suspended just out of reach.

Motionless on the ground Martha was still able to
watch what was going on. She hardly dared to believe

what she thought must be in Salem's mind. "Do it, Salem, do it," she thought desperately to herself.

Salem steadied himself on the swing, bunched his powerful leg muscles and sprang. When he was at maximum height he shot out his front paw to swat the bell. He hit it squarely, shaking loose some snow and ice and raising a sort of clunk. Then as he came down he fell back onto the icy porch. Salem repeated this maneuver nearly a dozen times as Martha watched.

"Oh thank you, Salem, thank you," she whispered to herself. Someone would surely hear the sound and come to the rescue. Sure enough, eventually a neighbor ventured outside to discover the cause of the repeated clanging.

In good time, Martha was transported to a local hospital, where she was treated for a fractured hip and an injury to her left temple. Salem, meanwhile, was rewarded with several bowls of warm milk, a weekly serving of gourmet food and a handsome plastic ball fitted with a tiny bell, which he swatted around the floor to his heart's content.

Eric Swanson

The Cowboy

My mother acquired him as a skinny little puppy. He'd been neglected, starved of everything, including love, but he grew to be a fine dog. He was a redbone bloodhound, sleek and handsome, his coat a deep, rusty red. He had the hound's musical bay, and a tendency to sleep through the heat of the day and roam at night. We called him Duke. He loved us all, but he adored my mother.

When Duke was about two years old, we lived in Tennessee, in a small motel on the outskirts of some easily forgettable town. Our front yard was two lanes of blacktop highway. Across this fast street was an immense cow pasture, and about forty yards in from the blacktop was a small creek covered by towering shade trees. We, the four young children, were forbidden to go there because of the bull, but it was hard to resist and we had snuck over a few times during that hot summer. We considered it safe if the cows weren't out.

On this particular hot and muggy day, here and there, cows dotted in the field and the hill. Normally, the sight of them would have ended our hopes of a dip in the stream, and we would have played in the sprinkler instead. But someone was washing a car so there was no sprinkler.

Even though the cows were out, we could not see the bull. We crossed the road and peered into the distance. He would not be hard to miss: huge, black and angry, an earthquake with each step of hard, heavy hoof. We leaned on the fence casually, watching the cows flick their tails at flies, waiting for the bull to make his presence known. After about five minutes, Kim sat on the fence and speculated that the bull may have stayed inside because of the heat. We waited for Kim to make up her mind: She was the oldest at ten, and we deferred to her.

After a moment, Kim jumped off the fence and onto forbidden ground. We waited, breath held, but there was no roar of outrage and no shaking earth. We scrambled after Kim in order of age: me, the eight-year-old, then Jeff, who was six, and Donna last, an impish and pouty three. Duke raced ahead and scattered cows.

I was scared but excited. I imagined I was behind enemy lines; I had to blow up the dam and destroy the bridge. I pulled my invisible gun and slunk toward the trees, my eyes darting across the landscape. I barked an order at Jeff because I didn't dare bark one at Kim, who strode imperiously ahead of our little column. Donna complained about the distance and asked where we were going.

Soon we were in the dark cool shade under the trees. The stream ran over stones and old branches, sluiced into deep, quiet pools. We entered quickly, pausing only to kick off socks and sneakers. The water cooled us, the earth squeezed between our toes, and the heat could not penetrate the darkness of the shade. We felt safe in that cool little pocket of the world. We built a dam, destroyed it, then built it again. We fought wars in which we won, and lost and won again. We scratched out plans of attack in the wet earth. We were captured and escaped.

We played like that for hours until we got hungry. Pulling socks over wet feet and stuffing them into sneakers, we prepared to head home. I called for Duke, who had not been seen for hours, but got no answer. We started across the field, four tired, hungry children.

We had covered about half the distance when I heard the bull, and my plodding stopped with my breath. I turned slowly and there he was: big, black and glaring. His head was lowered, and he struck the earth in front of him with one large hoof. The others saw him, too. Jeff sprinted for the fence with amazing speed, but Kim and I were slower: We were pulling Donna between us, half dragging her across the ground. It seemed that the more we pulled, the longer her little arms got.

We were running for our lives; we knew it because we could hear him, snorting and coming for us. And we could feel him in the tremendous shaking of the earth under our feet. There was no doubt in my mind: We would not make it. The field was too large and we were too small. There was a roaring and a rushing sound in my ears, blood propelled by fear. I could see the fence, so close, and yet I knew the bull was closer. Jeff was already over, and I envied him. I could be safe, too, but I would have to let go of Donna's small hand. For one second, I contemplated it, but even at eight I knew I wouldn't be able to live with the guilt. I gripped Donna's hand harder and threw a glance back.

That was when I tripped. My foot went into a hole and I went down, pulling Donna and Kim with me. I hit the ground and dry grass and dust went up my nose. For a moment I lay still, sensing the speed of his approach, and wondering how much time I had before he reached me. I flipped over and saw him bearing down on us like a freight train. He was only fifteen yards away; in a moment, he would trample us into the ground. I already felt the pounding of each hoof reverberate in my body. He was looming. He was large. He would hurt me. Yet I could not close my eyes.

And that is why it still mystifies me that I never saw Duke. There was only the faintest impression of red, moving across the surface of my vision—a blur, a streak that seemed to hit the bull and flip him off his feet. He rolled over, and that was when I really saw Duke for the first time, rolling with him. They came to a stop, the bull on his side, his feet dangling and his eyes rolling wildly, a reddish froth around his mouth. Duke was standing over him, his muzzle latched onto the bull's nose.

I grabbed Donna's hand and yanked her to her feet. Kim and I practically carried her the ten yards to the fence. We were slow and I was limping, my ankle twisted by the turn in the hole. But Duke and the bull never moved. When we were safely over I called to Duke and he came at a dead run, as if he expected the bull to rush after him. But the bull remained lying there for a few minutes, dazed. He had been defeated; suddenly he wasn't so huge or terrifying to me anymore. I was even a little sad to see that side of him disappear. He had been capable of causing such terror, but now he only snuffled through a bloody snout as he stumbled to his feet.

We didn't tell my mother, of course. None of us wanted a month's allowance docked and restriction to the motel courtyard to remind us who made the rules. And Duke seemed unaware of his role as our savior. He wagged at our silent attention, drank water, laid in the shade and went to sleep.

Many years later, a cowboy explained to me that the reason they put a ring in a bull's nose is to control him. "You twist that ring, that bull's head will follow, and you can lay him on the ground with it before he'll pull against you," he said.

But I could have told him that, because I'd seen it done in spectacular fashion. We had a cowboy in our family— and his name was Duke.

K. Salome-Garver

The Cat Who Needed a Night Light

On a warm August day, a dainty little cat named Dolores was receiving a special award: the American Humane Association's William O. Stillman award for bravery. The association gives the award to people who risk their lives to save animals from danger, and to animals who face down danger to save the lives of people. Either way, the winners are heroes, whether they're take-charge, fearless sorts of people, or extroverted, devoted pets like Dolores.

Dolores hadn't always been an extrovert. And she hadn't seemed very devoted to anyone, either. In fact, she'd been what most people call the quiet type. When she first came to live with her owner, Kyle, Dolores rarely had anything to say. And most of the time, she didn't like being touched.

Kyle didn't know why Dolores was so standoffish. And he didn't understand something else about her: why she always became upset whenever the lights were turned out. But Kyle didn't care. Something about the cat's quiet, unassuming manner appealed to him. So, at night, he just left all the lights on in the apartment where he and Dolores lived, even when it was time to go to sleep. And if Dolores wanted to keep her distance—well, he could respect that. Maybe, if he was patient, Dolores would someday decide to come to him, to talk to him, to be friends.

So for the next year, Kyle loved Dolores for exactly who she was. He let her keep her distance, and he didn't ask for more than she could give.

Then, one May evening, everything changed. The night started like any other. And, at evening's end, Kyle checked—as usual—to make sure all the lights in his apartment were on. Then, he went to sleep.

Sometime later he woke with a start. Something was jumping on his head! Paws were scratching his face! And, when he opened his eyes, his apartment was no longer brightly lit; instead it was filled with black smoke. But he could see who was doing the jumping and scratching: Dolores.

The little cat was all Kyle could see. But she was enough.

Together, the two made their way to the only available exit from the apartment—the back door. Kyle felt his way along the walls. At the same time, he felt for Dolores with his feet and followed her. Finally, the pair reached the back door. Kyle pulled on the knob to open the door, only to have the knob fall off into his hand. The door remained firmly shut.

Making his way to the door had taken every bit of strength and oxygen Kyle had, and he collapsed to the floor. But, once again, he felt those insistent paws scratching his face. Kyle mustered his last bit of strength to hurl himself against the door, break it down and run outside to fresh air and safety. Once there, he looked around for the cat who'd saved his life.

She wasn't there.

With sickening clarity, Kyle realized that Dolores was still inside the apartment. He ran to one of the firefighters.

"My cat's still inside my apartment!" he exclaimed. "Can you find her?"

The firefighter promised to try.

Now all Kyle could do was wait. He knew Dolores's chances weren't good, but still—maybe, just maybe, she would be found alive.

An hour or so later, the firefighters brought the blaze under control. And one firefighter brought Kyle a bundle wrapped in a towel. Kyle held his breath. Inside the bundle was Dolores—eyes seared shut, hair singed, but alive.

The firefighter explained that Dolores had collapsed just inside the door and that a fireman had stumbled on her when he entered the apartment. After removing her from the apartment, paramedics gave the cat CPR and oxygen before bringing her to Kyle.

The fire changed Kyle's life dramatically. He'd lost all his clothes, furniture and other possessions, and had to go live with his mother for a while. His cat had changed, too.

The once-quiet Dolores was now a talker who meowed and purred almost constantly. Even more surprising was her new desire to be touched and cuddled—preferably while she was lying on Kyle's lap.

Now, just four months later, Dolores was being recognized for her bravery. But Kyle knew he'd gotten a bigger prize. He'd never asked for more than Dolores could give—and then found she was willing to give him everything she had.

Susan McCullough

Flight over Little Egypt

March 18, 1925. Though only five years of age, I well remember the day the great tornado swept over "Little Egypt," as the southern tip of Illinois is called. The little coal-mining town in which we lived lay directly in its path. Our house trembled as if it had convulsions, bricks from the chimney tumbled about wildly, the roof ripped apart and the windows blew out. The howling wind sounded as if a dozen locomotives were roaring past. We huddled in the kitchen as the roaring filled our ears and seemed to shake our very bones.

The huge, dark funnel swept devastatingly across the ground. The "mother cloud," the cloud above the funnel, was a turbulent, boiling mass of blackness. In its wake lay death and destruction.

Suddenly it was over. The quietness felt unnatural and an eerie, uneasy feeling gripped us. "Children, please stay where you are," said Mother, her voice barely audible. "I've got to look outside."

Reluctantly, we obeyed. Opening the door, my mother stood transfixed as she gazed upon the awful scene. Debris lay everywhere. The street was impassable. People, some obviously in shock, milled around like cattle, unsure of what to do. The strange silence was suddenly broken by a subdued, pitiful whining at Mother's feet.

Trembling violently, a wet and frightened little poodle lay wedged between the door and the screen.

"My stars," my mother said, bending over. "Wherever did you come from?"

The bedraggled little dog timidly wagged his tail and began licking Mother's hand.

Jacky, as we named him, accepted our large family without reservation. We in turn lavished our love upon the displaced but lucky little poodle.

Almost immediately we realized Jacky was an exceptional dog—a very smart one. Surrounded by masses of curly hair, his dark inquisitive eyes sparkled with life. He often followed us on his hind legs from room to room or all around the yard begging for a biscuit. Actually one could say he skipped along. His balance and agility were hard to believe. And we were sure he understood every word we said.

"I wish he could talk," said Marshall, my older brother. "I'll bet he has a story to tell. I'd like to know where he came from. He sure isn't from around here because no one has asked about him. I'm glad. I couldn't stand to give him up now."

Jacky made friends with almost everyone, especially if they drove a car. He loved to go for rides. The strange thing was he wanted to ride *on* the car, rather than in it. Whenever a car pulled away he jumped up on the hood. After riding a few blocks, he'd jump off as the car slowed down or stopped, and then he'd run right home, a pleased look on his intelligent face.

The little dog had been a part of our family for about two years when a hobo knocked at the back door and asked if we could give him something to eat. The request wasn't at all unusual. In those days, many hobos stopped

at our corner. Mother brought a plate of food to the porch
where he waited.

As he sat down to eat, we boys gathered around him.
He began telling us about all the places he'd been and the
many things he'd seen. We were spellbound by his tales.

All of a sudden he stopped. We looked in the direction
he was staring, and there stood Jacky. For several
moments they looked at one another. Then a huge smile
came across the old hobo's face.

"You little rascal," he said, calling him by some strange-
sounding name. "What are you doing here?"

The little dog became hysterical with joy. He was all over
the hobo, barking and jumping as if he would never stop.
There was no doubt he knew the hobo and knew him well.
After caressing and talking to Jacky, the old hobo uttered a
brief command. Immediately, Jacky controlled his enthusiasm and lay down obediently at the old man's feet.

"Boys, where did you get this dog?" asked the hobo.

"We found him lodged between the door and the screen
during the big tornado of '25," said my brother.

"Yes, sir. It adds up," said the hobo. "I was with a circus
in Missouri in March of '25. That was sure some blow. The
big tent was ripped to shreds. Everything was demolished. Cages and animals flew every which way. Some
of the animals were recovered, a lot of 'em weren't. I don't
hanker to go through anything like that again. No sirree.

"This poodle was the number-one top show dog. He's
so valuable he was insured for hundreds of dollars. Lucky
dog, he is. Blowed all that distance and not gettin' hurt.
Just how far is it to Missouri from here?"

"It's sixty miles to the Cape. That's the first town in
Missouri," answered my brother.

"Boy, I been most everywhere and I done seen a lot of
things, but I ain't never seen a miracle before. This little
dog proves they do happen. I can hardly believe it," he

said, shaking his head in amazement.

We were trying to take in the fact that our little dog had been blown at least sixty miles by the tornado, when suddenly the hobo asked, "Do you have a barrel hoop, boy?"

"Sure, I'll get you one," said my brother. Running quickly to an old barrel he lifted off one of the steel bands. He dashed back and handed it to the hobo.

From beneath his old battered hat the hobo's blue eyes sparkled. A smile broke through his heavy gray beard.

"Watch this," he said. "'Less you boys been to a circus you ain't never seen anything like this."

He walked out into the yard and held the hoop a couple of feet above the ground.

"Get ready," he said to Jacky, again using that strange-sounding name. Jacky trembled with excitement. On command he sprang forward and leaped through the hoop—forward, then backward. As commands continued, he hurled through the hoop, turning end over end. He danced on his hind legs, then on his front legs. My brothers and I stared in awe as the knowledgeable old hobo put Jacky through his circus tricks.

"He's a little rusty on some of 'em, but he sure ain't forgettin' any of it," said the hobo. "Sure is great bein' together again. Brings back memories, don't it little friend?" he said fondly as he patted Jacky's head.

Then with a forlorn look about him, he straightened up.

"I guess I best be goin'," he mumbled and headed slowly towards the gate. Without hesitation, Jacky followed at his heels.

"Jacky, come back!" all three of us called. But it did no good. Tears trickled down our cheeks. We knew we had lost him.

Then the hobo paused. Looking down at Jacky, he said, "Our circus days is over, friend. Over and done. And the tramping life's no life for you. You best stay here." Jacky stood, watching the hobo walk away, still poised to follow.

Reaching the gate the man stood motionless for several seconds, then slowly turned around. "Boys, a circus dog never forgets the big top," he said. "You'd better lock him in the house till mornin'. I'd hate to see you lose him."

So we did. Jacky lived with us for many years, and although he was the smartest dog we ever had, we could never persuade him to perform his circus tricks again. We figured he'd taken the hobo's words to heart and put his circus days behind him once and for all.

G. Edgar Hall

"He must be very secure in his masculinity."

8

SAYING GOOD-BYE

For the soul of every living thing is in the hand of God . . .

Job 12:10

"Well, in or out?"

The Christmas Angel

When my daughter Rachel was six years old, we went to the local shelter, looking for the perfect cat. We liked a lot of the cats we saw there, but we were especially taken with a mother and her kittens. All the kittens were entirely jet black, except for one. She had a small white tip to her tail, like one bright light in the night sky. We brought her home and called her Star.

Starry was a charmer. Rachel admired her proud manner and enjoyed even more the secret knowledge that it was all an act. Starry could only appear aloof for so long before leaping up into Rachel's arms to be cuddled and stroked. As time went by, Rachel and Starry adopted certain routines. At night when we watched TV, Starry crawled into Rachel's lap, and stayed there, purring contentedly. Starry always rubbed her face along Rachel's chin, ending the love fest with a gentle nip on Rachel's nose. Sometimes I couldn't help but feel the injustice of this. I was the one who took care of the cat, feeding, cleaning, grooming—yet, Starry was clearly Rachel's cat. Eventually, I came to love watching their cozy bond.

My little girl grew up, went to junior high and finally high school. Starry was ten and Rachel was sixteen. Starry and Rachel were still close, though Rachel spent less and less time at home. Starry spent most of her day sitting on the sideboard in the dining room, looking out of the window into the backyard. I loved seeing her as I'd pass, her glossy black coat almost sparkling in the sunlight she loved to seek out, the white tip of her tail brilliant against the shining black of her curled body.

One Sunday morning, early in November, Starry got out the door before we could stop her. When Rachel's friend came over to study that evening, she came in the door with a worried expression. "Where's Starry?" she asked.

When we told her we didn't know, she had us come outside with her. There was a black cat lying in the street.

It was Star. The cat's body was warm and she didn't appear to be injured. There was no blood or wounds that we could see. It was after hours, but our vet agreed to meet us after our distraught phone call. Rachel was upset, but holding it together. My husband Burt and I told her to stay at home while we took Star to the vet.

Burt and I picked Starry up carefully and rushed her to the vet's office. The vet examined her briefly before looking up at us and saying, "I'm sorry, but she's gone."

When we got home, Rachel could tell by our faces that Starry was dead. She turned without speaking and went to her room.

It had been a hard year for me. My father had died not long before, and I hadn't totally come to grips with the loss. Rachel and I were in the midst of the delicate dance mothers and teenaged daughters everywhere find themselves performing—circling, pulling away and coming together in odd fits and spurts. I took a chance and knocked at her door. When she said come in, I sat with her on the bed and we cried together. It was a good cry, clearing out some more of the grief I couldn't face about my father and bringing Rachel and I closer as we shared our sadness about Starry.

Life went on. Thanksgiving came and went. Rachel and I both found ourselves mistaking black sweatshirts strewn on chairs or floors for our newly missing black cat. The sideboard looked desolate, empty of the warm presence glowing with life I'd come to expect there. Over and over, little pangs of loss stung our hearts as the weeks went by.

I was out Christmas shopping, when I saw it. It was a Christmas tree ornament in the shape of a "cat angel." A black cat with white wings and a red ball between her paws. I had to get it, but bought it wondering if it would be a happy remembrance of the cat we'd loved or a chilling reminder of our loss.

When I got home, I painted a white tip at the end of the angel cat's long black tail and hung the ornament on our tree.

That evening, when Rachel came in, she flopped on to the couch. She sat staring at the Christmas tree, "spacing out" after a long day at school and after-school sports. I was in the kitchen when suddenly I heard her gasp. "Mom," she called. "Mom, come here!"

I walked in and found her standing in front of the tree, looking at the cat angel with shining eyes. "Oh, Mom. It's Starry. Where did you find an ornament with a tail like hers?"

She looked about six again. I gathered her into my arms and wonderfully she didn't resist. We stood together, looking at the tree, feeling our love for Starry and for each other.

Our charming, nose-nipping cat was gone, but now Starry, the Christmas angel, would be a part of our family tradition for years to come.

Sometimes you can make your own miracles.

Pamela S. Zurer

Shorty

It doesn't seem like that long ago, but it has been nineteen years since a little ball of joy (and fluff) came into my life and changed it forever. I was working for a property management firm in San Francisco and was asked to relocate to Texas to oversee an apartment complex there.

Soon after my wife Linda and I arrived, the building maintenance man discovered a little mutt in a recently vacated apartment. The dog was in a closed closet with no food or water. The maintenance man and his wife were unable to keep her, so Linda asked me if we could do so, "Just for a little while," I reluctantly agreed, but added, "Just for a few days."

I nicknamed the dog Shorty. And Shorty took to me like you wouldn't believe. She followed me everywhere. She was closer than a shadow and when she lay beside me on the couch or in bed you couldn't get a dime between us. Both Linda and I quickly knew that a "little while" was going to become a lifetime.

When our time in Texas came to an end, we returned to San Francisco where Shorty adjusted to being a city dog. We'd take her to the park and for walks around town, but it wasn't the same as when she and I went running out in the fields together just enjoying the day and one another. That was truly our favorite time.

In San Francisco, Shorty learned how to play baseball. She absolutely loved it. Linda pitched, I hit and Shorty fielded the ball. She would catch it in the air or at the most on one hop, trot up to Linda, give her the ball and then run back to the outfield and bark as if to let us know she was ready for more.

As time went on, Linda wished she had a dog that was as devoted to her as Shorty was to me. So one day we went to the SPCA. Sitting in the back of a cage was a terrier-mix a little bigger than Shorty but with the same coloring. He had the biggest brown eyes and was just begging to be taken home. And he was.

Shorty and Buddy took to each other from the beginning and people used to think they were brother and sister.

Some years later, we rented a little house with a fence and room for Shorty and Buddy to play in. By then in her old age, Shorty started losing her teeth, and her tongue used to hang out of the side of her mouth. She also lost her sight and her hearing.

But Buddy became her eyes and ears. He knew that when Shorty went to the front door and barked once, the way she had always done, she wanted to go outside. But now she needed assistance, and Buddy knew exactly what to do. He would take her ear in his mouth and gently guide her down the steps to the lawn where he would lie down and watch her roaming around smelling everything she could. When she was ready to come into the house, Shorty would stand motionless, bark once and again Buddy would go to her, take her ear and guide her up the stairs to her bed.

One evening the door was open, and Shorty somehow made it down the stairs unattended but she collapsed at the bottom. I carried her to her bed and she lay there for a day whimpering, just as she had seventeen years earlier in that dark closet. I told Linda that it looked like it was about time.

Linda knew what I meant and nodded. We took Shorty to the vet that night and as expected there wasn't anything that she could do. She helped us feel better by asking us to think of all the positive things that Shorty had brought into our lives. I will always feel grateful for that.

I decided to remain with Shorty. The vet left us alone in a room, and I stood just stroking her. I think we both gathered some comfort in being with each other. When it was over I cradled her, not ever wanting to let her go.

Linda and I had Shorty cremated and today her ashes and her picture sit atop our dresser.

When the time comes, I've requested that I too be cremated. And Linda has promised me that she will scatter my ashes, together with those of Shorty, in the biggest field she can find.

Then Shorty and I will go running together once again.

Larry Monk

[EDITORS' NOTE: *Larry Monk passed away suddenly just three weeks after writing this story. In accordance with his wish, Linda Monk scattered Shorty's ashes, along with her husband's, in one of their favorite fields.*]

Prince's Golden Season

I first met Prince on a dark Thanksgiving Eve eight years ago when I returned from the city for the long weekend and went as always to feed my daughter's mare. Following a few steps behind the mare came a giant face out of the darkness, a head hanging like a broken branch from a crane-like neck, a concave back and a pace so slow that each step seemed painful. I had no idea how he got there, this caricature of a horse, nor where he should have been.

"It must be Prince," my daughter Jeremy said as we left him with a wafer of hay at his feet, his great neck lowering slowly. "My riding teacher told me about him. His owners are going to sell him at next week's auction. They've already stopped feeding him."

At sunrise on Thanksgiving I went to the corral to look at Prince. There, between me and the rising sun, he was even more incongruous. His color was orange, his winter coat long and standing out from his body, his sagging back holding the ball of the new sun. His face was camel-like below a straw-colored forelock, and his eyes, even as I approached, were tightly closed, as if another morning was too much to face. Tear streaks marked crooked paths along his nose. He walked only when absolutely necessary with an arthritic stiffness, and his conformation by any human measure of horse beauty was hopelessly wrong.

Over the long weekend, Jeremy and I fed and groomed Prince with gentle hands he seemed to enjoy. He accepted his first carrot, his private pile of hay with cautious disbelief. We called our blacksmith who put shoes on his front hooves to even out his sloping posture and to relieve the painful tilt caused by too much weight in front.

Of course, we could not just keep the horse. Nor could we return him to owners so utterly uninterested in his welfare. I called to find out what price he would have brought from bidders at the auction. The answer came quickly; Prince's price was $112. At the end of Jeremy's Saturday riding lesson I gave a check to her teacher. (I never knew nor wanted to know the identity of Prince's owners.)

As the winter weeks passed, Prince began to change. Doggedly he followed Jeremy's mare up and down the pasture, deeply in love. Now his eyes were open, russet pools in his barren homely face, and he stepped a little faster to keep up. He still looked like a huge, shaggy toy; a horse exaggerated for a laugh, but he held his head higher, he swished his tail as if it mattered, and the rows of his ribs, which once had corduroyed his flanks, began to disappear.

In March our mare gave birth to a pure white colt in a drenching rain. It was our firstborn horse, a memorable event for my daughter and me, but a much more satisfying one for Prince. Although gelded, Prince was certain the colt was his, and fatherhood became the final miracle. Now he led the mare, guided the wobbling colt and walked tall. It was he who chose their path, the patch of shade at noon, the green puddle of burr clover. He also found his voice, a deep ahem, and at mealtimes he rattled the aluminum gate with one shoe, impatient if we were late.

As his adopted son grew strong and challenging, Prince took over his discipline, never bothering to chase him, for nothing was worth the hurry, but administering necessary nips along the way. There was no longer any doubt that he had been properly named long ago when someone's hopes for him were high.

As the days of spring warmed, his winter coat fell away in tufts, each to be carried off to line the nests of larks and red-wing blackbirds. He put up with little girls straddling his scooped-out back and now and then would carry them a few steps before stopping to close his eyes.

And so he lived, a once-again Prince, his self-respect restored, his days of ignominy long forgotten. He suffered Saturday shampoos, standing in a cloud of suds, feeling the squirt of the hose, drying off by noon. He stood long hours at the fence corner gazing off toward the mountains, then resting his chin on a fence post to nap. Caught for a moment each evening between me and the setting sun, he seemed a golden horse, a misshapen Pegasus pausing between heavenly adventures.

I returned early from a trip last summer to find Prince noticeably thinner. Tests revealed the presence of worms, which were quickly eliminated, but his weight continued to drop. A rich diet of mixed grains and molasses was added, served three times a day in a bread pan to fit his jaws. Still he shrunk before my eyes, his ribs reappearing, the sag of his back emphasizing the emerging crags of his quarters. He still walked toward me, but he allowed me to do most of the walking, and he chewed each mouthful with less and less enthusiasm. The pill he now took once a day, powdered and mixed with his grain, had no effect. He spent his days in deep grass seldom reaching down to graze, and more and more I saw his eyes turned toward the mountains far away. I spoke quietly at such times, reminding him how fortunate we both were, reassuring him that all would be well. He, as I, knew better.

The great orange horse was fading before my eyes, and nothing I did made any difference. His mare and colt stayed near, but they seemed forgotten. He seemed already to have left them. His tear streaks lengthened, and as I dried them with my sleeve to keep the flies away, he bowed his head to allow me to scratch his forelock.

On a morning in mid-October, Prince returned to the corral and lay down at last. By then he was the shadow horse I had seen long ago. He could not raise his head to nibble at the sweet-smelling breakfast I brought, and I called John, my friend and veterinarian, who skipped his own breakfast to come to us. There in the corral Prince went to sleep. It was all we could do for him, a gentle push toward the mountains he now could climb.

* * * *

We who choose to surround ourselves with lives even more temporary than our own live within a fragile circle, easily and often breached. Yet, we still would live no other way. The life of a horse, often half our own, seems endless until one day. That day has come and gone for me, and I am once again within a smaller circle, still unable to believe that this evening I will not see Prince against the setting sun, head lowered, eyes half closed, tail a golden fall. He was, and is again, a prince to us.

Irving Townsend

Hondo

The one best place to bury a good dog is in the heart of his master.

Ben Hur Lampman

The years have aged Hondo; the winter has taken its toll. Spring snows thaw and summer flowers bloom, but for Hondo, only one season remains.

Our old black Lab has been unable to climb the deck for three days. He sleeps in the shady grass beneath a tree. We have carried his rug onto the grass, and he rests there. The cast-iron skillet that has been his food dish for more years than I can remember is next to him. But this morning he no longer tries to lift his head. He will not drink; he cannot eat.

I bring a currycomb up from the barn and sit on the grass next to Hondo. He has not completely shed his winter coat. Clumps of dusty gray fur come loose. We talk. I pretend he hears me, holding his head in my hands and kissing his forehead. I lift a paw and gently touch the cracked, hard pads of his feet.

Our lives revolve around his dying. We are given the weekend, days we can be home together. I pull a clump of

Hondo's hair from the comb and toss it into the breeze. The wind snatches the hair, carrying the clump away, past the driveway and into the tall grass.

Vivid scenes of Hondo over the years come to mind— Hondo sitting sentry in the front yard for two days, waiting for my husband Mark to return from fighting forest fires; Hondo and my daughter, Sarah, lying curled up together, like two leaves from a single tree; Hondo and Matt, my son, splashing together in the shallow stock pond, lunging at slick tadpoles.

And the two of us? The puppy I once cradled in my arms taught me to follow the deer trails, to listen to the call of the red-tailed hawk, to catch the smell of sage in the moaning wind. I learned to appreciate the smell of freshly turned earth, of damp fibrous roots, of sodden wood alive with insects.

The rain comes, large single drops that splash against the windows and the leaves of the trees. They fall on Hondo but he does not move, only blinks his eyes. I go down to the barn again and find an old horse blanket and lay it on top of him. He wags his tail and blinks again.

Mark helps me carry the picnic table to the lawn. We carefully set it over Hondo, making a shelter for him.

"Should we carry him inside?" I ask Mark.

"I think he is where he wants to be."

Later, looking through the window, the rain has stopped and I see Mark sitting on the grass next to Hondo. The horse blanket moves slightly as Hondo lifts his tail. Mark rests his hand on Hondo's head. He rubs behind the ears. They sit, man and dog, best of friends, constant companions.

During the course of the day Matt and Sarah stop to sit beside Hondo, each in turn, in their own time. Matt lies down next to him. Sarah lifts the blanket and strokes him.

By bedtime Hondo is sleeping quietly beneath the horse blanket, which covers all but his head. Our private good-byes have been spoken, our private tears shed.

Twinges of guilt tug at me, thinking maybe we should bring Hondo inside to sleep by our bed. But somehow we cannot confine him to four walls. We cannot bring ourselves to hide the stars from his eyes. We want the moonbeams to guide him to the heavens and the night crickets to lull him to sleep.

Dawn comes. Light pink colors the eastern sky. Dewdrops perch upon the grass blades. I sit on the wet grass in my nightgown. Hondo has just taken his last breath. I lay my head upon his massive chest, where his devoted heart now lies still, and I breathe his familiar dog-scent one last time.

When the sun has risen, and the early-morning songs of the chickadees and the robins and the bluebirds have quieted, I pull the old horse blanket completely over Hondo and go in the house.

Later, we carry Hondo to the grave.

"Mom, I want to pick some flowers for him," Sarah says. She scoots away in search of anything wild and pretty.

Matt wants to find a stick. "Would that be a good thing to bury with him?" he asks.

"Yes, Matt," Mark answers with a quavering voice, "a very good thing."

Sarah returns with wild dandelions, a few long purple asters, lots of white yarrow, two bluebell stalks and red clover blossoms.

"How are these, Mom? They're the prettiest I could find."

Matt returns with a smooth weathered stick about twelve inches long.

"It's perfect," Mark nods his head.

The four of us circle Hondo's grave and hold hands. Out loud, we take turns saying a short prayer.

"Dear God," Matt asks simply, "please take Hondo to heaven and make him young again."

We place a large heavy stone on top of the mound of dirt, and Sarah tucks her remaining flowers under the rim of the rock.

It is done.

We turn to go, walking shoulder to shoulder, lost in our own memories. As we pass the corner of the barnyard, Mark slows his pace and turns away. I hear a gut-deep, heartrending sob escape his tough exterior. Mark is leaning on the corner post of the fence that surrounds the barnyard, great sobs shaking his manly frame, and though I have seen tears discreetly spill from Mark's eyes before, this is only the second time I have ever seen such anguish escape him.

The next few days were as illusive as shadows. Then one late afternoon, fog enveloped the ranch. Mark and the kids were gone, so it was my night to do chores. I went to bring in the sheep and followed the fence, eventually coming to where they grazed. Like a shepherd's staff, my voice reached through the fog and urged them on until finally the grayness of the barn emerged—a port in the storm.

Once the sheep were safely corralled, I eased my way up the path. I searched the fog, wanting Hondo to glide through it and stand by my side. My hand reached out instinctively to pet his glossy blackness but found nothing to cling to—only the whiteness, and my grief.

Then, very quietly at first, I heard myself call him—a thin, high-pitched wail floated across the field, lengthening and thickening in the fog.

Hooonnndooo.

The ridge caught my cry, held it for a moment, then returned it to me—softer, partly absorbed, not totally mine any longer. And from somewhere in the white, colorless distance, a coyote answered.

Page Lambert

A Gentle Good-Bye

*She was, if possible, dearer in her decrepit old
age than in her radiant youth. . . . Calmly she
accepted her infirmities, depending upon me
with implicit faith.*

Eileen Gardner Galer

Several years after my mother was widowed, she
decided a cat would be the perfect companion. Since I
shared my home with two cats, I was considered the
feline expert. When my veterinarian told me about a litter
of six-week-old kittens that had been dropped off on his
clinic steps, I helped my mother pick out the perfect kitten, whom she named Cameo. From that point on, the sun
rose and set on this black and white cat, who, unlike my
cats, could do no wrong. Cameo quickly became my
mother's pride and joy.

For the next eight years, Cameo lived as an only cat.
Since Mommala and I lived near each other, we frequently
exchanged visits and cat-sitting chores. When I visited
Mommala accompanied by my golden retriever guide dog
Ivy, Cameo would go into hiding as soon as we entered

the apartment. After being unharnessed and unleashed, Ivy would go looking for a playmate, but Cameo would retreat further under the bed.

During my frequent travels, my two cats stayed at Mommala's house, and the three cats established a comfortable relationship. However, when Mommala traveled and Cameo came to stay with us, her shyness caused her to spend much of the time behind the stove or on the closet shelf. Frequently, the only sign of her presence was the emptied food bowl I set out for her at night while keeping the other cats enclosed in my bedroom. Although Ivy was gentle with cats, Cameo never learned to be comfortable around her.

At Mommala's death, Cameo's world turned upside-down. I had told Mommala that if anything happened to her I would adopt her beloved cat. Because I had recently married and moved from New York to California, Cameo's first hurdle was a coast-to-coast flight. To my delight, she traveled with hardly a meow in the carrier I placed under the empty seat next to me. Ivy, like most guide dogs, occupied the space for carry-on luggage under the seat in front of me. Following our arrival in Fresno, Cameo had to adapt to a strange new world, including one new cat and my husband's guide dog, Kirby. It had been bad enough dealing with one golden retriever, but now there were two of these playful creatures to reckon with!

As anticipated, Cameo went undercover for three weeks. It was her passion for food that eventually drove this timid creature out of hiding and into family life.

As a blind cat lover in a multi-cat household, I identify each cat by a distinctive-sounding collar bell. For Cameo, I selected one with a tiny tinkle that seemed to go perfectly with her petite and cuddly persona. The day I heard the tinkle of her bell hitting the food bowl, I knew we were entering a new phase of togetherness.

Whenever I sat in my favorite lounge chair listening to a book on tape and knitting, I knew immediately when it was Cameo who chose to share my lap. After a while she would butt her head into my hand indicating it was time to stop these other activities and begin brushing her. Delighting in being groomed, Cameo rewarded me with purrs and kneading paws. Occasionally, I felt her body stiffen, and I'd know one of the dogs was approaching.

During the first few months Cameo was with us, when Ivy or Kirby approached, she jumped off my lap and leaped onto a table, counter or the refrigerator. Soon realizing that dogs, although large, could easily be dominated by a powerful hiss or smack, she no longer relinquished lap time and administered doggy discipline as needed.

Over the next few years, Cameo coexisted peacefully with her canine and feline siblings. When the alarm clock went off in the morning and the dogs were invited to join us, she learned to make room in the bed for the canine corps. As time passed, she thought nothing of jumping over a dog for a cuddle from a favorite human.

When progressive loss of vision forced Ivy's retirement from guide work, and my new guide-dog partner, Escort, entered the family, Cameo met this challenge with newly acquired feline aplomb.

Escort, a young, playful and energetic golden retriever, was put in his place by hisses, spitting and, if needed, a smack on the nose. Like Ivy and Kirby, he learned that this small creature could readily communicate her desire to be left alone, particularly when she occupied my lap.

Although Cameo and my beloved guide dog Ivy lived together for six years, they could not be called friends. They resembled siblings, who, for the good of other family members, had agreed to live together but basically ignore each other's foibles.

During the year of Ivy's retirement, her health continued

to deteriorate. The day came when the quality of her life had worsened to the point where I knew our partnership had to end.

I made the dreaded call asking our veterinarian to come to the house to euthanize my friend, helper and companion of eleven years. When the doctor arrived, my husband, our friend Eve and I sat on the floor in a circle around Ivy to provide comfort in her last moments. At this time, Cameo was fast asleep in her favorite chair. What happened next showed me a totally new and unexpected side of her personality.

She awoke with a start, and the sound of her tinkling bell alerted me she was on the way. Jumping over Eve, she joined the circle. Purring loudly and rubbing up against her human companions, she provided the comfort we so desperately sought in this emotion-laden situation. She seemed to adopt the role of grief counselor. At one point she flung herself into my arms, sending me a clear message that she felt my pain and was there to comfort me. No more aloof feline reserve for her.

And as Cameo walked back and forth between us all, it was obvious that she was no longer indifferent to her long-term house partner. Several times she stopped and licked Ivy's face, something she had never done before. As I held Ivy in my arms and reached out to touch Cameo, I felt Cameo's tiny paw touching Ivy's large paw. Cameo seemed incredibly attuned to the importance of touching the old dog, who was now totally blind.

But Ivy could still hear, and it comforts me to realize that the last sounds my treasured teammate heard as she slipped quietly into a gentle death were my murmured endearments and Cameo's soothing purrs.

Toni Eames

Banjo

*The final cause of dogs having such short lives
. . . is in compassion to the human race; for
if we suffer so much in losing a dog after an
acquaintance of ten or twelve years, what
would it be if they were to live double that time?*

Sir Walter Scott

Banjo came to me by way of a paper bag deposited on
my doorstep, apparently the unwanted runt of a litter of
German shepherd puppies. At the time, I was single,
pushing thirty and living in the country, so I was able to
take on the responsibility of a new pet. But did I want
one? I had recently decided not to have another dog after
losing Chad, a collie who had been my companion for
nearly thirteen years. Chad had been a mature animal,
easy to live with. Now here I was holding a tiny creature
that would demand a lot of time, energy and patience.
Was I prepared to deal with the torn shoes, the gnawed
table legs, the destroyed flowerbeds? Was I willing to
spend the time it takes to properly train a dog?

These questions disappeared the moment I lifted that

black and brown furball into my arms. And in the years that followed, I never regretted my decision.

Later when I married, my wife Sandy didn't share my feelings about Banjo. She made it abundantly clear that she wasn't fond of dogs. To her, Banjo was simply the cause of hair on the couch and mud in the carpet, and a nuisance to make arrangements for whenever we went away.

But in time, I noticed a change. It began with her insistence that she had accidentally added too much milk to her cereal, and instead of wasting it, she might as well give it to Banjo. (She continued this ritual "accident" until the morning Banjo died.) Next, my grooming technique for Banjo suddenly became unacceptable, and Banjo and I found ourselves going on regular visits to the beauty parlor.

Sandy's love for Banjo truly blossomed during the second year of our marriage when my work took me away from home for ten weeks and Banjo became entirely her responsibility. Banjo never had it so good. The two of them did everything together, becoming better friends than Sandy ever dreamed, although there had never been any question in Banjo's mind.

Sandy has never been accused of spending too much time in the kitchen; yet, as I later found out, she and Banjo would spend their evenings baking gingerbread and blueberry muffins. Then they would top the treats with whipped cream and homemade jams and sit in front of the fire, leaning against each other, licking clean fingers and plates. Since I was more strict as to what was and wasn't considered dog food—and I never once baked Banjo his very own birthday cake—sharing dinners and desserts when I was away was a conspiracy they both relished.

Our life together with Banjo continued for ten happy years. Then Banjo's health began to deteriorate. When he was diagnosed with cancer, Sandy and I reached the painful realization that Banjo was leaving us.

In the weeks that followed, we were glad for every extra moment we had with Banjo, but we couldn't shake the sadness we felt. We were concerned when Banjo's dear face told us he wasn't feeling well, yet we were unable to make the decision that the time had come to help him along. And although we prepared ourselves for the inevitable, the end was no less painful, no easier to accept. It was still too soon.

The day Banjo died, he walked unsteadily over to me as I was pulling on my coat. I believe he was asking me to stay. I knew why. So I helped him outside one last time, then took him next to the fire and held his head on my lap. We talked about a lot of things, alone in the quiet, just as we had in the beginning, ten short years ago. After all, it seemed like only yesterday Banjo was curled up in the crook of my arm making contented little grunts, a sound only a puppy can make. It seemed like just last week I was explaining to him for the umpteenth time that the rawhide bones were his and the furniture was mine. If I had any regrets, if I thought I could have done certain things better, if I wished I'd been a little more under-standing with a young, rambunctious puppy, none of this mattered now as Banjo and I were ending our relationship the same way we started it: just the two of us holding each other close.

He was in pain, and as the glow of the fireplace enveloped us I kept telling him it was okay to let go. And he finally did, leaving me feeling very alone in the middle of the living room, wondering how the last ten years could have possibly gone by so quickly.

The line between life and death is but a fragile second, and watching Banjo cross it was profoundly moving. I held Banjo a bit longer than I probably should have, run-ning my fingers along the black stripes that accented his eyes. Though his life had slipped away, he was still Banjo, still my friend, and I wasn't ready to give him up. All I could think of, as tears ran down my cheeks, was that I wanted him back.

I wanted him waiting for me at the door, barking up a storm and acting as if after ten years he was still amazed that I actually came home to him every day. I wanted to see him wriggling down the hill behind our house on his back, making the first tracks in a freshly fallen snow. I wanted to hear that long, moaning sigh as he fell asleep next to our bed, a sound that clearly said, "This is a fine place to be."

I could have gone on forever with the memories, but Sandy would be home soon and it was important to me that her last time with him be as dignified as possible. So I folded a blanket around Banjo, arranged his head across his thick pillow, and left him lying peacefully in front of the fire.

When Sandy came home and walked through the front door, she knew by the expression on my face that it was over. I believe her heart broke even more deeply than mine.

We stayed with Banjo for a long while before composing ourselves and carrying him into the woods where he so loved to run. We buried him, covered his grave with pine bows and placed flowers against a hastily made cross.

And then the forest grew silent, except for the wind that pushed through the winter trees. When we finally turned to walk away, Banjo's gravesite seemed small, so small for a dog so large in our hearts.

* * * *

A few months have passed since we stood in the snow and said good-bye to Banjo, and I still miss him every day. But an outpouring of love during the ensuing weeks helped Sandy and me deal with our loss. Cards came through the mail, flowers arrived at our door, friends stopped by to offer their condolences. Even neighborhood children, who knew me only as "Banjo's Dad," came around to say how sorry they were. It was a warm feeling, knowing Banjo had touched so many lives, in however small a way, and that people understood and cared about what Sandy and I were going through.

I'd like to think Banjo and I shared an extraordinary kinship, one worthy of being recorded and remembered. But frankly, there was nothing unique about it. The world didn't spin differently because of us. The simple truth is we liked each other, and that's all that really mattered.

Now, the morning cereal bowls with their leftover milk sit in the kitchen sink, the front door opens without fanfare and I find myself once again saying, "No more dogs; I can't go through that again." But deep inside, it's a different story. I know exactly what will happen when the next puppy shows up on my doorstep.

David C. Hoopes

The Cantor's Cat

Imagine the head soloist, the music minister and the associate pastor of a house of worship. Now imagine one person taking on all those functions. That's about half of the job of a cantor.

Cantors commemorate every stop on the Jewish life-cycle. We chant the blessings that bring a child into the congregation; that celebrate the arrival of those children to young adulthood; that bind two lives together; and that pronounce a person's journey from life into death. We rejoice with the celebrants, as well as mourn with the bereaved. But how do we respond when somebody loses a loved one with four legs instead of two? And how do we handle this situation when it happens to us?

Some years ago, a silver tabby named Petey plopped into my life. We were a team from the get-go. Petey was large and cuddly and had the charming ability to hold hands with me, using a firm, tensile-pawed grip.

When I met my future husband, Mark, I was about to ask him the important question—did he like cats?—when he mentioned Julia, his own tuxedo puss. The first time Mark and I sat together on my sofa, Petey stretched out to his full length in order to sit on both our laps simultaneously. Then he looked at me with a face that said, "Can I keep this one?" And so our household numbered two cats, and two people who were allowed to live with them as long as they paid the rent.

On the first Sabbath in our first home, we suddenly noticed Petey and Julia sitting on the kitchen floor, watching our every move. We lit and blessed the candles together. They stayed at attention during *kiddush* and *motzi,* the prayers before the wine and food; and then they walked away. The following Friday, using the Yiddish word for Sabbath, we hollered, "Hey, *Shabbos* cats!" and they came into the kitchen and sat quietly during the blessings as they had the previous week.

Jewish law mandates caring for the animals in one's household, including feeding them before we feed ourselves. Being good Jewish pet lovers, we ran our household accordingly, and all of us thrived on the love that grew from this four-way relationship.

Many happy years passed. At fourteen, Petey started to lose his luster but none of his love. However, like an old man who doesn't quite understand why life doesn't continue on the way it did when he was young, he had his crabby moments. Still, he was my beautiful boy, and we all moved to Albuquerque from New York when I took a pulpit out West. Both cats seemed to thrive on the changed atmosphere and seemed extremely happy in their new home.

One Monday, some months after the move, I took Petey to the vet to try to find out why he couldn't keep his food down. The doctor prescribed an enzyme powder, and Petey valiantly continued to eat, but to no avail. By Friday night, he was miserable. No matter how hard we tried to make him comfortable, he cried like a baby with the effort of walking, of settling in my lap, of pressing next to the windowpane's cold glass. We ached for him and for ourselves. Clearly he was saying goodbye, but he wasn't about to go easily.

At last, too exhausted to fight any longer, he slept fitfully in our bed between Mark and me. He held my hand between the still-strong grip of his paws as I held him in my arms and whispered my thanks and my love. All night long, I struggled between fighting to keep him and facing the reality of letting him go. In the morning we rushed him to the vet, but Petey had other ideas. He died as soon as we got him inside the office.

His death destroyed us. The price of love just then was the deepest pain imaginable as we wept uncontrollably. To make matters harder, Sabbath services would begin in two hours. How could I serve professionally when my heart had just been ripped in two? Only those who have had an animal in their home can fully understand that loss, no matter how much they sympathize with it. Would the rabbi and the congregation understand my sorrow over a cat?

But begging off was out of the question. We needed to be with our congregation in our spiritual home that morning.

When I arrived at the synagogue, Mark mourned in my study, calling friends and family who knew and loved Petey. I went to the rabbi and told him what had happened. His eyes were gentle and full of understanding, and I felt the genuine quality of his words of comfort. To my surprise, he said, "Do as much as you can this morning, and I will fill in when you falter. You need the support of your congregation today. And I think we should let people know what's happened after the service." His support buoyed me enough to manage through the service. My notes soared, but my customary ebullient sparkle was severely diminished. The rabbi knew that this would be noticed, and we would meet the consequent inquiries with honest answers.

Afterwards, I hesitated to greet the congregation one-on-one. I still wasn't sure how they would react to my grief over the loss of a cat. After all, I was their invincible cantor. With a slight sinking feeling, I noticed Mrs. Gold approaching me. For the last few months, I'd been directing her son in his religious studies and I found the Golds to be the most demanding, least flexible family I'd ever worked with. But as she got nearer, I saw compassion in her eyes. She took me gently into her arms, saying, "The rabbi told me about your Petey. I'm so sorry. It's hard to lose a dear friend."

When she released me, we smiled at each other, and both our faces were shining with tears.

And so it continued, members of the congregation clasping my hand or embracing me, as they spoke kind words of condolence. I saw that Mark was having the same experience. This wave of comfort poured over us like warm honey as we began to feel our grief over losing Petey.

And though we had lost a loved one, we'd found something, too—the people in our congregation, a large and loving family to share our lives with. While Petey lived, he brought people together, and our *Shabbos* cat continued to do so—even with his passing.

Jacqueline Shuchat-Marx

Circle of Love

Before my husband and I purchased a small ranch in Idaho that included fifty head of Herefords, I never really knew much about cows. I used to think they were large, not particularly bright creatures who spent peaceful uncomplicated lives grazing in green fields or napping in the sunshine. But once we started living on the ranch, I started to pay closer attention and learned to appreciate them on a deeper level.

I soon began to recognize the cows by their different markings, personalities and habits. I gave them all names, and they became my "pets"—in a wild sort of way. Two of my favorites were Freckles and her calf, Spunky.

Freckles first came to my attention early one spring. The cattle had spent the winter months on our lower pasture along the river, but when the cows started calving, we decided to move them to one of the upper pastures near our house. The move was uneventful, except that we discovered that one cow was missing. It was Freckles. We weren't alarmed because we assumed that she had probably given birth and was hiding in the thick patch of willows near the water. The birthing process is a private matter for most cows, and when labor begins they are quite clever at finding a hiding place away from the rest of the herd.

As we got near the bottom of the hill, Freckles came running out of the willows and headed across the field. A look of fury flashed in her eyes, as if to scold us for intruding. Her belly was considerably smaller since the last time I had seen her and her udder was swollen with milk. These were both signs that she had calved. My husband went after Freckles to coax her back, and I headed toward the willows to find her baby.

The calf was so still I almost tripped over her. Nestled in a soft hollow of spring grass was the most beautiful little creature I had ever seen. The calf was a dark russet color with a white spot on her forehead and a tuft of white at the end of her tail. She was curled up like a fawn and looked up at me with enormous brown eyes. I slowly knelt down and spoke softly as I reached out to stroke her velvety coat. She quivered under my touch, but she didn't move. She wouldn't even raise her head. She couldn't have been more than twenty-four hours old, but she had already learned how to stay put and be quiet.

My husband managed to guide Freckles back toward the willows and when she saw me she bellowed for her baby. In a flash, the little calf understood the command, bolted from her nest and ran bawling toward her mother. We stood back to watch as they came together. The calf reached for the comfort of warm milk while her mother licked her reassuringly.

Once they had calmed down, we walked them up the hill to join the herd. With her head held high and her tail bobbing like a pump handle, the calf pranced behind her mother. We laughed and christened her Spunky—a fitting name, as she turned out to be our liveliest and most mischievous calf that spring.

As we got closer, the other cows started calling to

Freckles. They bellowed back and forth, again and again, as if to guide her back to their new location, and they were all waiting by the fence when we arrived. As soon as we closed the gate behind them and moved away, they surrounded Freckles, and with nodding heads and soft lowing sounds they gently greeted her and inspected Spunky. Apparently satisfied, they slowly drifted apart and began to graze. A sense of peace and harmony was restored to their little community.

I was puzzled the first few times I saw a single cow surrounded by several little calves, until I learned that cattle herds establish unique baby-sitting co-ops. Once again, I was amazed at their ability to communicate. How did they decide who would be the baby-sitter? And how did the mothers tell the babies not to move while they wandered away, sometimes for several hours?

One day, I glanced out my kitchen window and was astounded to see Red Man, our huge twenty-five-hundred-pound bull, lying in the pasture with a group of calves. The cows had somehow persuaded him to baby-sit that day. At least fifteen tiny calves surrounded Red Man, all of them content to lie lazily in the sun, except for Spunky, who had obviously grown tired of nap time. She slowly stood up. Her rump came up first, followed by a long stretch extending to the tip of her tail. Then she shook her head, flicked her tail and seemed about to go romping across the field when Red Man lifted his massive head and gave her a disapproving glare. I watched, entranced. Would the tiny calf defy the giant Red Man? Not that day. Spunky gazed at the bull for a long moment, and then her legs seemed to melt back into the ground, once again the docile baby waiting for her mother to return.

One night, we woke up to the terrifying sounds of a pack of coyotes on the hunt. Barking and howling, they raced down the hill behind our ranch and into the pasture where the cattle had settled for the night. Young calves were their favorite prey. The cattle stampeded in their panic to escape from the pack. My husband grabbed the shotgun and ran outdoors. A few shots fired into the air were enough to scare the coyotes, and we stood there listening to them yip and howl as they disappeared into the night. The herd had been badly frightened and their restless bawling went on for hours. But other than that, all was well.

Or so we thought. At daybreak we went out to check. All the animals were unharmed—except for one. We found a dead calf near some rocks, apparently killed in the stampede. My heart nearly stopped beating when I saw the white spot on its forehead, but it wasn't Spunky. It was a younger calf with similar markings. We carried the little body close to the gate and covered it with a tarp until we could bury it.

A while later, I heard a cow bawling. I looked around and saw the mother of the dead calf nudging it with her nose. Then I watched as Freckles and eleven other cows slowly walked over and formed a circle around them. One by one they began to bawl with the mother. The low, mournful tones of their lamentation drifted across the land as the morning sun rose.

As I watched them, I, too, became a member of their circle; I was one with them in their grief for the little life that had been, and was no more.

The cows stayed in that circle of love for over an hour. Finally, the mother backed away, turned and walked to a far corner of the pasture. Only then did the others end their vigil and move quietly away.

I stood rapt and motionless in the now-silent pasture, feeling the depth of their compassion in my own heart. Filled with awe and admiration for these animals, I turned back towards the house—that rare and tender scene firmly etched in my mind.

Maria Sears

One Last Gift

"Mom, I'm taking Snowflake to the vet on Saturday." My son slumped in the high-backed chair next to my hospital bed. "He doesn't seem right to me. I think he's got a cough, and he won't eat."

"I'll be home before then," I told him. "The doctor has promised you and Dad can bring me home tomorrow." I knocked hopefully on the plastic bed table strewn with get-well cards and half-finished glasses of stale ginger ale.

We'd had Snowflake for ten years. He was a black Lab with just enough setter in him to give him long legs and a scrap of white hair on his chest. We brought him home in a snowstorm just before Christmas, all huge puppy feet and a black tail far too long. We named him Snowflake for the storm and for the bit of white hair. He arrived just after my first bout with colon cancer when I was still struggling to make sense of the new and terrifying challenge in my life.

During the next months, Snowflake became my friend and companion. No matter how frightened or depressed I was, he needed to be cared for. We walked together through that snowy winter, his leash tangling around my legs. I watched him bound through snowbanks that nearly buried him. I swear he learned to grin at me as he dug through the snow, shaking the icy flakes off his whiskers.

I got better. I thought less of cancer and more of living. Snowflake got tall and leggy. He learned to walk at heel, although he never was very good at coming when called. He'd come within a few feet, toss me his catch-me-if-you-can look and wait until I got close before he ran just out of reach. I'd turn around to go in the house, and he'd finally follow, refusing to be ignored—a good dog, but one with an independent streak, a little like me.

He loved to run through the woods on the state land near our house. He galloped in wide circles while I walked and daydreamed or picked blueberries. Snowflake would find a stick for me to throw, or a rabbit to chase back into its hole.

It was eight years before the cancer returned. A new tumor in my colon sent me back to the hospital for more surgery. I began a year-long series of weekly chemotherapy injections that left me feeling sick most of the time. Early in the morning, Snowflake walked with me along an old canal towpath. The steady walking relaxed me, and the fresh morning air settled my stomach.

He had long since outgrown the bounding leaps of puppyhood. He walked more sedately now. I'd let him off his leash, and he'd take up a position about eight feet ahead of me, keeping pace and returning immediately to my side when I called. The old game of catch-me-if-you-can was gone, almost as if he knew I had little energy to chase him now. Occasionally he ran down the canal bank barking madly at a passing duck, but mostly he walked steadily ahead of me, turning every so often to check that I was keeping up.

So we walked through that spring and into the summer and into a new diagnosis. I found a lump in my breast that proved, after more surgery, to be breast cancer. I resumed chemotherapy and began daily radiation treatments. For several months I was too exhausted for our morning walks. Snowflake lay beside my bed, his brown eyes half closed.

Toward the end of winter, I began to feel stronger. The dog and I returned to the canal in the morning, walking carefully along the snow-covered towpath.

It was eighteen months before cancer struck again. A new tumor appeared on an ovary. So after Christmas, I left Snowflake once again to go into the hospital. As usual, he begged to go in the car. His white hair was no longer confined to the bit on snow on his chest. His face was almost entirely white and arthritis made his back legs stiff.

I woke from the anesthesia to hopeful news. The cancer appeared not to have spread. There was a good chance that I could get well. But I kept having the thought that there are only so many chances, only so many times to dodge a bullet.

Still I did all the things necessary to recover from surgery. I blew into a small plastic tube designed to exercise my lungs. I got painfully out of bed. I shuffled down the hall pushing my IV pole. I graduated from ice chips to sips of ginger ale and bites of lemon Jell-O.

Now, almost ready to go home, I listened to my son's worries about Snowflake's cough, his lethargy and refusal to eat.

"Don't worry," my husband said. "Maybe he just misses you."

The next day my husband packed me and my awkward baskets full of get-well flowers into the car. It was icy cold outside, almost zero, and snowing.

Snowflake was at the door, of course, almost his old self, wagging his tail and rubbing his ears under my hand. "He hasn't been coughing today," my son told me. "I think he might be better."

I curled up on the sofa in the bright winter light from the big windows, and the dog lay down beside me. My husband made a fire and fell asleep in the recliner. So we spent that first afternoon home.

That evening I went to bed early, tired from the effort of leaving the hospital, but I couldn't fall asleep. In my head I went over the doctor's words again and again. I thought about the first colon cancer and the second one, the breast cancer, and now ovarian cancer. I thought about dying and how afraid I was.

"Kate," my husband called from the living room about eleven o'clock. "I think you should come here. Something's wrong with the dog."

Snowflake was lying on his side in front of the fire. His breathing was harsh and slow. When he saw me, he lifted his head and moved as if to get up, but his legs crumpled under him.

I sat down on the floor and put his head in my lap. His huge brown eyes looked up at me, and his breathing seemed to ease a bit. I sat there no more than ten minutes, silent in the firelight with Snowflake's head in my lap. Then, with a sigh so soft I nearly missed it, he closed his eyes and stopped breathing.

"You waited for me to get home," I whispered.

I sat there for a long while, the dog motionless in my arms, thinking of the gentleness and peace of his death, the silence that had filled us both. For the first time since I had been diagnosed with cancer, I felt no fear.

"You waited for me," I whispered again, tears in my eyes, "to show me not to be afraid."

Kate Murphy

$\overline{\underline{9}}$

ON COMPANIONSHIP

In order to keep a true perspective of one's importance, everyone should have a dog that will worship him and a cat that will ignore him.

Dereke Bruce

"Look at that crazy cowboy, Butch,
he's talking to his horse."

Soldier Dog

During the monsoon season of 1968, after several months of combat following the Tet Offensive, my army unit was moved from the mountains of northern South Vietnam to the coastal plain, north of Da Nang. We had been assigned to provide security for a battalion of Seabees. It rained torrentially for most of each day and night, but we tried to stay as warm and dry as we could.

As a medic, my life was pretty good at this assignment. I didn't have to pull guard duty, just hold sick call and do radio watch for a couple of hours each night. Sure, I was halfway around the world, separated from my family and my home, but the Seabees had supplies. We even got fresh food, which sure beat the freeze-dried and canned rations that were issued for consumption in the jungle. But best of all, I could buy a beer each evening and relax and try to forget the terror that had been with me since the beginning of the Tet Offensive.

I was aware of the dramatic changes my personality had undergone in the short time I had been in Vietnam. I distrusted everything and everyone I came in contact with. Like the times when I treated Vietnamese civilians in their villages for their ailments.

This was an attempt by the army to win the hearts and minds of the local population. The army's public information officer wanted some photographs showing that the First Brigade of the 101st Airborne, the toughest of the tough, was also the most caring. On such occasions, the villagers would lay out a meal, sometimes consisting of rice and meat, with great formality. This was intended as a respectful greeting to me, and courtesy demanded that I eat first. But I was suspicious, and fearing that the food might be poisoned, I always insisted that the Village Chief be the first to take a bite, thus managing to thoroughly offend our hosts. But I didn't care; my sole concern at that time was surviving to make it home.

One night, after some revelry in the galley, I walked back to our camp and knelt down to slide into my damp living space. As I crawled in headfirst, I felt a wet, furry body brush my forehead. I grabbed my pistol and my flashlight and prepared to kill the rat in my bedroll.

But it wasn't a rat. In the light, I saw before me a shivering brown puppy that looked like a Chihuahua. Its big eyes were imploring, as if it knew that its life was almost over. I reengaged the safety catch and picked up the little body, so cold, so wet and so scared. *We're a lot alike*, I thought.

I dug around in my gear and found a can of beef slices from an old meal unit. I opened the can, broke up the meat into little bites, and put it in front of this intruder, who snapped it up quickly. Then I rinsed the can out and filled it with clean water so he could drink.

That night, when I curled up to go to sleep, I wasn't remembering the girl back home; I had a living, breathing being snuggled next to me trying to gain security and warmth from my existence. And I didn't dream of the girl back home, either. Instead I dreamed of my beagle, who always curled up at the foot of my bed when I came home from school on vacations, and who went with me everywhere.

The next morning, I went to breakfast and got extra eggs, bacon and sausages. My new little friend wolfed them down.

I decided to name him Charger, after our battalion commander. Every time I called out "Charger!" I offered him a tidbit of food, so he learned his name in no time. He also learned some simple tricks, and seemed to grow very attached to me. Wherever I went, that little ring-tailed mutt of dubious parentage was right there with me, and I grew very fond of him.

One day I was in the nearby village of Lang Co, where I went every day except Sunday, to treat the villagers for their various ailments, which ranged from ringworm and pinworm to elephantiasis. While I dispensed different pills and salves, I noticed my little friend frolicking with the fire team that had accompanied me for security. As I watched him darting after the sticks they threw for him and prancing proudly back with the stick clamped firmly in his teeth, I had to smile. I turned back to the Vietnamese child I was examining, and I saw an answering smile light up his small face. Little Charger was effecting a remarkable change in my personality. I realized that I had begun to care about the local people. I really wanted to cure their illnesses, whereas earlier I had just been going through the motions to please the army public relations machine. Charger was helping me to recover some of the humanity that I feared I had lost.

I was soon to be separated from my new friend, however. After a few short weeks, my company was ordered back to the mountains. After numerous inquiries, I was able to find someone in the mortar platoon at our battalion fire base to adopt Charger. I left him there, knowing that I would miss him but trying not to look back as I

walked with my company toward the jungle, returning to
the harsh reality of war.

I served more than seven months with the infantry,
before I was reassigned to a medevac unit. I had not forgotten Charger, and as I came through the fire base on my way
to my new assignment, I had already decided that I would
bring my little friend with me to my new unit. We recognized each other instantly, and our reunion was ecstatic.

I spent the day at the fire base and soon noticed that
something was different there. Talking with the soldiers, I
registered that the level of profanity and vulgarity had
dropped. And the men seemed more caring towards each
other. A large number of them called to Charger as he
trotted by, often stopping to scratch his head or give him
a treat or two in passing. Charger was working the same
magic for his new friends in the mortar platoon that he
had worked for me.

With my heart breaking, and on the verge of tears, I left
Charger with his newfound friends, for they seemed to
need him even more than I did.

That was the last time I ever saw Charger. My medevac
chopper was shot down about two months later. I was
evacuated, and regained consciousness in a hospital in
Japan. I tried to find out about Charger, but only heard a
vague rumor that he had been taken back to the States. I
hoped it was true.

I still remember him now, more than thirty years later.
He lives on in my heart. And whenever I think back to
that rainy and miserable night in Vietnam when our paths
first crossed, it seems impossible to know just who rescued whom.

Ron St. James

Mr. Reed

People often ask me why I've devoted half of my fifty-eight years to working with pet birds. I usually answer by recounting the story of Mr. Reed.

We first met in the early 1980s. Back then Mr. Reed was like many of the elderly people I encountered in nursing homes and senior citizen residences near the pet store I run. The Great Depression had stripped Mr. Reed early in life not only of his money and pride but also of his ability to trust in mankind. As far as I knew, he had never married, he had no children, and after four decades of isolation in different institutions, he was withdrawn and uncommunicative.

Now in his eighties, Mr. Reed hid his loneliness behind thick black-rimmed glasses that dwarfed his weathered blue eyes. He shuffled about inside the quiet nursing home, unwilling to smile or converse with anyone. Mr. Reed's only companions, it seemed to me, were whatever memories he kept to himself.

Yet, despite his aloofness, Mr. Reed was always quite interested in the activities going on in the nursing home lobby. On this particular day I arrived with a pair of gregarious green lovebirds. They were about five inches long, chunky in stature, with blue rumps and bright peach-colored foreheads.

I was scheduled to deliver the two lovebirds for placement inside this nursing home's lobby, where I hoped they would enliven the sterile surroundings. Although the nursing home's staff was officially responsible for the care of the animals, lonesome patients looking for companionship often assumed the feeding and other responsibilities themselves. Birds made particularly suitable pets in a location like this because they stayed caged, were often chatty and could eat almost any type of people food without fear of upset tummies. Looking after the birds often instilled a sense of purpose in the patients' otherwise monotonous lives. As for the birds, they were blessed with attentive care from people who had few other obligations.

That fall day I situated the pair of lovebirds in a semi-circular silver cage, which I hung against a wall next to a fading picture of the home's rather stern-looking founder. Underneath the cage, I placed a small book about their care. The barren, medicinal-smelling lobby quickly warmed with the delightful sound of their chirping and wing-flapping.

Seniors passed by with their walkers and canes, peering at the creatures. Although a few residents seemed wary, most could barely conceal their curiosity, pointing wrinkled fingers at the cage and grinning when the birds jumped about.

Mr. Reed, meanwhile, circled the room nervously, keeping to himself and trying to conceal his interest in the excited lovebirds. Finally, after the room cleared out for lunch, he stopped directly beside their cage. Glancing to see who was watching, he picked up the bird book, eased into a nearby chair and began reading. For hours he remained by the birds' side, studiously examining the guide.

When my day's visit ended, I approached him cautiously. "Would you like to help take care of these birds for a few days?" I asked. He looked up, his dulled eyes flickering behind his glasses. Then he nodded, a tiny tentative smile creeping onto his lips.

As the weeks progressed, I learned from the nursing home staff that Mr. Reed had gradually assumed all the care and feeding of the lovebirds. One morning I received a call from the home saying Mr. Reed felt the birds were ready to mate. I drove over to check, and indeed, Mr. Reed's diagnosis was correct—it seems he'd learned a great deal from studying the little book I'd left behind. Together, Mr. Reed and I offered the lovebirds a small wooden box, which they gladly accepted and began filling with shredded newspaper and other materials to create a nest. Throughout the afternoon, as Mr. Reed watched protectively, the carefree birds sang love songs and bustled about constructing a fine crib for their eggs.

A few days later I stopped by to appraise the lovebirds' progress and noticed a very odd white and brown material lining the nest. "What a strange-looking nest, Mr. Reed," I noted. "Do you mind my asking what's in there?"

"Toast," he replied in a proud voice. "Every morning I save a piece of my breakfast toast for the birds. They seem to like it."

I nodded and marveled at the profound change in this man. Not long ago he had been tired and reclusive; now he interacted regularly with the staff while caring for these lovebirds with the devotion of a conscientious innkeeper. Watching them eat and nest, he would chuckle as they bobbed their heads about, dancing as if they knew it brought him pleasure. After years of speaking only when spoken to, Mr. Reed would invite other residents to witness the lovebirds' antics.

These creatures, I realized, had become much more

than transient boarders passing through Mr. Reed's life. If their relationship had begun as tenant and landlord, the birds and Mr. Reed were now each other's only family. Through some mutual agreement struck gradually over mornings of shared breakfast and evenings of simple conversation, the birds had decided to keep Mr. Reed, and he in turn agreed to spend his remaining years with them. It seemed a fair bargain.

Soon the lovebirds produced two charming babies whom we moved into Mr. Reed's room, along with their mother and father. The babies also attached themselves to Mr. Reed, and we trimmed their wing feathers so they could venture outside their cage to interact with him.

Several times I saw him gently placing one of the baby birds in the trembling hands of other senior citizens, assuring them that the birds would cause no harm. Every Sunday there was at least one resident whose family would fail to show up for a visit as promised. Mr. Reed always made certain the lovebirds spent extra time cuddling in the arms of that senior. In many ways Mr. Reed became the center of social activity at the home.

One winter evening, after a pleasant dinner with his chattering charges, Mr. Reed went to bed, as usual, at nine o'clock. The next morning, when the lovebirds cried for his attention, he did not wake up, for sometime in the predawn hours, Mr. Reed had died peacefully in his sleep.

To this day I keep a picture of Mr. Reed in my store. In the photo, the little lovebirds are cuddling beneath the crisp collar of an old man's shirt, their green heads peeking out to rest on his fuzzy black cardigan. But it is his face that my eye always returns to. It is alight with affection and love—the face of a man surrounded by his family.

Ruth Hanessian with Wendy Bounds
Excerpted from Birds on the Couch

A Moggy for Michael

By associating with the cat, one only risks becoming richer.

Colette

One summer evening, about eight o'clock, the phone rang. "Sherlock Bones, here," I said.

"Are you the man that looks for lost cats?" a child's voice asked.

"That's right," I replied. "What can I do for you?"

"I want you to help me find Sam. He's gray with black stripes. My mom gave him to me, but he's been gone four days."

"I see. Could I talk to your mom for a minute?" Whenever kids call me, I make sure to talk to their parents and let them know what's going on. In a minute, a man came to the phone.

"I'm Mike's father," he said. "My wife has passed away. We already put an ad in the paper. I told Mike we couldn't afford anything else. That kid's pestering the daylights out of me over that cat."

"Well, kids get attached to their pets," I said. "Especially since his mom gave him Sam, he's probably—"

"That's just it," he replied. "When she died, he was a regular little soldier—no crying, nothing. I was real proud of him. It's been almost six months now, and he's been doing fine—until this business with the cat. Look, I gotta go to work."

Mike got back on the phone. I asked him where he lived. "Why don't I stop by and we can talk some more about Sam?"

"Okay," he said eagerly. "And about what my dad said . . . well, I've got some money saved up, almost twelve dollars. Is that enough?"

In my career people have offered me hundreds and even thousands of dollars to find their missing pets, but no one had ever promised me everything he had. I could see this was a case I was going to have to take.

Mike answered the door. He was a small, dark-haired kid, maybe ten years old, with pale skin and big brown eyes. With his mother recently dead, and his father working at two jobs, Mike was on his own most of the time. No wonder the kid was so anxious to get his cat back.

Mike told me Sam hadn't been wearing a collar, but he did have a distinguishing feature—an egg-shaped white spot on his chest.

"That's what we'll put on the poster," I said and explained about putting up posters and checking the animal shelters. "I'll let you know as soon as I hear anything," I said, walking to the door.

He looked so forlorn I said, "Hey, Mike, tell you what. You can be my assistant, and I'll give you a reduced rate." We spent the day working together.

The next day I was putting up a poster in the window of a supermarket when I noticed it had an old-fashioned meat counter—the kind with a butcher. When I was a kid, our butcher knew the name of every pet in our neighborhood.

"Excuse me," I said, "have you heard of anyone finding a cat recently? Gray with black stripes, white spot on its chest?"

"Have you talked to the cat lady?" the butcher asked me. "She comes in once a week and loads up on fish scraps and bones for her cats. She must have a houseful."

That afternoon, I went to the cat lady's house and rang the doorbell. The door opened a crack, and a voice called out in a strong English accent, "Yes, ducks, what is it?"

I handed her one of my cards, and said, "I help people find missing pets."

"Do ya, now?" she said amiably and opened the door. "Mind me moggies," she warned.

Once inside, I saw them: on the stairs, on the table, on the floor, on the chairs, scampering out of my way, crouching watchfully—there were cats everywhere.

She led me into the kitchen. "Have a seat, luv," she said. "I'm Mrs. Bentwhistle, and I'm goin' to make us a nice cuppa."

"My," I said, unable to avoid commenting on the obvious, "you certainly have a lot of cats."

"You like me moggies, do ya?" she said with a bright smile.

"Moggies?"

"That's right, moggies. Me mum come from Lancashire, and that's what she called 'em, and so do I."

She was a short, wide woman somewhere in her late sixties, I judged. Her gray hair was caught in the back with a couple of combs. Bright pink lipstick and rouge were enthusiastically if erratically applied.

She poured in the tea, and handed me mine. I took a sip and almost gagged.

"How do ya like it, then?" she asked.

"Oh," I replied weakly. "It's . . . um . . . tasty. Very unusual."

"Nothin' like it," she agreed, taking a good swallow.

"Mrs. Bentwhistle, I'm looking for a cat—gray with black stripes."

"Gaw!" she exclaimed, "I got millions of 'em. Why don't ya have yourself a look? It's almost feedin' time." She lifted the lid of an enormous pot and a terrible aroma escaped.

"Come on, grub's up," she yelled.

Suddenly the place was alive with furry bodies. Within five minutes the food was gone and so were the cats.

"There," she said with satisfaction. "Did ya find the one ya were lookin' for, then?"

"I'm afraid I didn't," I said. I explained about Mike and his cat. "He was very brave," I said. "*Too* brave."

"Oh, it's a crying shame," Mrs. Bentwhistle said sympathetically. "Here, why don't ya come back tomorrow and have another look? I get new ones every day."

The next day, over tea, Mrs. Bentwhistle told me that she and her husband had come to this country toward the end of World War II from their home in bombed-out East London.

"We had a good life here, Ernie and me. He's been gone now almost ten years, rest his soul. Still, I've got me moggies to look after. But poor Mikey, all these moggies, and none of 'em Sam."

With her permission I called in to the office for messages. Someone had seen the body of a cat in some bushes not far from Mike's house. Dejected, I hung up and told Mrs. Bentwhistle I was afraid I had come to the end of my search.

I found the cat where I had been told to look, and its markings matched Sam's exactly. I gingerly placed the body in a box, and with a heavy heart drove to Mike's house.

Mike answered the door. "Hi," he said eagerly. "Did you find Sam?"

"I have some bad news for you, Mike. Sam's dead."

The blood drained from his face.

Mike said nothing as we went about laying Sam to rest. I was worried and didn't want to leave him by himself. Then I thought of something.

"Tell you what, Mike," I said, "there's a nice lady not far from here who's got quite a few cats. How's about we pay her a visit?"

"Okay," he replied passively.

"Mrs. Bentwhistle," I said quickly when she answered the door, "I brought Mike. We just buried Sam."

"Come in," she said. "You're just in time for a lovely cuppa tea."

As soon as Mike sat down, a small black cat jumped up on his lap, and he stroked it mechanically.

"Now then," she said affably, passing out the tea and settling into her chair, "you lost your moggy, is that it?"

"That's what Mrs. Bentwhistle calls cats, Mike," I explained.

"Yes," he said in a frighteningly matter-of-fact tone. "He was hit by a car."

"Ain't that a shame," she sighed, sipping her tea and shaking her head. "And to think your mum gave Sam to you. Ya know, lad, it reminds me of me own mum."

Mike looked up.

"Right before she died she gave me a set of dishes. Beautiful blue dishes, they was, me pride and joy, and I kept 'em in the front room where everyone could see 'em. Well, wouldn't you know, one afternoon one of Hitler's bleedin' buzz bombs up and smashed half the house. But all I cared about was them dishes. I just felt so bad, because me mum give 'em to me."

Mike stopped stroking the cat.

"Course it wasn't me fault," she continued, "but I still felt bad. It's a bit like you and Sam, ain't it? Now he's been done in, but it weren't your fault. Your mum knows that. Your mum still loves you, just like me mum loves me," she said softly. "Well, that's enough about that. Can't hang your hat on the past, as ya might say." She paused. "What about the moggy on your lap? How would you like to have him?"

Mike didn't say anything.

"Come on now, lad," she insisted. "Do you want him?"

Mike shook his head vehemently. "I don't want him," he cried. "I want Sam!"

And Mike bolted out of the room. I started after him, but Mrs. Bentwhistle stopped me.

"Leave him be," she said. "He needs a good cry. Lads has got to be on their ownsome when they cry. I know a thing or two about lads as well as moggies."

Soon Mrs. Bentwhistle got up and limped down the hall. Finally, they reappeared, Mike red-eyed, and Mrs. Bentwhistle with her arm around his shoulder.

Mike glanced at me and almost smiled. "Mrs. Bentwhistle told me I can help her feed the cats whenever I want to."

"I think that's a fine idea," I said. I wondered what it was Mrs. Bentwhistle had said to Mike; he no longer seemed to be carrying such a heavy burden.

"And did you know Mrs. Bentwhistle had a little boy once?" Mike said. "He got killed in the war."

"Hush now," she interrupted. Then to me she said, "You can run along now. It's time for Mikey and me to feed the moggies."

I drove home with my head full of awe at the unseen forces that had used the tragedy of a boy's dead pet to bring two lonely people together.

A few weeks later, I gave Mrs. Bentwhistle a call. "How's everything?" I asked.

"Couldn't be better, luv," she replied cheerily. "Mikey's a lovely lad. He helps with the moggies and goin' to the store. Don't know what I did without him. Oh, and he took that little black moggy home with him." She laughed. "He said it was just for a bit, but he don't fool me. He's a stubborn one, he is."

"Mike stubborn?" I said.

"Oh yes!" she exclaimed. "He won't drink me tea! Did ya ever hear the like? But don't you worry, he'll come 'round. We'll make a proper lad of him yet, just you see."

John Keane (a.k.a. Sherlock Bones)

Double Duty

Life + a cat . . . adds up to an incalculable sum.

Rainer Maria Rilke

As a member of a "dog family," I had long been conditioned to believe that cats simply didn't possess the ability or desire to be loving companions. This belief was so deeply ingrained that, while I didn't actually dislike cats, I found them, for the most part, uninteresting.

Arriving home from work one afternoon, I discovered a cat at my doorstep. I ignored him, but apparently he was not offended, because he was there again the following day.

"I'll pet you," I told him, "but there's no way you're coming in."

Then one night soon after, as the rain beat down and thunder clapped, I heard a faint meow. I couldn't take it anymore; I became a cat owner.

My new roommate, now named Shotzy, quickly became more than just a stray cat to feed. I liked the way his soft purring greeted me every morning and the way he nudged his head against my leg when I came home each day. His playful antics made me laugh, and soon Shotzy seemed more like a longtime friend than a pet I hadn't really wanted.

Although I suspected Shotzy had been an outdoor cat for a good portion of his life, he seemed perfectly content to stay inside, except for one remarkable exception. As if an alarm had gone off, at about six o'clock every night he'd cry to go out. Then, almost exactly one hour later, he'd be back. He did this for several months before I finally discovered what he had been up to.

One day a neighbor who knew about Shotzy showing up at my doorstep told me she thought the cat might belong to an elderly woman who lived down the street. Worried that I had mistakenly adopted someone's pet, I took Shotzy to the woman's house the next day.

When a white-haired woman opened the door, Shotzy bolted from my arms, ran into the house and made himself at home in a big recliner. The woman just threw her head back and laughed, saying, "Jimmy always did love his chair."

My heart sank—my Shotzy was obviously her Jimmy.

I explained I had taken him in and only discovered the day before that he may have already had a home. Again, the old woman chuckled. She invited me in and explained that the cat did not belong to her.

"But, I thought you called him Jimmy," I questioned.

The woman, who said her name was Mary, explained that Jimmy was her husband's name. He had died about a year before, just a few months after being diagnosed with cancer.

Before Jimmy died, he and Mary would eat dinner at five o'clock every night.

Afterward, they would retire to the living room, Jimmy to his favorite chair, to talk about the day's events. The couple had followed that routine every night for the sixty years they were married. After Jimmy's death, with no other family nearby, Mary said she just felt lost. And more than anything, she missed their nightly after-dinner talks.

Then one night a stray cat meowed demandingly at her screen door. When she cracked open the door to shoo him away, he ran straight to Jimmy's chair and made himself comfortable, as if he had lived there forever.

Mary, who had never had a pet in her life, found herself smiling at the animal. She gave him a little milk and then he cuddled on her lap. She talked to him about her life, but mostly about Jimmy. At about seven o'clock, at which time she normally turned on the TV and made herself some hot tea, the creature slipped off her lap and went to the door. At six o'clock the next evening, the cat was back. Soon, Shotzy and Mary had their own routine.

"Now, I believe in the Good Lord," Mary told me. "I don't know about all that reincarnation stuff, but sometimes it feels just like I'm talking to Jimmy when that little cat is here. I know that sounds strange, and I guess what's important is that the cat is a real comfort to me. But it's interesting to think on, all the same."

So Mary and I continued to share Shotzy. At my house, he revealed to me the many daily joys that come with living with a cat. At Mary's, his presence served to fill the six o'clock hour with happy companionship.

Our marvelous cat seemed to have an uncanny knack for always being in the right place at the right time.

Lisa Hurt

An American Cat in Paris

When people think of pets in France, they think dogs. Dogs being served little platters of steak tartare in fine restaurants. Tiny, fluffy poodles poking their heads out of fashionable pocketbooks.

As for my wife and me, when we think back on the two years we lived on rue St. Didier in Paris, we think of a very different sort of pet. We think of Chuck. Our Rhode Island-bred, orange-and-white, tiger-striped, lazy, hungry and sometimes biting cat, Chuck.

Not long before moving to our cramped sixth-floor Parisian apartment, we were introduced to Chuck at the Providence Animal Rescue League. Unlike the kittens there who eagerly poked their paws through the bars of their cages, Chuck just sat on a little shelf in the back of his pen and looked up at us with a wounded expression. "I know you're not going to choose me since I'm a full-grown cat," he seemed to be saying, "so I'm not going to try and sell myself."

But when my wife gently lifted him out and gave him a hug, Chuck allowed himself to purr very softly, and we adopted him on the spot. A few months later, when it became clear that we would have to move overseas because of her job, most French people we talked to urged us to bring our new pal along. But our American friends did not agree.

"It wouldn't be fair to him," said one friend. "He's just getting used to life as a housecat." Still, it didn't take long for us to decide that Chuck was now a full-fledged member of the family, and where we went, he went. I think we said something like, "Chuck is used to our routines, and we don't want to break that up." Inside, we knew that it was the two of us who were used to *Chuck's* routines, and we badly wanted his comforting presence in a big, foreign city where we knew not a soul.

During those first few months in Paris, when we could understand little that was said to us, were afraid to speak up in stores and restaurants, and felt like strangers right down to the soles of our shoes, Chuck's new European-style habits gave us much-needed laughter and encouragement. He was delighted with French food—*Friskies au boeuf,* to be exact—and he cheerfully rode the bus to his veterinarian in a cat carrier that allowed curious passengers a full view of his impressive orange-and-white mane.

"*Il est superb!*" exclaimed one delighted French matron with a boxy hat and high-necked Chanel suit. A construction worker from Madrid gravely examined and lightly prodded him then, despite our objections, declared that "he *must* be Spanish." Chuck even developed a nodding friendship with a nightingale that sang its song each evening from on top of a nearby hotel. And he made us realize, seeing his round, fluffy shape up in one of our many windowsills, that we were not, in fact, alone.

We soon found out, however, that the French windows Chuck loved so much could swing wide during a windy night, as could the French doors that led to our minuscule balcony. When my wife awoke for work one morning and saw those doors banging in the wind, she instinctively began to search the apartment. Chuck wasn't in any of his usual hiding places and since the drop from our balcony was probably a fatal one, we feared and expected the worst.

The sidewalk below held no clues, nor did the neighbors we questioned in nervous, flailing bursts of English and French. We tried taping cardboard signs with a crayon drawing of Chuck and our phone number up and down rue St. Didier, but as the day passed by, we felt more and more hopeless. An indoor cat whose claws had been taken out by a previous owner, Chuck wouldn't have known what to do or where to turn if he had found himself without a roof over his head. And now it was getting dark. *"Bon courage,"* said our concierge clasping her tortoiseshell cat Violette in strong arms, *"bon courage."*

The hours dragged on that night, and eventually my wife and I came to terms with the simple fact that we had lost our best friend.

"It's my fault," I said again and again. "I should have put in locks or something so he couldn't get out."

"No, it's both our faults," said my wife. "We should have let Chuck stay in Rhode Island where he would have been safe. I can't get over how empty it feels in here without him, and this is how it's going to be from now on."

The apartment seemed to hold nothing but useless Friskies boxes, sweaters with orange-and-white hair on them and cat toys that jingled as we accidentally brushed past them. My wife tried taking a bath, but it wasn't a *real* bath without Chuck there to jump up on the bidet and watch the water foam and gurgle as it swirled down the drain. I tried flipping through *Paris Match,* but what was the point without the fat, furry body that always inserted itself if you spread open a magazine or book.

It was early the next morning when the telephone jangled us out of sleep. "I theenk I have your cat," said the voice, and proceeded to give an address at the far end of our long St. Didier block. Though I didn't believe it could possibly be Chuck, I grabbed his basket and ran as if pushed along by little jet-puffs of hope.

I can't remember now what the building looked like or the elevator that took me to the seventh floor. All I can recall is the image of the chubby, long-haired pet we had brought to Paris from Providence lounging casually in the corner of this stranger's bedroom and looking about as pompous as I had ever seen him.

"Chuck jumped through the bedroom window of a sleeping Frenchman," was how my wife ended up describing the whole thing at work the next day, "after leaping from balcony to rooftop to balcony to balcony." Several times she and I walked along rue St. Didier pointing skyward to trace the truly impossible route. Several times we agreed that there was just no way a shelter cat with no claws should have been able to traverse so many slippery rooftops.

When visitors came to our small apartment in the weeks and months after that, they never failed to comment on the green garden fencing that was sloppily nailed over each of our lovely French windows. Most also noticed the rickety wooden gate I had hammered into place to block the door to our balcony. "Why are you obscuring these beautiful views?" they would ask. "And why did you put that fence in front of such an ornate, Parisian patio?"

When my wife and I heard this we would simply smile at each other and explain nothing. But as a certain orange friend purred safely down in the crack between two couch pillows, we would think, "Chuck has had *his* Paris adventure. Now it's time for him to stay put, so we can have ours."

Peter Mandel

Waiting at the Door

My grandmother became a widow in 1970. Shortly after that, we went to the animal shelter to pick out a puppy to keep her company. Grandma decided on a little terrier that had a reddish-brown spot above each eye. Because of these spots, the dog was promptly named Penny.

Grandma and Penny quickly became very attached to each other, but that attachment grew much stronger about three years later when Grandma had a stroke. Grandma could no longer work, so when she came home from the hospital, she and Penny were constant companions.

After her stroke, it became a real problem for Grandma to let Penny in and out because the door was at the bottom of a flight of stairs. So a mechanism using a rope and pulley was installed from the back door to a handle at the top of the stairs. Grandma just had to pull the handle to open and close the door. If the store was out of Penny's favorite dog food, Grandma would make one of us cook Penny browned beef with diced potatoes in it. I can remember teasing my grandmother that she loved that dog better than she loved her family.

As the years passed, Grandma and Penny became inseparable. Grandma's old house could be filled to the brim with people, but if Grandma went to take her nap, Penny walked along beside her and stayed by her side until she awoke. As Penny aged, she could no longer jump up on the bed to lay next to Grandma, so she laid on the rug beside the bed. If Grandma went into the bathroom, Penny would hobble along beside her, wait outside the door and accompany her back to the bed or chair. Grandma never went anywhere without her faithful companion by her side.

The time came when both my grandmother and Penny's health were failing fast. Penny couldn't get around very well, and Grandma had been hospitalized several times. My uncle and I lived with Grandma, so Penny was never left alone, even when Grandma was in the hospital. During these times, Penny sat at the window looking out for the car bringing Grandma home and would excitedly wait at the door when Grandma came through it. Each homecoming was a grand reunion between the two.

On Christmas Day in 1985, Grandma was again taken to the hospital. Penny, as usual, sat watching out the window for the car bringing Grandma home. Two mornings later when the dog woke up, she couldn't seem to work out the stiffness in her hips as she usually did. That same morning, she began having seizures. At age fifteen, we knew it was time. My mother and aunt took her to the veterinarian and stayed with her until the end.

Now the big dilemma was whether to tell Grandma while she was still in the hospital or wait. The decision was made to tell her while she was in the hospital because when we pulled up at the house, the first thing Grandma would look for was her beloved Penny watching out the window and then happily greeting her at the door. Grandma shed some tears but said she knew that it had to be done so Penny wouldn't suffer.

That night while still in the hospital, Grandma had a massive heart attack. The doctors frantically worked on her but could not revive her. After fifteen years of loving companionship, Grandma and Penny passed away within a few hours of each other. God had it all worked out— Penny *was* waiting at the door when Grandma came Home.

Barbara J. Crocker

Flying Free

For the first twelve years after I took over this farm of ours, there wasn't a goose on the place. Then one June morning, a sad-faced lad of ten came up the road with five downy goslings peering over the rim of a basket, "The old man says we got to move again," he said. "To town this time. These here's pets. They'd follow me to hell an' gone."

I paid ten dollars for the lot, and before the day was out they were following *me* to hell an' gone. It could be quite funny to have them always tangled around your feet if you could take the time to laugh at it. But it was down-right exasperating when you had to get somewhere.

Soon the goslings grew saucy, roamed farther afield, and their feather stubs began to stab through the yellow and gray down. They became gawky and insatiably curious about everything on the farm. Across the road, my neighbor, Walter, began to watch the goslings instead of television. Walter was reporting to the doctor rather often now and wore a pacemaker. He didn't move too fast or too far anymore.

"I've seen geese before," he said, "but these are different. They're really clowns, these. I sit here half the afternoon sometimes just laughing at them."

He'd been an outdoorsman all of his life. It seemed to me that a man who used to be so very much alive couldn't have many things left to laugh at when he had to be content with watching the world through his window.

"And they're clever, too!" Walter told me. "You know what they do now every time the dogs come near them? They beat it for your porch and line up outside the front door. They know bloody well a dog isn't going to try any shenanigans there!"

It seemed no time at all before the geese were acting as though they owned the place. They threatened, bullied, shrieked obscenities at every new face and nothing could keep them out of the garden. One September morning I found them in Walter's garden, and they had made a mess of it. I wanted to pay for it, but Walter wouldn't hear of it.

"Could've stopped them myself if I'd wanted to," he said. "But they were havin' an awful lot of fun thinkin' they were deep in sin. And besides, the doc had me in for a checkup yesterday. He told me not to get in an uproar over things."

Looking at Walter, I thought he was much grayer than usual. "How did the checkup go?" I asked.

"The doc switched me onto a new medicine," he said. "But he told me not to start readin' any more continued magazine stories."

It was awkward trying to laugh with him. A man like Walter ought to live forever.

November blew down on us, and one night when the wind was throwing the moon around, my geese began to holler. A minute later my phone rang.

"You wonder what's got into your geese?" Walter asked. "There's a flock of Canadas goin' over. Guess yours are tryin' to flag them down."

When I went outside I could barely see the Canadas. There were thirty or forty of them maybe. In a few minutes, Walter came over and we watched them together.

Meanwhile, my five earthbound geese were tilting their heads at the sky and calling at the top of their lungs.

They kept up their silly calling long after the sky was quiet and empty. We turned to go in and Walter said, "Something kind of special about a flock goin' over. Kinda sad, too. You know it's gettin' near the end."

He was right. We had seen the last of the Canadas and also the last of autumn. Next day the first flints of sleet came bounding down, and before the week was out snow covered everything. My geese had to give up foraging now, and they parked on the front doorstep. They seemed strangely quiet.

I didn't share Walter's excitement when he told me that those fool geese of mine were now teaching themselves to fly.

"Craziest thing you ever saw," he said. "Every morning about sunup they line up over in the corner of your front pasture. And then they rev up and point their noses into the wind and go whoopin' across the whole bloody field. And I swear they're gettin' now so's their feet don't hardly touch bottom!"

Then one morning when I was rounding the corner of the barn with a couple of pails of calf feed, I met a goose who was sufficiently airborne to knock my hat off. He and the others were ridiculously awkward at first. Even after the geese could gain enough altitude to clear the treetops, they still made comical mistakes, landing in the middle of the cattle, or on the roof of the barn and then tobogganing down over the edge and onto the manure pile below.

Then, suddenly, the awkward comedy was over. Their flying became sure and triumphantly beautiful, and when they floated by over my head, there was a grace and a majesty to them that made my throat tighten.

Walter said he saluted every time they went by his window. He spent a good deal of the time on his back now, but he had rolled his cot alongside the window so he still saw more of the geese than I did. And it was he who reported the tragedy to me.

"Better go out and look behind your lilac bush," he told me one night when I got home. "Your springer and your pointer—well, the geese came down right in front of them, and they sort of ganged up on one. It couldn't lift out of the way fast enough, I guess."

Because I was pretty sure those dogs would do the same thing again first chance they had, I took my pail of oats into the machine shed that night, and when the geese followed me I shut the door on them. "That's all for this year," I told them. "You'll just have to stay put."

I hadn't been thinking about Walter at all, I guess, that night I locked up the geese. But one morning, when I went in to split some kindling for him, I noticed that his couch was no longer by the window.

"Oh, but the days do be long now!" he told me. "I keep thinkin' about them geese of yours," he said. "I do miss seein' them go by the window! I keep thinkin' if I was a goose and you was to give me the choice between bein' a safe prisoner or flyin' free, and maybe gettin' my neck bit off, I know what I'd choose!"

Next morning I let the geese out of the shed, and I locked up the dogs. And the geese took off and went shrieking around the farm and over the house and through the trees till I thought they would drop from sheer fatigue.

"Heck no, they're not *tired!*" Walter said. "Can't you hear them laughing up there?"

He had his couch smack tight to the window again. *I'll go in one morning,* I thought, *and find him dead on that couch.*

But I was wrong about that. They found him one soft, misty, green morning in April about halfway back to the woods. He had a little pack on his back and a pair of field glasses.

Mae, if some of you happen to cross over before I do, you might tell Walter for me that the geese are still flying free. He shouldn't be hard to find, because if things are like they say they are over there, he'll have had no trouble making it all the way to the woods this time.

H. Gordon Green

Of Dogs and Angels

During my years in animal welfare work—I served as the president of the American Society for the Prevention of Cruelty to Animals—I have heard wonderful stories about the power of the human-animal bond. One of my favorites is about a girl and her very special dog.

When the girl was born, her parents were stationed with the U.S. Army overseas. The tiny baby spiked a fever of 106 degrees and when they couldn't help her at the military base, the baby and her family were flown home to the United States where she could receive the proper medical care.

The alarming fever kept recurring, but the baby survived. When the episode was over, the child was left with thirteen different seizure causes, including epilepsy. She had what was called multiple seizure syndrome and had several seizures every day. Sometimes she stopped breathing.

As a result, the little girl could *never* be left alone. She grew to be a teenager and if her mother had to go out, her father or brothers had to accompany her everywhere, including to the bathroom, which was awkward for everyone involved. But the risk of leaving her alone was too great and so, for lack of a better solution, things went on in this way for years.

The girl and her family lived near a town where there was a penitentiary for women. One of the programs there was a dog-training program. The inmates were taught how to train dogs to foster a sense of competence, as well as to develop a job skill for the time when they left the prison. Although most of the women had serious criminal backgrounds, many made excellent dog trainers and often trained service dogs for the handicapped while serving their time.

The girl's mother read about this program and contacted the penitentiary to see if there was anything they could do for her daughter. They had no idea how to train a dog to help a person in the girl's condition, but her family decided that a companion animal would be good for the girl, as she had limited social opportunities and they felt she would enjoy a dog's company.

The girl chose a random-bred dog named Queenie and together with the women at the prison, trained her to be an obedient pet.

But Queenie had other plans. She became a "seizure-alert" dog, letting the girl know when a seizure was coming on, so that the girl could be ready for it.

I heard about Queenie's amazing abilities and went to visit the girl's family and meet Queenie. At one point during my visit, Queenie became agitated and took the girl's wrist in her mouth and started pulling her towards the living room couch. Her mother said, "Go on now. Listen to what Queenie's telling you."

The girl went to the couch, curled up in a fetal position, facing the back of the couch and within moments started to seize. The dog jumped on the couch and wedged herself between the back of the couch and the front of the girl's body, placing her ear in front of the girl's mouth. Her family was used to this performance, but I watched in open-mouthed astonishment as the girl finished seizing and Queenie relaxed with her on the couch, wagging her tail and looking for all the world like an ordinary dog, playing with her mistress.

Then the girl and her dog went to the girl's bedroom as her parents and I went to the kitchen for coffee. A little while later, Queenie came barreling down the hallway, barking. She did a U-turn in the kitchen and then went racing back to the girl's room.

"She's having a seizure," the mother told me. The girl's father got up, in what seemed to me a casual manner for someone whose daughter often stopped breathing, and walked back to the bedroom after Queenie.

My concern must have been evident on my face because the girl's mother smiled and said, "I know what you're thinking, but you see, that's not the bark Queenie uses when my daughter stops breathing."

I shook my head in amazement. Queenie, the self-taught angel, proved to me once again how utterly foolish it is to suppose that animals don't think or can't communicate.

Roger Caras

More Chicken Soup?

Many of the stories and poems you have read in this book were submitted by readers like you who had read earlier *Chicken Soup for the Soul* books. We are planning to publish five or six *Chicken Soup for the Soul* books every year. We invite you to contribute a story to one of these future volumes.

Stories may be up to twelve hundred words and must uplift or inspire. You may submit an original piece or something you clip out of the local newspaper, a magazine, a church bulletin or a company newsletter. It could also be your favorite quotation you've put on your refrigerator door or a personal experience that has touched you deeply.

In addition to future servings of *Chicken Soup for the Soul*, some of the future books we have planned are *Chicken Soup for the Grandparent's Soul, Divorced Soul, Man's Soul, Grieving Soul, Laughing Soul, Writer's Soul, Expectant Mother's Soul* and *Sports Fan's Soul*.

Send a copy of your stories and other pieces, indicating which edition they are for, to the following address:

Chicken Soup for the *(Specify Which Edition)* Soul
P.O. Box 30880 • Santa Barbara, CA 93130
phone: 805-563-2935 • fax: 805-563-2945
e-mail: *soup4soul@aol.com*
Web site: *www.chickensoup.com*

We will be sure that both you and the author are credited for your submission.

For information about speaking engagements, other books, audiotapes, workshops and training programs, please contact any of the authors directly.

Problems with Your Pet?

Do you have a pet that continues to bite, bark, dig, chew, scratch or make messes despite repeated warnings or punishment? Have you thought about kicking it out of bed, out of the house, or worse?

Unrealistic expectations and lack of understanding about pet behavior has resulted in millions of innocent pets being taken to shelters and euthanized each year, along with the accompanying human guilt and grief.

The key to understanding your animal's behavior is to first understand that it's not "a little person" but a proud member of another species. All animals instinctively act like they would in the wild, unless we teach them otherwise. Without proper training, it's just a matter of time until the pet behaves in a way that is natural to them, but that runs counter to people's wishes. Sadly, the pet pays the ultimate price.

There are solutions! If you or someone you know has a pet with a behavior problem, ask your veterinarian where to obtain accurate information and referrals to trained behaviorists.

Individuals who have raised and trained animals for decades are getting better results with new, gentler methods. People are learning that they can teach an old cat new tricks, such as using a scratching post or a litter box. They're also learning that love, patience and kindness are far more effective tools for training a dog than a belt or the back of a hand.

Join us in eliminating the needless killing of pets for treatable behavior problems. Ask your veterinarian for advice or referral, or contact:

American Society for the Prevention of
Cruelty to Animals
Behavior Hotline (212) 876-7700 xHELP (#4357)
www.aspca.org

American Veterinary Medical Association
(847) 925-8070
www.avma.org

American Veterinary Society of Animal Behavior
Referrals to a veterinary behaviorist
Martinala@juno.com

Animal Behavior Society
Listing of certified applied animal behaviorists
Fax (812) 856-5542
www.animalbehavior.org (select applied behavior section)

More Resources

Television

When you land on Animal Planet, you're in for a surprise. It's everything you love on TV but with an animal twist! Action. Adventure. Comedy. Pet care shows. Even sports. Shows like *Emergency Vets, The Crocodile Hunter, Petsburgh U.S.A.* and the world's most fascinating wildlife documentaries. Animal Planet . . . it brings out the human in us. Visit them at *www.animalplanet.com* for great tips on pet behavior problems.

Magazines

Rodale's *Pets: part of the family* focuses on all aspects of the people-pet partnership—emotional, physical and spiritual. It also provides specific ways of improving problematic behavior that can ruin this relationship. There is a book series and Public Television series also called *Pets: part of the family*. Hosted by Gary Burghoff—"Radar" on the *M*A*S*H* series, the show covers a wide variety of heartwarming and practical segments on all kinds of pets. For more information visit their Web site at: *www.petspartofthefamily.com*.

Products

For behavior management information or for a referral, visit *www.gentleleader.com*.

Organizations Dedicated to Helping Pets

In an ongoing effort to return a portion of the priceless gifts that pets give mankind, part of the proceeds from *Chicken Soup for the Cat and Dog Lover's Soul* will be donated to the following organizations. Contact them directly for more information and join us in supporting them generously.

American Veterinary Medical Foundation (AVMF)

Committed to the special relationship between people and pets, the American Veterinary Medical Foundation (AVMF) fosters animal health and well-being by funding treatment for animals injured in disasters, promoting the bond between people and animals, supporting studies to save and improve the lives of animals, and enhancing veterinary education.

Disasters pose a huge threat to the bond we share. Fortunately, the AVMF can be a source of help and hope as floods, hurricanes, fires and tornadoes continue to devastate our country each year. A partnership between the AVMF, the American Veterinary Medical Association and the American Red Cross is helping to establish the resources and networks to address this issue.

You can support the AVMF by sending a contribution to: 1931 N. Meacham Rd., Schaumburg, IL 60173-4360. You can also reach them by calling 800-248-2862, ext. 207, by e-mail at *AVMFMail@aol.com*, or by visiting their Web site at *www.avma.org/avmf.*

Actors and Others for Animals

Actors and Others for Animals is a powerful and tireless force against animal cruelty worldwide. Using celebrity power, but supported entirely by donations, this nonprofit organization provides spay/neuter outreach, disaster relief, in-school humane education programs, pet-assisted therapy, help-line referrals and emergency veterinary subsidies. Support Actors and Others for Animals: P.O. Box 33473, Granada Hills, CA 91394, 818-386-5870.

Best Friends Animal Sanctuary

There are never fewer than eighteen hundred dogs and cats and other animals at the sanctuary and, once they come to Best Friends, these once-sad little faces are guaranteed a life that makes up for whatever went before. Support the Best Friends Animal Sanctuary: Kanab, UT 84741-5001, 435-644-2001, *info@bestfriends.org, www.bestfriends.org.*

The American Humane Association (AHA)

Since 1877, AHA has been the national leader in identifying and preventing the causes of animal abuse and neglect. Programs include: advocacy to improve welfare of pets; promoting adoptions and curbing pet overpopulation; supporting animal shelters with training/grants/educational materials; emergency animal relief during natural disasters; legislation to protect pets, wildlife and lab animals; and protecting animal actors in film and TV productions. Support the AHA: 63 Inverness Dr. East, Englewood, CO 80112, 303-792-9900, *www.americanhumane.org*.

The Argus Center

Colorado State University, in Fort Collins, has created an innovative program called The Argus Center to develop Bond-Centered approaches to the practice of veterinary medicine. The Argus Center aims to support and train veterinarians in expanding their roles as healers to include providing pet owners with education, resource referral and emotional support thereby helping to create and strengthen Bond-Centered Families. Support The Argus Center; W102 Anatomy, College of Veterinary Medicine and Biomedical Sciences, Colorado State University, Fort Collins, CO 80523, 970-491-5786.

The Ark Trust

The Ark Trust, via its annual Genesis Awards, honors outstanding individuals in the major news and entertainment media for spotlighting animal issues with courage, creativity and integrity. The star-studded gala, airing as a TV special on Animal Planet, reflects The Ark Trust motto: Cruelty Can't Stand the Spotlight! The Ark Trust, founded by Gretchen Wyler, also takes direct action on animal-protection issues, propelling them into the media spotlight throughout the year. Support The Ark Trust, Inc.: 5551 Balboa Blvd., Encino, CA 91316, 818-501-2275, *genesis@arktrust.org, www.arktrust.org*.

The People-Pet Partnership (PPP)

The PPP continues founder Dr. Bustad's Bond work through its community service programs and through its research on animal-assisted therapy for special populations. In addition to taking the Bond into care facilities, volunteers provide therapeutic riding lessons for people with disabilities. They also, "get 'em while they're young" through a K-6 curriculum guide *Learning and Living Together: Building the Human-Animal Bond.* Support the PPP: Box 647010, WSU, Pullman WA 99164-7010, 509-335-4569, *fmartin@vetmed.wsu.edu, www.vetmed.wsu.edu/depts-pppp.*

Who Is Jack Canfield?

Jack Canfield grew up surrounded by animals of every kind. There were always at least one dog—mostly collies and German shepherds, along with an occasional mutt—and two or three cats, plus hamsters, gerbils, rabbits, parakeets, white mice, box turtles, tropical fish, racoons, a horse, a cow, a goat, and eventually a kennel full of rambunctious Afghan hounds. This love of animals led to an adult life filled with a series of wonderful dogs—a Samoyed, an English sheepdog and a golden retriever—as well as too many cats to keep track of, all of which have always become members of the family with full run of the house. Jack is currently the proud owner of one dog, two cats and two pet rabbits, as well as a pond full of magnificent koi and goldfish.

Jack Canfield is one of America's leading experts in the development of human potential and personal effectiveness. He is both a dynamic, entertaining speaker and a highly sought-after trainer.

He is the author and narrator of several bestselling audio- and videocassette programs, including the twenty-six-book *Chicken Soup for the Soul* series, *Dare to Win, Self-Esteem and Peak Performance, How to Build High Self-Esteem, Self-Esteem in the Classroom* and *Chicken Soup for the Soul—Live.* He is regularly seen on television shows such as *Good Morning America, 20/20* and *NBC Nightly News.*

Jack is a regularly featured speaker for professional associations, school districts, government agencies, churches, hospitals, sales organizations and corporations.

For further information about Jack's books, tapes and training programs, or to schedule him for a presentation, please contact:

The Canfield Training Group
P.O. Box 30880 • Santa Barbara, CA 93130
phone: 800-237-8336 • fax: 805-563-2945
Web site: *http://www.chickensoup.com*
to send e-mail: *soup4soul@aol.com*
to receive information via e-mail:
chickensoup@zoom.com

Who Is Mark Victor Hansen?

Mark Victor Hansen is a professional speaker who, in the last twenty years, has made over four thousand presentations to more than 2 million people in thirty-two countries. His presentations cover sales excellence and strategies; personal empowerment and development; and how to triple your income and double your time off.

Mark has spent a lifetime dedicated to his mission of making a profound and positive difference in people's lives. Throughout his career, he has inspired hundreds of thousands of people to create a more powerful and purposeful future for themselves while stimulating the sale of billions of dollars worth of goods and services.

Mark is a prolific writer and has authored *Future Diary, How to Achieve Total Prosperity* and *The Miracle of Tithing*. He is coauthor of the *Chicken Soup for the Soul* series, *Dare to Win* and *The Aladdin Factor* (all with Jack Canfield) and *The Master Motivator* (with Joe Batten).

Mark has also produced a complete library of personal empowerment audio- and videocassette programs that have enabled his listeners to recognize and use their innate abilities in their business and personal lives. His message has made him a popular television and radio personality, with appearances on ABC, NBC, CBS, HBO, PBS and CNN. He has also appeared on the cover of numerous magazines, including *Success, Entrepreneur* and *Changes*.

When Mark was a child, he only had one family dog. He was not then aware that his heart and home would eventually expand to include the forty-six animals that currently inhabit the Hansen compound, including four cats, three dogs, two birds, two horses, several goldfish, one bunny, one duck who thinks he is a chicken, and twenty-five chickens, all of which have names.

Mark is a big man with a heart and spirit to match—an inspiration to all who seek to better themselves.

For further information about Mark write:

P.O. Box 7665
Newport Beach, CA 92658
phone: 714-759-9304 or 800-433-2314
fax: 714-722-6912
Web site: *http://www.chickensoup.com*

Who Is Marty Becker, D.V.M.?

What Jacques Cousteau did for the oceans and Carl Sagan did for space, Dr. Marty Becker is doing for *The Bond*. He has made it a mission to enthusiastically celebrate, protect and nurture this powerful, life-enhancing relationship we share with our pets.

As a veterinarian, best-selling author, university educator, media personality, professional communicator, devoted pet lover and Good Samaritan for pets, Dr. Marty Becker is widely recognized as the "best loved family doctor for pets" in the world.

Dr. Becker is widely acclaimed as the veterinary contributor to ABC-TV's *Good Morning America*. In addition, he stars in a variety of segments for Walt Disney Television's series *Petsburgh, U.S.A.*, now entering its second season on Animal Planet. Dr. Becker is a contributing editor for *Pets: part of the family* and has been featured in *USA Today, USA Weekend,* the *New York Times, TV Guide, National Enquirer, Prevention Magazine's Guide to Dogs and Cats, Dog Fancy, PetLife* and many other leading newspapers and magazines.

Having been a doggedly persistent communicator on six continents and in over sixty countries, Dr. Becker has helped pioneer the way we interact with and take responsibility for our pets. Dr. Becker has lectured at all twenty-seven of the veterinary schools in North America and has delivered keynote addresses on *The Bond* to groups ranging from national organizations and corporate boardrooms to the Smithsonian Institute in Washington, D.C.

When he isn't traveling the globe passionately speaking about the importance of *The Bond*, Dr. Becker devotes his life to his family at Almost Heaven Ranch in northern Idaho, which includes his beloved wife of over twenty years, Teresa, daughter Mikkel and son Lex, along with their other kids: Scooter, a wire-haired fox terrier; Sirloin, a Labrador retriever; cats Turbo and Tango; and Gabriel, Pegasus, Sugar Babe and Chex, their four quarter horses.

For more information, please contact Marty Becker at:

250 2nd Ave. South, Ste. B2
Twin Falls, ID 83301
phone: 208-734-8174
fax: 208-733-5405
Web site: *www.BondWorks.com*
e-mail: *thebond@aol.com*

Who Is Carol Kline?

Carol Kline has been a pet lover her entire life. She is the co-director of the Noah's Ark Animal Foundation Dog Rescue Program, in Fairfield, Iowa, a volunteer effort that saves lost, stray and abandoned dogs.

Carol spends many hours a week monitoring the fate of animals that are brought into the city pound. She also walks, feeds and "socializes" the dogs at the Noah's Ark facility, a cageless shelter for cats and dogs. "The gratitude and love I receive from these animals are more fulfilling than any paycheck I could ever receive. Volunteering time with the dogs fills my heart, and brings great joy to my life."

A freelance writer for twelve years, Carol, who has a B.A. in literature, has written for newspapers, newsletters and other publications. She is also coauthor of *Chicken Soup for the Pet Lover's Soul*. Recently, she has contributed stories and her editing talents to other *Chicken Soup for the Soul* books.

In addition to her writing and animal work, Carol is also a speaker, self-esteem facilitator and certified instructor of the parenting skills program, *Redirecting Children's Behavior* (RCB). The first RCB instructor in Iowa, Carol presents workshops and in-service programs for childcare providers, and teaches a five-week program for parents. She has also been a counselor at a self-esteem camp in Missouri for teens and kids. Since 1975, Carol has taught stress-management programs to the general public. In 1990, she studied with Jack Canfield, and since then has assisted as a facilitator in his annual Train the Trainers program. Her dynamic and engaging style has won her enthusiastic receptions from the various audiences she addresses.

Carol has the good fortune to be married to Larry Kline, and is proud stepmother to Lorin and McKenna. Carol's former "foster dogs," Jimmy and Beethoven, have found a permanent home with Carol and join Hannah and Larry's new dog, Beau, as cherished members of the family.

To contact Carol:

P.O. Box 1262, Fairfield, IA 52556
phone: (515) 469-3889
fax: (515) 472-3720
e-mail: *ckline@lisco.com*

Contributors

Many of the stories in this book were taken from books
we have read, which are acknowledged in the Permissions
section. If you would like to contact authors for information on their books, tapes or seminars, you can reach them
at the addresses and phone numbers provided.

Many of the stories were also contributed by readers
like yourself, who responded to our request for stories. We
have also included information about them.

Janine Adams is an award-winning dog writer who has published dozens of
magazine articles about pets in a variety of animal-related publications
nationwide. She lives in Brooklyn, New York, with her husband and their
standard poodles, Kramer and Scout.

Bryan Aubrey is a former professor of English and is the author of two books
and numerous articles and reviews. He is English, but has lived in Iowa since
1981. In 1993, he was joined by his German-trained, British-mannered cat,
Prince Peter. Bryan can be reached at 1100 East Madison Ave., Fairfield, IA
52556 or by calling 515-472-2224.

Charles Barsotti has been a cartoonist with the *New Yorker* magazine for
twenty-seven years. His work has appeared in the *Atlantic,* the *New York Times,
USA Today, Fast Company, Texas Monthly, Playboy, Barron's* and many other publications. He has published four books. Visit his Web site at *www.barsotti.com.*

Barbara Bartocci is an award-winning author and speaker. Her latest book is
Midlife Awakenings: Discovering the Gifts Life Has Given Us (Ave Maria Press,
Notre Dame). She speaks before women's conferences and business audiences
throughout the United States and Canada. For more information, call toll-free
877-214-9625 or e-mail *BBartocci@aol.com.*

Carol Ann Baum is a New Jersey-based freelance writer, retired from her previous career as a driver of a large school bus for a private carrier. She is married and the mother of two grown sons. She has always written, but not
seriously until recently.

Ellen Perry Berkeley, formerly senior editor of the *Architectural Forum,* is author
of the heart-warming and fact-filled *Maverick Cats: Encounters with Feral Cats.* For
an autographed and personalized copy of this acclaimed and award-winning
book, send a check for $12.95 to Ellen at Box 311, Shaftsbury, VT 05262.

Martha Campbell is a graduate of Washington University School of Fine Arts,
and a former writer-designer for Hallmark Cards. Since she became a freelancer

in 1973, she has had over twenty thousand cartoons published and has illustrated nineteen books. She can be reached at P.O. Box 2538, Harrison, AR 72602 or by calling 870-741-5323.

Roger Caras a prolific author and broadcast correspondent on animals, wildlife and the environment, became president of the American Society for the Prevention of Cruelty to Animals (ASPCA) in October 1991. It was the latest challenge for a man whose career in animal welfare began at age ten. Caras, a mainstay in the movement to promote adoptions and stop the killing of retired greyhounds, owns four greyhounds and eight other dogs, nine cats, five horses, two cows, a llama, two alpaca and assorted other animals on his farm/retreat in western Maryland.

Dave Carpenter has been a full-time freelance cartoonist and humorous illustrator since 1981. His cartoons have appeared in *Barron's*, the *Wall Street Journal, Forbes, Better Homes & Gardens, Good Housekeeping, Woman's World, First,* the *Saturday Evening Post* and numerous other publications. Dave can be reached at P.O. Box 520, Emmetsburg, IA 50536 or by calling 712-852-3725.

Cindy Podurgal Chambers is a freelance writer, editor, photojournalist and advertising copywriter with hundreds of magazine and newspaper articles to her credit. A well-known public speaker specializing in humorous and motivational topics, she is frequently featured at seminars, as well as on television and radio talk shows. She is currently putting the finishing touches on a collection of humorous reminiscences entitled *Growing Up in the Sixties and Other Tales of Horror.* She can be reached by e-mail at *Oka2@aol.com.*

John E. Cooper, D.T.V.M., F.R.C.V.S., was the lead veterinarian for the Mountain Gorilla Veterinary Project (MGVP) in central Africa from 1993 to 1995. The project provides veterinary care and monitors the health of the highly endangered mountain gorillas. Dr. Cooper obtained his Bachelor of Veterinary Science degree from Bristol University in 1962 and was granted membership to the Royal College of Veterinary Surgeons in 1966. He lives in England with his wife, Margaret. Morris Animal Foundation's Mountain Gorilla Veterinary Project is one of just a few projects in the world that provides health care for an endangered species in its natural habitat. To contribute to or help Morris Animal Foundation call 800-243-2345, visit the Web site at *www.morrisanimalfoundation.org* or send a tax-deductible donation to 45 Inverness Dr. E., Englewood, CO 80112.

Jo Coudert is a freelance writer, a frequent contributor to *Woman's Day* and *Reader's Digest,* and the author of nine books, among them the bestselling *Advice From a Failure* and *Seven Cats and the Art of Living,* and her most recent, *The Good Shepherd.* She lives on the bank of a small river in western New Jersey with one person, one dog, and six cats, and there she gardens and paints watercolors.

Christie Craig is a writer, photographer and teacher. With over three hundred magazine credits and one published novel, her work has appeared in magazines such as *Reader's Digest, Pet Life, Cats* and *Bird Time.* Known for her inspiration and encouragement, she teaches writing classes in Houston, Texas. For information, call 281-376-6474.

Barbara J. Crocker lives in Flat Rock, Michigan. She is a paralegal for Adams & Pope, P.L.L.C. Her husband, Michael, is an electrician. They have a twenty-two-year-old daughter, Amy, and a two-year-old Labrador retriever named Amber, who thinks she is in charge! Barbara and her family enjoy camping, boating, going to northern Michigan, taking the dog for long walks and Detroit Red Wings hockey. In her spare time she enjoys crocheting, counted cross-stitch, working in the yard and reading. She is a Sunday school super-intendent and a Sunday school teacher at her church.

Lisa Duffy-Korpics is a high-school social studies teacher and freelance writer from Dutchess County, New York. Before becoming a teacher, she worked for the Peekskill Police Department as their animal control officer, an experience that provided her with a lot to write about! She enjoys spending time with her husband, Jason, her five-year-old son, Charles, and two-year-old daughter, Emily. She can be reached at *Memleigh@aol.com.*

Toni Eames is an author and lecturer who writes a column for *Dog World* magazine. Among her books are *A Guide to Guide Dog Schools* and *Partners in Independence: A Success Story of Dogs and the Disabled.* In 1998, she was inducted into the National Hall of Fame for Persons with Disabilities.

Alicia Karen Elkins shares her north Alabama home with two cats. She is the only female to receive service-connected disability for a bareback-bronco rodeo wreck on army time. A columnist for Native American and farm publi-cations, Karen also enjoys writing poetry, covering events and being a stock-yard barnhand at Fisk/Allison.

Jane Eppinga is a Tucson-based freelance writer. Her book, *Henry Ossian Flipper: West Point's First Black Graduate,* was part of the petition presented to President William J. Clinton, who posthumously pardoned Henry O. Flipper. A racially biased court-martial removed Flipper from the military in 1882. Currently, she is working on a book entitled *Arizona Folklore.*

Benita Epstein's cartoons appear in hundreds of publications such as the *Wall Street Journal, Barron's* and *Better Homes & Gardens.* She has three cartoon collec-tions: *Suture Self, Interlibrary Loan Sharks* and *Seedy ROMS and Science of Little Round Things* (McFarland & Co.). Benita can be reached by calling 760-634-3705 or by e-mail at *BenitaE@aol.com* Visit her Web site at *www.reuben.org/benitaepstein/.*

George Feifer is the author of eleven books of fiction and nonfiction. The *New York Times Book Review* named his book on Okinawa, *TENNOZAN,* a Notable Book of 1992. His articles and essays have appeared in magazines such as the *Atlantic, Harper's,* the *New York Times, New Republic,* and the *Boston Globe.*

Mary Bucher Fisher composed "A Gift Exchange" for her 1987 Christmas card. She is a retired copyeditor who now freelances. Her credentials include B.A., cum laude; M.A., journalism; Phi Beta Kappa; Mensa; listings in *Literary Market*

Place and three volumes of *Who's Who* (women, Midwest, communications); and technical editing awards. Mary can be reached at 100 Glenmont Ave., Columbus, OH 43214 or by calling 614-262-5628.

Debbie Freeberg-Renwick and her husband, Tim, design and build everything from period costumes to custom cabins on wheels. Their motto, "Nothing is too good for our kitties," led to the creation of the ultimate scratching post: a seven-foot faux marble classical column wrapped with matching rope. Jeeves and Poppy enjoy watching these activities and occasionally lend a paw. Jeeves mastered toilet training through the excellent book, *Ray Berwick's Complete Guide to Training Your Cat.* Deb and Tim can be reached by e-mail at *timdeb@kdsi.net.*

Joe Fulda has been into purebred dogs for more than thirty years, as well as being a breeder, exhibitor, trainer, groomer and kennel operator. Joe has been an AKC judge and is a past president of the Tacoma, Washington, Kennel Club. He authored an award-winning weekly pets column for *Tacoma New Tribune* for eleven years and has contributed articles to major dog magazines since 1967. He was twice vice president of the Dog Writers' Association of America. Joe also was the talk-show host on KLAY as "The Pet Professor" in Lakewood, Washington, for three years. He is the author of *Maltese, A Complete Pet Owner's Manual* (Barron's, 1996).

Randy Glasbergen has had more than twenty-five thousand cartoons published in magazines, books and greeting cards around the world. He also creates *The Better Half,* which is syndicated to newspapers by King Features Syndicate. You can find more of Randy's cartoons online at *www.glasbergen.com.*

H. Gordon Green was known at the time of his death in 1991 to readers of his weekly columns in the *Toronto Star* and Montreal's the *Gazette.* H. Gordon Green will also be remembered across the country for his regular commentaries on more than thirty radio stations, including CBC, and for his twenty years as contributing editor of the now defunct *Family Herald,* Canada's most widely read magazine.

Jim Grove and daughter, **Amy,** live in Winter Park, Florida. Amy is ten years old and a fourth-grader. Jim and his wife, Leslie, have been married for eighteen years and have two other children, David and Jennifer. They also have a dog named Flower; two rabbits, Oreo and Thumper; a leopard gecko named Tiger and a new hamster, Sunshine. Jim, a financial advisor, enjoyed a twenty-year career as a sports writer and editor at four daily newspapers. Hopefully, his writing career is just beginning. He can be reached at 3063 Ash Park Loop, Winter Park, FL 32792, by calling 800-356-3009, ext. 3009, or by e-mail at *jegrove@juno.com.*

Liz Gunkelman, D.V.M., is a 1987 Graduate of Iowa State College of Veterinary Medicine. She lives on an acreage near Glenwood, Iowa, with her husband, two sons and various critters. Dr. Gunkelman works part-time at Best Care Pet Hospital in Omaha, Nebraska. Her full-time job is "Mom." She can be reached at Best Care Pet Hospital at 3030 "L" St., Omaha, NE 68107 or by calling 402-734-1494.

G. Edgar Hall is a University of Arizona retiree and a member of the Society of Southwestern Authors and the Southeastern Arizona Christian Writers Fellowship. His publications have appeared in nostalgic, religious, outdoor and historical magazines and newspapers. He is seventy-nine years old, married and has seventy-two grandchildren. Presently, Edgar is working on a book of family stories entitled *Hall Family Footprints*.

Vincent Hans is the national sales and marketing manager for Vanguard Records. During his free time, he enjoys giving tours at the William S. Hart Museum in Newhall, California. **Norma Hans** is a full-time college student majoring in business. She is also an aspiring actress. Vince and Norma reside in Valencia, California, and have been soul mates since 1987. They are very grateful to Dr. Tracy McFarland (The Cat Doctor) of Newhall, California, for keeping Ragamuffin healthy for the past seven years. Vince, Norma, Ragamuffin and Maggie can be reached by e-mail at *vh3@ix.netcom.com*.

Ellen Harvey is a writer and publicist with the United States Trotting Association, the registry for Standardbred horses. Raised on a horse farm in western Pennsylvania, her father and brother are both racehorse trainers. She can be reached at HRC, 41 Rt. 34, Colts Neck, NJ 07722, by calling 732-780-3700 or by e-mail at *HRCNews@aol.com*.

Jonny Hawkins is a nationally known cartoonist whose work has appeared in the *Saturday Evening Post, National Enquirer, Barron's* and over 175 other publications. His syndicated comic feature, *Hi and Jinx*, runs in many U.S. newspapers.

Bill Holton is a freelance writer living in Key West, Florida. He can be reached by e-mail at *bholton@reporters.net*.

David C. Hoopes lives, works and writes in West Chester, Pennsylvania, with his wife Sandra and his pal, Wolfgang, a 115-pound German shepherd. He is currently seeking representation for his first novel, while working on his second.

Lisa Hurt is an assistant editor at the *Connecticut Post* in Bridgeport, Connecticut. After growing up in West Point, Kentucky, she graduated from Western Kentucky University and has since worked at newspapers and magazines in Kentucky, Florida, Hawaii, New York and Louisiana. She lives in a New England coastal town with her fiancé, Steve, and their four cats. She can be reached by e-mail at *Lisazkozar@aol.com*.

Pam Johnson-Bennett is a well-known feline behaviorist and author of several books, including *Psycho Kitty* (Crossing Press) and *Twisted Whiskers* (Crossing Press). Her newest book, *Think Like A Cat* (Penguin Books), will be available in January 2000. Pam frequently appears on national TV, on such networks as CNN and Fox News Channel.

Tim Jones is a former newspaper and magazine editor who left behind the confines of a more urban life in Anchorage, Alaska in 1980. He has been a boat captain on Prince William Sound and built homes in Baldez. He has written four other books and also has edited several books. His articles have appeared in numerous magazines.

Bil Keane created the *Family Circus* in 1960. It now appears in over fifteen hundred newspapers and is read by 100 million people daily. A new all-color hardcover book the *Family Circus—By Request* is available from Gayle Keane, 4093 Jefferson St., Napa, CA 94558.

John Keane has spent twenty-five years helping pet owners recover their lost and stolen pets. His California-based business Sherlock Bones, Inc. provides nationwide and local services to help lost-pet owners quickly and efficiently "get the word out in their surrounding neighborhood about their missing pet"—the key to finding lost or stolen pets. To enjoy more stories of lost and found pets, visit his Web site at *www.sherlockbones.com* If you have stories you want to share with him, he can be reached by calling 800-942-6637 or by e-mail at *sherlock@sherlockbones.com*.

Jim Kerr is the director of the Colorado Boys Ranch Horsemanship Program. For the past twelve years, he has instructed and nurtured hundreds of boys as they learn about horses. Prior to CBR, Jim also worked with young people as a teacher and coach. Colorado Boys Ranch is a nonprofit, residential treatment facility for young people with severe emotional and behavioral problems. Their horsemanship program and other special program opportunities for young people are funded through the generosity of contributors. For further information, please write to P.O. Box 681, La Junta, CO 81050 or call 719-384-5981.

Joe Kirkup is the author of approximately sixty nonfiction essays published in various periodicals and paperbacks, including two in *Chicken Soup for the Pet Lover's Soul*. *Life Sentences,* an anthology, can be purchased through *MudTurtle.com* on the Internet, or by calling 860-572-0079 or sending an e-mail to *JoeKirkup@compuserve.com*.

Cynthia Knisely grew up in Grand Rapids, Michigan. She moved to Arizona in 1978, where she was a reporter for the *Arizona Republic* until 1984. She brought Cassie with her from Arizona in 1989. Cassie's health is declining rapidly now, but she is not suffering. Should it become necessary, her veterinarian, Dr. Weiss, will go to her house to put her to sleep. Cynthia is disabled and has fibromyalgia. She is the mother of a five-year-old and a special-needs six-year-old. Her husband's fifteen-year-old daughter also lives with them.

Stephanie Laland, a well-known speaker on animal-related issues, is the author of *Peaceful Kingdom: Random Acts of Kindness by Animals* and *51 Ways to Entertain Your Housecat While You're Out*. A workshop leader for people wishing to increase their connection to animals, she and her husband and many animal friends live in Felton, California.

Page Lambert, author of *In Search of Kinship* and *Shifting Stars,* and contributor to *Chicken Soup for the Woman's Soul,* is a Colorado native. She now lives on a small ranch in the Black Hills of Wyoming, where she loves to walk the deer paths with their new dog, Duke. A facilitator of unusual writing retreats, she can be reached by calling 307-283-2530 or by e-mail at *plambert@mcn.net.*

Sharon Landeen, a retired elementary-school teacher, is the author and illustrator of two bilingual picture books, *When You Get Really Mad* and *Really, Riley.* She enjoys working with youth and was involved for twenty years with 4-H. She is a volunteer teacher in reading and art, but still finds the time for her writing as well as being "grandmother superior." She can be reached at 6990 E. Calle Arandas, Tucson, AZ 85750 or by calling 520-886-1194.

Aletha Jane Lindstrom of Battle Creek, Michigan, died May 4, 1998. She was born in 1908. She graduated from Olivet College and Western Michigan University. She was employed as an elementary-school teacher and later as an elementary-school librarian in the Lakeview school district. After retiring, she taught writing classes in the adult-education program at Kellogg Community College. She also was a freelance writer, who was published in *Reader's Digest, Catholic Digest, Guideposts* and many other publications. Aletha also published a children's book, *Sojourner Truth.* She married Carl in 1943; he died February 5, 1998. She is survived by her son, Carl Timothy, a grandson and her brother.

Mike Lipstock's stories have appeared in previous volumes of the *Chicken Soup for the Soul* series. They have also appeared in well over a hundred magazines and nine anthologies. He recently received his second nomination for a Pushcart Prize and a nomination for a story to be presented on National Public Radio. He lives in Jericho, New York and can be reached by calling 516-681-0171.

Peter Mandel is a writer of books about animals for both children and adults, and currently pet columnist for the *Providence Journal Bulletin.* He lives in Providence with his wife, Kathy, and cat, Chuck. Mandel grew up in Manhattan and graduated from Middlebury College and Brown University. He has a book entitled *The Official Cat I.Q. Test.* His more recent books include *The Cat Dictionary, The Official Dog I.Q. Test,* and a picture book entitled *Red Cat, White Cat,* which was named an American Bookseller "Pick of the Lists" and a Kirkus Reviews "Best of the Issue." He likes baseball, ocean liners, Chinese food and walking around in the city of Paris.

Terry Perret Martin is a freelance writer and a single mother of three-year-old Sophia. She runs her publicity/business-writing company from home with her cat on her lap and her two dogs sleeping under the desk! She and her father, an Emmy Award-winning comedy writer, have created the Professional Comedy Writing Correspondence Course. Terry can be reached at P.O. Box 1739, Agoura Hills, CA 91376-1739, by calling 818-707-0155, by fax at 818-707-0137 or by e-mail at *TerMartin@aol.com.*

Susan McCullough specializes in writing about pets and parenting topics. Her work has appeared in the *Washington Post, PetLife* and *Pets: Part of the Family.* She also has written for *Family Circle* and *Modern Maturity,* and has contributed to several pet-care books. She and her family live in Vienna, Virginia.

Cindy Midgette lives in eastern North Carolina with her husband, Buddy, and children, Brent and Allie. Cindy is an avid animal lover. She supports Airedale rescue. Cindy can be reached at *http://www.airedale.org.*

Larry Monk passed away November 15, 1998. He was married for twenty-five years. The last position he held was a realty specialist with 70th Regional Support Command. He spent ten years with the civil service.

Holly Manon Moore is grateful to be a full-time mom-and-wife-at-home in Fairfield, Iowa. She has a B.F.A. in art and an M.A. in education administration which happily qualifies her for her activities as artist, writer, organic gardener, tree and animal lover. She has been a teacher for the Transcendental Meditation program for over twenty-five years.

Kate Murphy is a writer and long-time cancer survivor. Her first bout with colon cancer was in 1983. Since 1993, she has been treated for colon, breast and ovarian cancer as well. She lives by a lake in upstate New York with her husband, three cats, and her golden retriever—and has no sign of cancer today. She is a founding member of the Colon Cancer Alliance.

Michael A. Obenski, V.M.D., is a 1972 graduate of the University of Pennsylvania School of Veterinary Medicine. He is the owner and chief veterinarian of the Allentown Clinic for Cats, which he founded in 1978. Located in Allentown, Pennsylvania, the clinic is a veterinary hospital devoted exclusively to feline medicine and surgery. Doctor Obenski has been awarded the Alumni Award of Merit from the University of Pennsylvania for his contributions to veterinary literature. To date, he has written over two hundred magazine articles and has served for more than twenty years as a contributing author to *D.V.M. Newsmagazine.* He and his wife, Martina, reside in Zionsville, Pennsylvania, with cats, Spiffy and Rocket, and dogs, Brindle and Howdy. They have three grown children, Chad, Rachel, and Bryson.

Sheldon Oberman is a writer, a storyteller of traditional Jewish tales and a high-school teacher. He is married, with three children and one young cat. His Web site, *www.mbnet.mb.ca/~soberman,* has many stories and creative guides. He can be reached at 822 Dorchester Ave., Winnipeg, Manitoba R3M 0R7.

Evelyn Olson has spent most of her eighty-seven years in, or near, Ogilvie, which is a small town in central Minnesota. She attended and graduated from the Ogilvie School, and St. Cloud University. For thirty-five years, she taught in nearby rural schools; then, for the next ten years, she taught handicapped children in the Ogilvie School. On retiring, she was honored and presented with an award by the Minnesota Board of Education for her forty-seven years of teaching service. She had many pets in her life, but Brownie was her favorite. This was probably due to his long life, and his devotion to her and her entire family.

Lori Jo Oswald, Ph.D., lives in Alaska with her three dogs, three cats and two horses—all rescues. She writes and edits *Alaska Pet News* (subscriptions $18 a year), which focuses on animal issues, pet care, reducing pet overpopulation and rescuing homeless animals. Lori Jo can be reached at *Alaska Pet News,* P.O. Box 231043, Anchorage, AK 99523 or by e-mail at *petnews@alaska.net.*

Jan Paddock and her husband, Brad, began their life together three years ago with the help of a happy golden retriever puppy named Cognac. At that time, the rest of the "Janimal" house included two rescued cats: an eighteen-year-old Siamese and a sixteen-year-old tabby. Brad brought to the family a blue-and-gold macaw named Calypso. In the last year, both cats have passed over the Rainbow Bridge. The family has recently grown to include a new golden retriever puppy named Zany.

Lynn Pulliam lives just south of Atlanta, Georgia, with her husband, two sons, four dogs and two cats. In addition to writing, she enjoys drawing, painting and gardening. She can be reached at *lynnwp@juno.com.*

Nancy Roberts's first book, *North Carolina Ghosts and Legends,* was published at the suggestion of Carl Sandburg. His praise launched twenty-five books and began her career writing true ghost stories based on interviews. *Southern Living* magazine calls Nancy "Custodian of the Twilight Zone." Among her twelve books of supernatural stories are *Animal Ghost Stories, Civil War Ghosts and Legends, Georgia Ghosts, South Carolina Ghosts* and *America's Most Haunted Places.* She is also an authority on pirates and is the author of *Blackbeard and Other Pirates of the Atlantic Coast* and *Blackbeard's Cat.* Roberts's books are available from Amazon or by calling 800-337-9420. A gifted storyteller and speaker, she can be reached by visiting her Web site at *www.nrobertsbooks.com* or by fax at 704-365-5309.

K. Salome-Garver is an aspiring writer who is studying for her B.A. in social work. She currently makes her living as a bartender, which is a good job if you don't drink, and a great job if you do—only one pays better. She lives in Austin, Texas, with her dog, Satchel Paige, and her two cats, Izzy and Slick. They are her children, and she loves them, even when they are bad. Kellie can be reached at *kjs@texas.net.*

Allen M. Schoen, D.V.M., is coauthor of *Love, Miracles and Animal Healing* and editor of three textbooks on complementary and alternative veterinary medicine. He is a world-renowned lecturer and pioneer in this field and continues to maintain a referral practice in large- and small-animal alternative and complementary medicine in New York and Connecticut. He is the founder and director of the Center for Integrative Animal Health, a division of Global Communications for Conservation, Inc., and a recipient of numerous grants to develop complementary animal health care.

Maria Sears is enjoying an active retirement. She's a busy wife, mother and grandmother who enjoys traveling, volunteer work, music, books and many crafts. In her spare time, she's writing her life stories. This story is part of the unforgettable experience of a city girl becoming a rancher's wife. She can be reached by e-mail at *Deriter@aol.com.*

Jacqueline Shuchat-Marx is cantor of Congregation Albert in Albuquerque, New Mexico, where she creates and implements classes and programs in religious school and adult education. She was invested at Hebrew Union College-Jewish Institute of Religion. Her compositions have been performed in several synagogues. She cocreated a musical and dramatic presentation for two youth choirs at a citywide birthday commemoration of Dr. Martin Luther King Jr., and lends her voice to CD releases by Cantor Benjie-Ellen Schiller and Rabbi Joe Black.

Shari Smyth is a religious-education teacher and storyteller. She is a contributing editor of *Guideposts* magazine and writes regularly for the devotional book, *Daily Guideposts.* She has also been published in *Reader's Digest, Yankee* magazine, *Happiness* magazine and numerous Christian publications such as the *Lookout* and *WITH.* Shari and her husband, Whitney, have four grown children. The nest, however, is lively and full with three dogs, three cats and cats' friends who hang out on the front porch. She can be reached at 557 Mt. Pleasant Rd., Kingston Springs, TN 37082.

Ron St. James, L.C.S.W., A.C.S.W., was educated in New York, Massachusetts and Connecticut. He is married, the father of two wonderful daughters and is a clinical social work supervisor in Maine. Since 1973, he has been owned by a succession of droops of basset hounds. He can be reached by e-mail at *stjames@cybertours.com.*

Renée Sunday lives in Knoxville, Tennessee, with her husband of twenty-four years and their two children (Timothy, eighteen and Kimberly, five). She is a mortgage loan originator for First American National Bank. Dolly is now twelve years old and getting on in age for a cockatiel. She loves to have her head scratched and she can still let out that wolf whistle!

Joan Sutula writes poetry, essays and fiction. Her work has appeared in *Lyrical Iowa, Capper,* and numerous anthologies, and she has taken first-place awards in state and national poetry societies. She and her husband, Joe, have four children, eight grandchildren, and enjoy riding the beautiful bicycle trails of Iowa. She can be reached at 319-266-6450 or by e-mail at *jjsutula@aol.com.*

W. Bradford Swift, D.V.M., retired from veterinary medicine years ago to pursue his dream of being a writer, speaker and personal coach. He founded and now directs Life On Purpose Institute, a resource and learning center on the World Wide Web for people interested in living meaningful and satisfying lives. He is the author of *The Human Being Service Manual* (available through his Web site) and *Coaching To Win: Building Your Business by Building Your Team.* He lives with his wife, daughter, two cats, a dog and a school of fish in Flat Rock, North Carolina. He can be reached at 828-697-9239 or by e-mail at *brad@lifeonpurpose.com* Visit his Web site: *http://www.lifeonpurpose.com* (The subject of his story, Chitra Besbroda, is in dire need of assistance to keep her humane work alive. For more information, contact: Chitra at Sentient

Creatures, Inc., P.O. Box 765, Cathedral Station, New York, NY 10025, or call 212-865-5998.

Patti Thompson and her husband, Stephen, are coauthors of *CAT HYMNS,* a book and CD written from a cat's point of view. The Thompsons enjoy traveling to promote their book. Patti has also written a stage play based on *CAT HYMNS.* She is the owner of Way-Fil Jewelry and can be reached at P.O. Box 361, Tupelo, MS 38802 or by e-mail at *thompson@cathymns.com* Visit her Web site at *www.cathymns.com.*

Christine Townend is a writer who has had poetry, short stories and five books published. She founded Animal Liberation in 1976 in Australia, and campaigned for animal protection until she became managing trustee of the Help in Suffering Sanctuary Jaipur, Rajasthan, in 1990. In 1992, her husband resigned from his law partnership and moved to India with her where they work together as volunteers.

Irving Townsend, (1920-1981), was a producer for Columbia Records until 1971. His first book, the *Less Expensive Spread: Delights and Dilemmas of a Weekend Cowboy,* was published in 1971. Mr. Townsend's essays about living with animals were collected and published in 1986 in *Separate Lifetimes.* Both titles are available from J.N. Townsend Publishing, which was begun by Townsend's daughter, Jeremy, in 1986. A free catalogue is available by calling 800-333-9883 or writing to J.N. Townsend Publishing, 12 Greenleaf Dr., Exeter, NH 03833.

Deborah Turner is the owner of Doggie in the Window, a pet-grooming salon with retail and in-store veterinary clinic in Long Beach, California. She speaks professionally and teaches seminars for the pet industry. She is very involved in pet rescue and works through her store to better the lot for homeless and abused pets. She has coauthored with her friend, Diana Mohler, a children's book entitled *How Willy Got His Wheels,* which describes the plight of one of her rescues and won the 1998 Maxwell Award in Children's Literature. She and the little Chihuahua have appeared on television and have been featured in newspapers and magazines. Deborah and Willy can be reached at 4106 East Anaheim St., Long Beach, CA 90804-4269, by calling 562-494-7085 or by fax at 562-494-7606.

Joan M. Walker was lucky to combine avocation and vocation in the areas of animal welfare and domestic violence intervention, having served her community both as director of a local animal shelter, and as a crisis counselor for the woman's shelter. She has a B.S. in business administration, and shares a home with her partner, five cats, a dog and three chickens. Based on their experiences at the animal shelter, Joan and her partner are developing a series of humane education stories. Joan can be reached by e-mail at *jwalker@oregon.uoregon.edu.*

Susan White is primarily engaged in philanthropic and educational pursuits and artistic endeavors. She is forty-something and is wife to Daniel and best friend to Buddhi, their newest pup Bhakti and Face, the feline. She learns everyday from them and cherishes the wonderful ways that animals model living life to its fullest, loving unconditionally, embracing the passion within and being totally in the present moment.

Rosamond Young retired from teaching high-school English to become a columnist for the *Dayton Daily News*. She is author of fifteen published books, and, since her retirement as a staff columnist, continues to write a weekly column for her newspaper. She lives in a Lutheran retirement home in Dayton, Ohio, although she and her cat, Edith, are Episcopalians. Edith appears in two books by Mrs. Young. Mrs. Young can be reached by fax at 937-436-7721.

Pamela S. Zurer lives in Silver Spring, Maryland, with her husband, Burt, daughter, Rachel, and tabby cat, Peeps. A doctorate in chemistry, she works as an editor and reporter at *Chemical & Engineering News*, the weekly newsmagazine of the American Chemical Society. She enjoys bicycling, gardening and quilting.

The Day We Almost Didn't Go. Reprinted by permission of Arthur Gordon. ©1999 Arthur Gordon.

Letters from Vietnam. Reprinted by permission of Joe Fulda. ©1999 Joe Fulda.

I Love You, Pat Myers. Copyright ©1991 by Jo Coudert. Reprinted by permission of The Richard Parks Agency.

Jake and the Kittens. Reprinted with the permission of Simon & Schuster from *Chocolate for a Woman's Heart* by Kay Allenbaugh. Copyright ©1999 by Kay Allenbaugh.

We Are Family. Reprinted by permission of Jan Paddock. ©1999 Jan Paddock.

Me and My Mewse. Reprinted by permission of Cindy Podurgal Chambers. ©1999 Cindy Podurgal Chambers.

Step-Babies. Reprinted by permission of Christie Craig. ©1999 Christie Craig.

Jet. Reprinted by permission of Lynn Pulliam. ©1999 Lynn Pulliam.

Obedience. Reprinted by permission of Lori Jo Oswald, Ph.D. ©1999 Lori Jo Oswald, Ph.D.

A Cat Named Turtle. Reprinted by permission of Ellen Perry Berkeley. ©1999 Ellen Perry Berkeley.

Woman's Best Friend. Reprinted by permission of Holly Manon Moore. ©1999 Holly Manon Moore.

Mighty Hercules. Reprinted by permission of Barbara Bartocci. ©1999 Barbara Bartocci.

Angie's Dog Always. Excerpted from *Animal Ghost Stories* by Nancy Roberts. ©1995 by August House. Reprinted by permission of Nancy Roberts.

Lesson in Love. Reprinted with permission from "A Lesson in Love" in *Psycho Kitty* by Pam Johnson-Bennett. ©1984. Published by The Crossing Press, P.O. Box 1048, Freedom, CA 95019.

More Than Medicine. Reprinted by permission of Liz Gunkelman, D.V.M. ©1999 Liz Gunkelman, D.V.M.

Wheely Willy. Reprinted by permission of Deborah Turner. ©1999 Deborah Turner.

The Education of Jeeves. Reprinted by permission of Debbie Freeberg-Renwick. ©1999 Debbie Freeberg-Renwick.

Silky's Test. Reprinted by permission of Christine Townend. ©1999 Christine Townend.

Cat's Paw and *Ding, Dong, Bell*. Excerpted from *Hero Cats: True Stories of Daring Feline Deeds*. ©1998 Eric Swanson. Reprinted with permission of Andrews & McMeel Publishing. All rights reserved.

Charity. Excerpted from *Animals As Guides for the Soul* by Susan Chernak McElroy. Copyright ©1998 by Susan Chernak McElroy. Reprinted by permission of Ballantine Books, a Division of Random House, Inc.

Pampered Persian. From *Cats Incredible* by Brad Steiger. Copyright ©1994 by Brad Steiger. Used by permission of Dutton Signet, a division of Penguin Putnam, Inc.

Three-Dog Night. Reprinted by permission of George Feifer. ©1999 George Feifer.

Ginny, the Dog Who Rescues Cats. Excerpted from *The Dog Who Rescues Cats: The True Story of Ginny* by Philip Gonzalez. Copyright ©1996 by Philip Gonzalez. Reprinted by permission of HarperCollins Publishers, Inc.

Jim the Wonder Dog. Reprinted by permission of Bryan Aubrey. ©1999 Bryan Aubrey.

The Cowboy. Reprinted by permission of K. Salome-Garver. ©1999 K. Salome-Garver.

The Cat Who Needed a Night Light. Reprinted by permission of Susan McCullough. ©1999 Susan McCullough.

Flight over Little Egypt. Reprinted by permission of G. Edgar Hall. ©1999 G. Edgar Hall.

The Christmas Angel. Reprinted by permission of Pamela S. Zurer. ©1999 Pamela S. Zurer.

Shorty. Reprinted by permission of Larry Monk. ©1999 Larry Monk.

Prince's Golden Season. Excerpted from *Separate Lifetimes* by Irving Townsend. Reprinted by permission of Jeremy N. Townsend. ©1986 by Irving Townsend.

Hondo. Reprinted by permission of Page Lambert. ©1999 Page Lambert.

A Gentle Good-Bye. Reprinted by permission of Toni Eames. ©1999 Toni Eames.

Banjo. Reprinted by permission of David C. Hoopes. ©1994 David C. Hoopes.

The Cantor's Cat. Reprinted by permission of Jacqueline Shuchat-Marx. ©1999 Jacqueline Shuchat-Marx.

Circle of Love. Reprinted by permission of Maria Sears. ©1999 Maria Sears.

One Last Gift. Reprinted by permission of Kate Murphy. ©1999 Kate Murphy.

Soldier Dog. Reprinted by permission of Ron St. James. ©1999 Ron St. James.

Mr. Reed. Excerpted from *Birds on the Couch* by Ruth Hanessian with Wendy Bounds. Copyright ©1998 by Ruth Hanessian and Wendy Bounds. Adapted and reprinted by permission of Crown Publishers, Inc.

A Moggy for Michael. Excerpted from *Sherlock Bones* by John Keane. ©1976 by John Keane.

Double Duty. Reprinted by permission of Lisa Hurt. ©1999 Lisa Hurt.

An American Cat in Paris. Reprinted by permission of Peter Mandel. ©1999 Peter Mandel.

Waiting at the Door. Reprinted by permission of Barbara J. Crocker. ©1999 Barbara J. Crocker.

Flying Free. Reprinted by permission of Cheryl Johnstone for H. Gordon Green. ©1999 H. Gordon Green.

Of Dogs and Angels. Reprinted by permission of Roger Caras. ©1999 Roger Caras.

MORE BEST SELLING PET STORIES IN

Chicken Soup for the Pet Lover's Soul

#1 New York Times
BESTSELLING AUTHORS
Jack Canfield
Mark Victor Hansen
Marty Becker, D.V.M.
Carol Kline

Chicken Soup for the **Pet Lover's Soul**

Stories About
Pets as Teachers, Healers,
Heroes and Friends

Code #5718 Paperback—$12.95

Do you talk to your pets like they were people?

Do you sign your cat's name to greeting cards?

Does your dog's wild "welcome home" make your day?

By sharing the remarkable relationships between people and animals, these inspirational stories prove that oftentimes our greatest heroes, healers and teachers are furry, feathered, or four-legged.

A New Season of Chicken Soup for the Soul

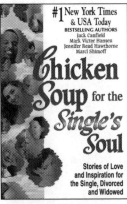
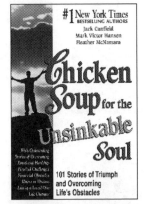
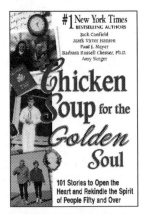